THE
POLITICS
OF
HEAVEN & HELL

CHRISTIAN THEMES
FROM CLASSICAL, MEDIEVAL AND MODERN
POLITICAL PHILOSOPHY

JAMES V. SCHALL

UNIVERSITY
PRESS OF
AMERICA

LANHAM • NEW YORK • LONDON

Library of Congress Cataloging in Publication Data

Schall, James V.
   The politics of heaven and hell.

   Includes indexes.
   1. Christianity and politics—History. I. Title.
BR115.P7S2683   1984   261.7'09   84-7409
ISBN 0-8191-3991-2 (alk. paper)
ISBN 0-8191-3992-0 (pbk. : alk. paper)

Brief citations from Plato's *Republic* are from the Modern Library Edition; those from Aristotle are from the Random House Edition of *The Basic Works of Aristotle,* Edited by Richard McKeon; those from Scripture are from the *Jerusalem Bible,* unless otherwise indicated. *WHAT IS POLITICAL PHILOSOPHY?* by Leo Strauss. Copyright © 1959 by the Free Press, a Division of Macmillan, Inc.

Cover Illustration, The Elect, from The Universal Judgement in the Church of Sant'Angelo in Formis, near Capua, Italy. XI-XIII Century, Italian Romanesque.

ACKNOWLEDGEMENTS

The author wishes to thank the Editors and Publishers of the following Journals for permission to reprint essays which previously appeared in their Journals. These have been rewritten for this book.

Communio, (Chapers VI and VII); Divus Thomas, (Chapter XI); The Downside Review, (Chapter IV); Fellowship of Catholic Scholars' Conference Proceedings, Catholic Social Thought and the Teachings of John Paul II, 1983, (Chapter XII); Homiletic and Pastoral Review, (Chapter I); Laval Théologique et Philosophique, (Chapter XIII); The Review of Politics, (Chapter VIII); The Thomist, (Chapters V and X); Worldview, (Chapter II).

TABLE OF CONTENTS

CHAPTERS:

PREFACE

The absence of widespread attention to the intellectual relation of religion and politics, particularly the Judaeo-Christian religion, in current academic political science curricula and scholarly journals, is rather curious in view of the impact the great religions have had and continue to have on public life. Paradoxically, in recent years, religion itself has become more and more politicized, so that it tends to have a growing ideological effect in public life, one that often seems, by traditional standards, to be more political than religious. The specific contribution of religion itself seems obscured.

Political philosophy, in particular, seems incomplete when what belongs to it and what belongs to religion are not clarified. Basically, there are many reasons for this neglect. One is the somewhat open claim of the university to its own autonomy. But another is the failure to understand how ideas, rooted often in religion, relate to classical political philosophy. How these ideas appeared in medieval and modern times, both in thought and in practice, has become obscured, as Sheldon Wolin pointed out in his Politics and Vision.[1]

However, Professor Glenn Tinder wrote, in his Political Thinking, that all political reflection is a consequence of the need to explain why men are estranged and at odds with each other.[2] Political thinkers, thus, divide over how they explain this and how they live with this estrangement, transform it, or remove it. It seems clear, then, that the way the Judaeo-Christian tradition in particular confronted ideas of creation, death, evil, law, hell, mercy, and final destiny can be a most fruitful source for understanding what Professor Leo Strauss called, following the classics, the limit of politics.[3] Aristotle had said that if man were the highest being, politics would be the highest science.(1141a20-22) But he likewise held that man was not the highest being, so that the relation of politics to metaphysics in understanding the political enterprise is an abiding problem which arises out of our political experience itself.

vii

The Politics of Heaven and Hell: Christian Themes From Classical, Medieval, and Modern Political Philosophy addresses itself to this crucial neglect in contemporary political philosophy. The consideration of these traditions and ideas is basic to understanding how political thought was formed. It indicates what must happen to political theory when they are neglected. The chapters and themes look both forward and backward. Ideas arising from classical or religious traditions are treated as living factors in political thought and public life, even though they may have originally arisen in the Old and New Testament periods or with St. Augustine or St. Thomas Aquinas. (Hereafter, St. Thomas Aquinas appears in the text as St. Thomas Aquinas, Aquinas, or St. Thomas interchangeably).

The death of Socrates and the death of Christ, which even Mill touched on in his famous essay, symbolically serve to introduce the deepest themes into man's study and thinking about the nature and limits of politics.[4] In dying at the hands of the state, both said something about death, politics, philosophy, and man's relation to law and the transcendent God. Oftentimes, in the modern era, political philosophy is seen as a substitute for or an alternative to these questions. That is, it becomes itself a kind of covert metaphysics, as Aristotle suspected it might. This is why it is doubly important that political theory recognize its relation to the Judaeo-Christian heritage as it is itself in turn related to Greek and later modern political theory, as well as to the way religion has transformed itself before politics, sometimes, unfortunately, even into politics.

Religion, political theory, science, history, economics, and philosophy must be touched by each other. All have human roots. All that has happened to mankind, including the question of whether a revelation has been directed to its intelligence and life, is pertinent to this issue. By broadening the vision of ourselves, we can hope to make an understanding of our political life more definite, more within its proper limits. Politics is an architechtonic science, Aristotle said, one that touches everything in the practical order, one allowing us to reach our contemplative end of what is. (1094a18-b11) The purpose of this book is to recruit the student to this broader scope. Yet he ought not to forget that those thinkers most likely to know about politics and its limits are those who have actually lived it, often suffered from it, those who recognize that when we know everything about politics, we do not yet know everything about man himself.

Finally, I wish to acknowledge the encouragement and critical attention given to this project by Mr. James E. Lyons, Managing Editor, University Press of America, the perceptive reading of the text and advising about its structure by Mr. Michael Jackson, the word-processing and guidance about the text generously given by Mrs. Joyce Kho, and the word-processing facilities in San Francisco provided by Father Joseph Fessio, S. J. For citations from classical authors, scripture, St. Augustine, and St. Thomas Aquinas, I have used standard references in the text itself. For the convenience of the reader, references occurring in more than one chapter are repeated in full in each chapter. Likewise, I have included references to other works of mine in which a given point is also discussed. In addition, after the first three Chapters, I have placed a small list of readings which I hope might be helpful to those not familiar with the matter under discussion.

James V. Schall, S. J.
Georgetown University,
Washington, D. C.
May, 1984

Footnotes:

1. See Sheldon Wolin, _Politics and Vision_, Boston, Little, Brown, 1960, Chapter I.

2. Glenn Tinder, _Political Thinking_, Boston, Little, Brown, 1979.

3. Leo Strauss, _What Is Political Philosophy?_, Glencoe, Free Press, 1959.

4. John Stuart Mill, _On Liberty_, Chapter II, London, Oxford, 1966, pp. 61-65.

INTRODUCTION

The current academic neglect of medieval political theory is itself a major problem in political philosophy. For too long, the methods of "modern" political analysis, the very presuppositions and definitions of its subject matter, have obscured the central and real issues upon which political thought is based. What is studied and what neglected, then, often provide the best possible outline of a university's or a culture's notion about the place and significance of politics in the world. Exactly where, in fact, politics is to be located in the intellectual order is an issue we have inherited from the Greeks, to whom the medievals, Jews, Muslims, and Christians alike, were also more than beholden.[1]

No doubt to some extent, at least, the appreciation of medieval trends and political ideas depends upon the status and self-comprehension of Christianity itself, in its relation to classical and Old Testament thought. But Christianity was also concerned with the theoretical status and meaning of politics. Indeed, just how this was so must be understood if we are to grasp anything about modern theory. McIlwain's famous thesis about the medieval origins of modern constitutionalism seems, if anything, more pertinent than ever for these very reasons.[2]

The normative but limited place of politics itself in medieval political thought makes its moral reflection pertinent in recent years when Small Is Beautiful, public morality, fair business procedures, war, and controlling state taxing and policing powers seem to have themselves become pressing elements of practical politics, elements whose origins seem to lie in medieval thought.[3] In this sense, then, medieval political theory has never seemed more capable of appreciative understanding and use as contrasted with modern theory which has been overly dominated by physical and psychological sciences, by the dubiously "scientific" claim of atheist humanism proceeding from the Marxist tradition.

Medieval theory was rejected by modern theory because the latter claimed ethics and religion to be themselves autonomous and consistent disciplines, not needing in their own orders any further basis but what is justified by modern scientific culture. The

xi

growing criticism and even rejection of the consequences of modern theory, with its premises in Machiavelli, devised specifically against classical and medieval ideas and values. They have made it imperative to reconsider more objectively medieval social and political ideals and ideas.

Professor Michael Walzer, in a valuable essay, "Teaching Morality," has called attention to the need of common, traditional, public ethical discourse in our universities and civic life. American liberal thought especially, which has so dominated our academic life, has led either to a radical subjectivity or to an empirical objectivity, both of which neglect, if not actually distort, the real force and content of morality. But there is, in fact, a public standard and code which men in society must discover and rediscover in each generation. There are norms that are not merely rooted in our private world or in mathematical formulae about utility.

Walzer wrote:

Moral language is shared even when we use it to talk about, and to disagree about, the most difficult issues -- in war, in politics, in personal life. According to that language, people are not only sincere and insincere, but good and bad; the decisions they make don't only involve costs and benefits, but rights and wrongs, justice and injustice.[4]

This means that moral, political reflections on justice, war, medical ethics, business practices, or the actual achievements of labor unions, lobbies, courts, and congresses are essentially human activities in moral terms. This endeavor has been "temporarily discontinued at American universities, at some cost." The effect of a renewed study of ethics and morality "presses us back to older moralities, or forward to newer ones, in which personal choice and utilitarian calculation are subject to the discipline of a public philosophy."[5]

The notion of a "public philosophy," of course, was used after World War II by Walter Lippmann at a time when the tragic abuses of political practice seemed obviously to have had intellectual roots in a widespread academic and theoretic rejection of common public standards.[6] The older medieval notion of a "philosophia perennis" suggested, likewise, that certain standards of the human good did exist and were discernable by reflective human minds. Thus, the function of education and moral life was to discover such norms and, more importantly, to live according to them. The medievals doubted if the latter, the living, could long exist without the former, the discovering. This is why they placed such a remarkable emphasis on rational reflection in private and public activity and its norms.

In our era, however, when objective ethics and morality have not been thought of except as a kind of historical analysis of what man once held, their very reconsideration will itself be a novelty over against the content of most curricula in political thought. Just as Professor Henry Veatch once suggested that we should treat Aristotle as a contemporary writer, so we should look upon medieval thought as something new and unheard of.[7] In fact, even when apparently objective morality again becomes popular, as with John Rawls' A Theory of Justice, it strives to hide itself within the name and confines of "modern" theory, perhaps because pure distributive justice does contain within itself unavoidable utopian claims that would reject a truly higher norm of critical judgment on politics.

In Western mentalities, however, the very novelty of a subject is often itself "liberal" over against what most people do or think, so there may be some more than ordinary impetus to look closely at ideas once held to be the common subject of political reflection. Indeed, without such reflection, in one sense, there really is no "political theory" at all, since these topics of morality and metaphysics were really the ultimate ones about the human condition as such, that very "human condition" Hannah Arendt saw so well as the proper subject matter of political philosophy.[8]

Yet, a reconsideration of medieval political theory will not merely be a question of renewed interest in ethics and morality. To be sure, medieval thought itself considered politics from this point of view. But modern theory has not. This means that subjects more properly, at first sight at least, religious and ontological have come to be subsumed into political theory. The problems of "hell" and "evil", for example, as I shall subsequently suggest, are among these. Their claim to restatement and reflection is one of political theory. Further,

xiii

modern theory, especially liberal theory, has on the surface tried to separate politics from other areas of life, an impetus stemming in part from the Christian tradition of limiting Caesar to the things of Caesar.

The growing control of the state over all areas of life, in bureaucratic, socialist, and modernization theory, however, is philosophically to be explained because we find nothing radically higher than or different from this same Caesar, however named. This means, in other words, that the key issue in any reflection on medieval political philosophy is the one that seeks to take from politics its all-embracing theoretic pretensions. The other side of this is a return of politics to the sphere of its own competency. From this point of view, the meaning of the Old Testament, the death of Jesus, and the position of St. Augustine, are of crucial significance. Their neglect is, indeed, the very justification for their inclusion in any fundamental analysis of political theory.

If one side of Christian and medieval theory seeks to recognize the reality and legitimacy of religion and metaphysics in determining the nature of political theory, the other side is to live with, draw the consequences from the proposition that the "good life," that search which began political philosophy in the first place with Plato, does not ultimately reside in the human <u>polis</u>. This is the conclusion St. Augustine drew forcefully for all authentically Christian reflection on classical theory. On the other hand, certain speculative consequences about this life and the next, a curious confusion of them, functions in theory itself. Many contemporary political ideas were remarkably discussed in Aquinas as aspects of the next life, a fact that causes a fundamental insight into the nature of classical and Christian political theory.

The idea that politics is in theory restricted to its own field, likewise, relates to the limits of law and the classical questions of the best and worst forms of rule. One of the main problems of political theory is what to do with the discovery that politics is <u>not</u> the highest science, that metaphysics is superior to politics. What becomes of the search for the Good? Is it to be forgotten, or denied, or repoliticized? Law, likewise, deals with men, for the most part, less than perfect. This is itself a theoretical proposition resulting from the public tradition itself. This will, as a result, have a direct effect on radical or utopian politics as well as on practical politics, which latter becomes dangerous when only the practice of what men "do" do is admitted. Medieval political theory is what best prevents us from making our own politics openly or covertly a kind of theology or metaphysics wherein all is explained by its own order.

The importance of medieval theory, then, is and remains what it teaches. Its value lies in its capacity to restate the kind of abiding reflection needed both to restore metaphysics to its proper place and justify morality in its own sphere. Medieval theory, in other words, is not merely historical or antiquarian, but itself a way of "theory," a way to think about what we mean when we say politics is properly "politics." Medieval theory teaches how man is "a social and political animal," as Aquinas translated Aristotle. This denied that man was "the highest being in the universe" or politics the absolutely "highest activity" open to him, without at the same time denying his special dignity as a microcosm of all that is or his dignity as a son of God. This kind of reflection always must begin and end political theory proper.

For this reason, then, we cannot, nor ought not to avoid medieval thought, for it remains the "perennial" reflection, the public philosophy which frees us from our individually constructed norms. Likewise, it checks science if it claims a single type of knowledge. As Stephen Miller wrote on this subject:

> The Sea of Faith has not quite receded.... Why? To my mind, the answer is obvious: the Enlightenment is over. It is not that most writers and thinkers are opposed to scientific and technological progress; rather, it is that they find it exceedingly difficult if not impossible to entertain the hope that in the future man will learn to live in harmony with his fellow man, a hope that glowed in the minds of many Eighteenth Century thinkers. Until recently -- until, really, the publication of The Gulag Archipelago -- some writers who were opposed to capitalism could dream that the magic wand of Marxian socialism would dispel alienation, anomie, oppression, and

xv

poverty. But Marxian socialism is now on the defensive, and the melancholy roar we hear is the roar of a receding faith in a socialist future.

We have lost too our faith in the wonder-working powers of education and psychology.... We have become utterly disenchanted with the preachers of liberation.... Most writers and thinkers, I suspect, regard it as foolish to assume that science will ever set our political or psychological house in order -- let alone make us more tolerant and humane. [9]

It is in this context, that "the intellectual climate of the 1980's is very different from that of the 1950's and 1960's," as Miller put it, that the religious tradition is again being seriously considered. This is why a more complete knowledge of it is of such importance.

In placing the political in its proper sphere, then, medieval theory enables us to have a reason for denying the validity of any "totalitarian" claim, no matter in what guise it might appear, even that of liberty, or fraternity, or, more recently, of equality, or distributive justice. Medieval theory will raise more ultimate questions today than any other theory. And it will have the advantage of recognizing them for what they are by not allowing them to hide behind the surface of merely "political" issues. This alone would probably justify its study.

But beyond this, medieval theory also maintains that there are answers, that the rational and religious enterprises are, in the end, also needed not just for themselves but for and in politics. Political theory ought finally be free enough to find and discover only itself and not some hidden metaphysics calling itself by the noble name of politics. The advantage of studying medieval political theory, then, is that it teaches us that to understand politics, we need to know about everything else, yet without calling anything else politics, but politics.

Footnotes:

1. See Ralph Lerner and M. Mahdi, _Medieval Political Philosophy_, Ithaca, Cornell University Press, 1963, Introduction.

2. See Charles H. McIlwain, _The Growth of Political Thought in the West_, New York, Macmillan, 1932; Heinrich Rommen, "The Genealogy of Natural Rights," _Thought_, Autumn, 1954, pp. 403-25.

3. See James V. Schall, "On the Teaching of Ancient and Medieval Political Theory," _Christianity and Politics_, Boston, St. Paul Editions, 1981; "Rethinking the Nature of Government," _Modern Age_, Spring 1979, pp. 158-66; also E. F. Schumacher, _Small Is Beautiful_, New York, Harper, 1975; _A Guide For the Perplexed_, New York, Harper-Colophon, 1977.

4. Michael Walzer, "Teaching Morality," _The New Republic_, June 10, 1978, p.13. See also Reo Christenson, _Heresies: Left and Right_, New York, Harper, 1976, Chapter I; Hadley Arkes, _The Philosopher in the City_, Princeton, Princeton University Press, 1981.

5. Walzer, _ibid._, p. 14. See John Hallowell, "Obstacles to the Recovery of a Christian Perspective on Human Nature," _Modern Age_, Winter, 1983, pp. 2-14.

6. See Walter Lippmann, _An Essay on the Public Philosophy_, Boston, Little, Brown, 1955; John Courtney Murray, _We Hold These Truths_, New York, Sheed and Ward, 1960; Ernest Cassirer, _The Myth of the State_, New Haven, Yale University Press, 1946; Jacques Maritain, _Man and the State_, Chicago, University of Chicago Press, 1951.

7. See Henry Veatch, _Aristotle_, Bloomington, University of Indiana Press, 1974.

8. See Hannah Arendt, _The Human Condition_, Garden City, Doubleday, 1959.

9. Stephen Miller, "Religion and the Intellectual: A Strange New Respect," _The American Spectator_, April, 1983, pp. 14-15.

CHAPTER I

THE OLD TESTAMENT AND POLITICAL THEORY

> As regards the correct opinions through which the ultimate perfection is obtained, the Law has given only their end and has called us to believe in them in a summary way -- namely, in the existence of the deity, the Exalted, His unity, His knowledge, His power, His will, and His eternity. All these are ultimate ends that do not become evident in detail and with precision except after knowing many opinions.... The Law has called us to adopt certain beliefs, the belief in which is necessary for the sake of the well-being of political conditions -- like our belief that the Exalted becomes violently angry with those who disobey Him and that it is therefore necessary to fear Him and to dread Him and to take care not to disobey. -- [Moses Maimonides, A Guide to the Perplexed, Part III, Chapter 28.]

During a period in which a great percentage of political news and media coverage is devoted to Israel, it comes as something of a shock to realize that few of the standard texts in the history of political theory pay more than a passing attention to the Old Testament.[1] To be sure, not much more concern is given to the New Testament, while that which is devoted to either often misses its main import to political thought. A book like Sir Ernest Barker's From Alexander to Constantine is a welcome corrective for both of these deficiencies, at least as regards the latter books of the Old Testament.[2] Certain issues intrinsic to history and political thought cannot be wholly avoided in academia because of Christianity. The most obvious area here is that of church and state, though as Charles N. R. McCoy pointed out, this interest in church and state usually neglects the more important philosophical contribution of Christianity to political theory.[3] Somehow, however, it is assumed traditionally that the Old Testament can be practically avoided altogether.

1

Of late, however, interest in the Old Testament has arisen from several rather ideological sources, ones which tend to obscure the issue of the political significance of the Old Testament. The first comes from the Christian liberationists who write of the Old Testament in terms of class struggle and a so-called more loving society, writing that often carries clearly Marxist origins.[4] But this use of the Old Testament to push a contemporary anti-capitalist ideology seems rather dubious both in time and in how it is selectively applied.[5]

The second reference to the Old Testament has come from Jewish scholars seeking to use the heritage of the Bible as an argument for the political support of present-day Israel. In this regard, Professor Aaron Wildavsky has written:

> America's national interest in the security and prosperity of Israel rests on this: any moral argument which condemns Israel applies equally to America itself and any cultural argument against Israel applies to all of Western civilization. In Israel we Americans are brought face to face with our own origins. By acting as if there were no American national interest in Israel, the United States would simultaneously be rejecting its own religious, moral, political, and cultural identity. America has a national interest in Israel precisely because no other nation invokes at one and the same time so many basic American values. What's in it for us? -- Our own purposes, values, self-worth, and any other reasons we Americans have for believing in ourselves.[6]

This approach does belatedly recognize the significance of the particular religious relationship of the Old Testament to Western and American culture. Yet, its argument here seems to be more one of self-interest than any appreciation of the value of the Old Testament itself as a philosophic issue.

Still a third analysis came from Erich Fromm whose <u>You Shall Be As Gods: A Radical Interpretation of the Old Testament and Its Tradition</u> tried to enlist the Old Testament moral passion and ethical vision in the cause of secular humanism for creating a just

2

society after radical models. Fromm, who admitted he was not a theist, still felt it possible to save some of the essence of this great vision in the name of this-worldly ends. This "secular humanism," of course, is the major type of analysis that confronts any theist tradition, such as found in the Old and New Testaments.[7] Hans Urs von Balthasar once remarked that these are really the only two philosophies contending the world -- the secularized Jewish messianism of this world and the Christian retention of the primacy of God within and beyond the world.[8]

When we come to the heart of the meaning of the Old Testament in political thought, then, we may well recall that Leo Strauss wrote a perceptive essay on "Jerusalem and Athens," while Matthew Arnold in the last century was much interested in the Hebrew mind as compared to the Greek, itself an issue of abiding significance in political thought.[9] Furthermore, certain writers important in political thought, Filmer and more especially Calvin, were much influenced by the Old Testament. The whole Puritan experience on all its planes, including the American one, had Old Testament overtones, as Max Weber noted on the economic side.[10] Sometimes, there are treatments of Philo, Josephus, or Maimonides, though these usually are considered in relation to Greek, Arabic, or Christian analyses. Too, practically any Christian author will see the Old Testament as part of his own tradition; the City of God of St. Augustine is only the most conspicuous example. Yet, as the passage from Maimonides suggested in the beginning, the relation of the Law to the order of politics is a fundamental consideration that we can by no means avoid. Does political philosophy judge the Law or does revelation also address reason even in its own sphere?

Undoubtedly, one of the reasons why students of political theory can receive their higher degrees without even a clue about what is in Deuteronomy, for example, is because the Old Testament is assumed to fall exclusively under the category of "religion," almost as if religion had no historical or intellectual impact on the discipline of politics. The mental bloc against religion in academia ought not to continue to pass unnoticed, of course, if only as a sign of intellectual prejudice. Moreover, many practicing Old Testament scholars, who write specifically on their own subjects, are not concerned with the political aspects of their material, except

3

perhaps as historical record, while the efforts of those who do try to apply the Old Testament to politics often result in a kind of covert ideology.[11] What the relation of the Old Testament to the area of political thought and its unity may be, does not normally lie in most Old Testament scholars' area of competence.

Indeed, the degree to which the Old Testament has been ideologized by both Old and New Testament writers in recent years is rather remarkable. Certain newer movements, such as liberation theology from Latin Europe and America, as I mentioned, have potentially great political significance and are directly influenced by the Old Testament. But this latter theology is often filtered through a kind of Marxist presupposition, which should not be surprising, as Marx himself was originally a Jew, while Hegel was a student of theology, so that many properly Marxist ideas are frequently but secularizations of Old Testament notions.[12] (See Chapter VIII) In any event, the connection between the end of Isaiah and the conditions of the "classless society" is more than coincidental, however dubious this relationship may in fact be.

To present the Old Testament as a legitimate, indeed necessary, element in any complete or even adequate understanding of the content and evolution of political theory and its consequences requires us to broaden our understanding of political thought to include political and cultural ideas that have in fact formed political communities, even though their origins may not be "scientific" by some limited contemporary academic standard.[13] The Old Testament remains one of the most widely read books in the history of man. And it was not only read but believed and acted upon, so that events in the world were brought about because of its existence and influence.

Moreover, the Old Testament presents not merely a concrete model of "theocracy" as a form of government or politics, as an answer to the classical problem of the best form of rule, but it stands at the bottom of the question about what is a "nation."[14] Modern political science has largely endeavored to construct the justification and organizing force of political life from rational or emotional sources requiring no further explanation but themselves. Aristotle and the Christian sources flowing from him have likewise tended to give a philosophical basis for political

4

foundations. This necessarily implied, however, some considerations about the nature and limits of reason itself as well as the relation between man's _final_ end and his final _political_ end. These were by no means the same things, however much they are directly interrelated in actual human lives.

Yet, there are few nation-states in the world today that are not affected by some notion of a special calling which stands at the origins of their formation and justifies their continued existence. And as the case of the Chinese demonstrates, not every historical embodiment of a "chosen people" concept needs to come directly from the Old Testament. The United States in many ways is itself unintelligible without the notion of the "City on the Hill," which the early Puritans came to establish on these distant shores.[15] We have tended, not wholly incorrectly, to explain foundation myths in the Platonic manner, in which there is a creative reason given about why particular people came to be, a reason, a "myth." In this the people are taught to believe or come to believe some explanation, historical or mythical, that accounts for the unique political presence and configuration of their nation in the world. A sense of political uniqueness is as much a human need as a sense of common humanity.

In this context, then, the Old Testament account of why Israel was founded as a unique "nation," as a people with a specific destiny, is perhaps even more fruitful an explanation than the Platonic one to explain why nations think they are founded and why they continue to exist. The mystery of the foundation of Israel forces us to wonder, intellectually wonder, if nations are solely the products of rational political philosophy.[16] Academics of every hue, to be sure, would be inclined to an exclusively rational position. Probably few actual members of a citizen body, however, would ever have so thought about themselves. One does not have to read very far in the literature about the founding of the almost one hundred nation-states since World War II, not to mention those founded earlier, to realize that rational political theory does not take us all the way in explaining fully why political entities come to be.

If we are to form a just estimate of the importance of the Old Testament in political theory, therefore, we must first form an intellectual place, or space, as it were, for its unique and far-reaching contributions. Even Aquinas, reflecting largely on the Greek problem of the best form of government, arrived at his theoretical solution of the ideal mixed constitutional form from precisely a consideration of the "Old Law." But this is probably not where the most fruitful approach to this question lies.(I-II, 105) The place to begin is undoubtedly where the Old Testament itself began, with Genesis. This is so because there is an Old Testament source for the unity of mankind, for the idea that all humans form one people. The idea is not just "rational," as with the Stoics. This is the real import of the creation account in Genesis. And connected with this is the Old Testament account of why men are not united, the account of the Fall.(Genesis, Chapters 3 and 4) This latter in a very real way has been as influential as Plato's Republic in describing the situation of the decline of states. We cannot begin merely with those monuments to political theory in Hobbes or Rousseau, which try to account for what has gone wrong with the human race, accounts which place the burden in property division or fear.

Moreover, the classic remedies proposed to cure the political and social ills -- property reform, labor, political structures, even the conditions of birth -- are already reflected in Genesis. Indeed, it can well be argued, that the Old Testament probably provides the best insight into that type of political philosophy that attributes human evil to social structures, particularly structures due to coercive government, property, and work. The secularized restoration of the Garden of Eden is about in political theory in one or another historical and intellectual form. Further, the Old Testament lies at the origin of the optimistic belief that men can establish a perfect society in the future of this world. In this sense, Isaiah and Daniel are probably more pertinent than Socrates.

Nonetheless, the first thing to note about Genesis, about its essential worldview, is its description of the condition of the cosmos -- that it is good -- and of the relation of man to the cosmos and this earth -- that he is to reduce them to order.[17] They are for him. The fundamental impact of Genesis lies in its denial of a god of evil, in its refusal to identify matter and creation with a perverse principle. (See Chapter VI) This means that man is a certain kind of being who is intrinsically

6

related to the world and yet that he also is properly the "image" of Yahweh, not merely just like other material beings. Already here is the beginning of that concept of human rights and dignity which sees in the human worldly enterprise itself an absolute value which men did not create or give to themselves but which is theirs to hold as a gift.

The Old Testament, in a sense, is an effort to prevent men and nations from settling for anything less than Yahweh. From this point of view, it is a much more graphic endeavor than that found in The Ethics of Aristotle with its relation to The Metaphysics or even in the first questions of the Prima Secundae of Aquinas' Summa Theologica about the location of human beatitude. The net effect, consequently, is to prevent the nation from being an idol, an absolute, even though it is a good. Already in the Old Testament, we are aware that the most dangerous threat to human worth and dignity will probably be from a political system claiming the prerogatives of Yahweh. This is the power to set up a nation's own definition of right and wrong, its own idols, of which itself, the nation, the political power, is the most perilous and the most tempting.

In point of fact, however, as the accounts in Deuteronomy (Chapters 5-7) and Exodus (Chapter 24) show, Israel is "chosen." The notion of a chosen people or race has been an explosive one, even a dangerous one. It can, though need not, cause envy and resentment. More than one political theory is designed to obviate just such a concept. And yet, if this chosenness be examined in the Old Testament, it contains some odd characteristics. It is clear that Israel was not chosen for any virtue or value of its own, so that the result of its choice was both a great challenge and a heavy responsibility to itself. Israel was to be measured not by itself nor by the nations but by its observance of the Commandments, that is, by being actually better men, better people, according to the strict norms set down by the Commandments themselves. Aristotle too had said that politics does not make man to be man, but taking him from nature, makes him to be good man.(1258a21-22)

This observance meant for Israel, however, as the Book of Jonah hinted, that the peculiar virtues of the nation were valid only insofar as the nation was a channel back to the object of creation in Genesis, the Fatherhood of Yahweh over all His people. Obedience

7

to Yahweh did not alienate man from himself, but restored him to himself. Contrariwise, the Old Testament contains the notion of a nation that does not obey the Commandments, a nation which is for that very reason punished for its wrong-doings, usually by the political enemies it finds about her. This is the meaning of the History Books of the Old Testament such as Chronicles and Kings. Israel is given Canaan not because of Israel's virtues but because of the injustices of these Canaanite people themselves. The Old Testament begins in fact the question of the relation of civic stability to personal and political morality.

Aristotle and Plato both held that political theory must account for the bad as well as the good forms of rule. The Old Testament's "bad" forms of rule are actual tribal or empire states. Revolution is more than a theory of justice. It also includes the reality of judgment. The Old Testament, thus, is full of rather bloody wars whose meaning is seen to be judgment on the sins of peoples. Man himself is a certain kind of a being, subject to Yahweh, not to himself, for what he is. Furthermore, Israel is the "least" of the nations. The theme of the lowly being exalted is a familiar one in the scriptures but it is, also, an essential element in the process in which we recognize that the lowly are to be the objects of rule and dignity in themselves. The theme of the "remnant" in the Old Testament, however, leaves the impression that even in the chosen people, not all, nor even most, are faithful.(Isaiah, Chapter 4; Jeremiah, Chapter 33) This theme again brings up the classic Platonic question of whether ultimate justice and good are to be found in any actual constitutional state.

And so within the Old Testament, this leads to the prophetic traditions -- to Amos, Isaiah, Jeremiah, and Ezechiel, to the source of judgment upon the performance of rulers and peoples. Nathan and Samuel judge the kings in the name of Yahweh. The chastisement of the rich in Amos, his sense that neither the poor nor even prisoners are to be abandoned, yet that they too sin as with the incident of the Golden Calf, this sheds light not only on the idea of slavery but on the transcendent worth of each human person. Human beings are not merely members of a species, as in Greek philosophy, but distinct individuals, chosen and called. The initial words in Jeremiah, therefore, contain some of the most powerful affirmations of human dignity in all its stages that

8

there are to be found in any literature or philosophical source:

> The word of Yahweh was addressed to me, saying: "Before I formed you in the womb I knew you; before you came to birth I consecrated you; I have appointed you as a prophet to the nations."
>
> I said, "Ah Lord Yahweh, look, I do not know how to speak: I am a child!"
>
> But Yahweh replied: "Do not say, 'I am a child.' Go now those to whom I send you and say whatever I command you. Do not be afraid of them, for I am with you to protect you -- it is I Yahweh who speaks!" (1: 4-8)

This is not a self-sufficient humanism of the strong but an affirmation that the weak and small, even those in the womb, are also, even primarily, God's spokesmen and children.

The prophetic tradition, therefore, the idea that a source of right and good exists outside the political society calling it, its leaders, and people to their own vocation, is a pregnant one. The Old Testament, of course, knew false prophets, just as it knew good kings. But the covenant with Yahweh acted as a political norm. Relations with Yahweh depended upon the treatment of widows and orphans.(Amos) It was not obviously a perfect society, or else there would have been no widows and orphans. In other words, there was a standard which men were called to observe in their private and public lives, so that an unjust state was no merely rational category, as it was in Greek formulations, but a real relation of moral disorder that demanded action in the name of Yahweh. His ways were to be followed, because of Yahweh and of His knowledge of what was best for and in man. This is undoubtedly the "public philosophy" that includes the least and the best, that knows the difference of right and wrong.

The Covenant, moreover, that treaty-like concept that was to have so much influence in the form of social contracts of various sorts -- an idea whose time seems to have come again in current political theory -- demonstrated the highly promissory basis of political and human life.[18] Throughout the Old Testament, the actors make promises and are expected to keep them. As Hannah Arendt was to point out, the promise-structure of this kind of thought in political theory was one of the most fruitful imaginable for shaping how a future is to turn out within the freedom foundations of all social order.[19]

It is this web of promises to be kept or broken, then, that really prevents political thought from being merely deterministic. In this sense, the Old Testament is crucial to understand any theory that would hold an order of good and justice within freedom. Thus, laws are covenants that appeal first and mainly to our willingness to accept them. Sanctions are seen as secondary, not primary, in the formation of the structure of Israel. On the other hand, promises are not merely arbitrary. They contain moral obligation, self-chosen, to be sure, but self-chosen in the light of a real good that is objective in the laws of Yahweh, designed specifically for the creatures' good.

The goodness of creation and man's place in it are the Old Testament's initial contribution. But if through the free Image of Yahweh, the man made "a little less than the angels," as the Eighth Psalm memorably said, summing up this relationship, if through man an account of evil must also be made, still the final heritage of the Old Testament is the Promised Land, the place where all the evils will be righted. Zion is not only chosen, singled out, but it has a future, evidently an earthly destiny. The Christian transformation of this result is important in its own context. But here it is necessary likewise to suggest that a people, a nation modeled on the Old Testament tradition rather than the Greek or rational philosophical traditions -- which themselves often also had chosen people ideas connected with them -- will conceive itself to have a worldly destiny which is to establish a unique and perfect justice in the concrete future.

To be sure, often this notion can be abused as merely self-aggrandizement, a cover for a nation's own self-interest, as modern political thought has usually insisted on interpreting this idea. Yet, the Old Testament itself saw Israel as not its own. It was rather a way of God, if it were faithful, to instruct the nations in His ways. Consequently, Israel was not its own, nor were its laws purely its own, but as Aquinas was later to elaborate, all was of Yahweh. This is why the other nations were seen as also

10

instruments of Yahweh's teaching and rule. It is also why all the nations are to be judged by Yahweh's rules, not their own self-made ones. All cultures, in other words, have an external criterion of judgment. This is the beginning of any transcendent meaning of human rights.[20]

Mankind, therefore, does not stand in isolation in its own categories of history or rule. All nations, consequently, are to be judged by an absolute standard to which some are more clearly conformed than others, because they follow explicitly or implicitly the laws of Yahweh. There is, then, a real and objective diversity of good and bad in the performance of individuals and nations. The destiny of the nations as such is that they achieve a concrete and good life, in which the scattering effect of original sin will be remedied. Part of this remedying, at least, is to be political.

This is the Old Testament promise, one that precludes, or perhaps transcends its effect on political thought when the same idea was to be seen with Christian eyes, particularly with those of a St. Augustine. But the point here is that the Old Testament notion of the nation in its origins, structure, norms, land, and destiny is one that has, more than any other almost, been the real sense of meaning people have given to their national experiences. There is both an historical and an intellectual reason for this. Historically, the Old Testament was part of the very mind of many of the key founders of Western political notions and ideas.

But intellectually, there is a concreteness to the Jewish tradition that grounds the particular political order of a people, whatever it be, to a transcendent meaning that establishes and founds nations not in any "myth" as in Plato, but in human and divine purpose. The very structure of Western theory is open to this idea, to the universal in the particular, to meaning in the world, meaning that is not vain or self-imposed. What is of value is the relation of this concrete Old Testament history to that context of political institutions formed and framed by classical Greek theory, to the search for the best form of political rule that required a right ordering not just of the political and of human life, but of all this towards something that transcends politics itself.

11

What the Old Testament taught was that all
nations were under Yahweh, whose ultimate rule was
alone capable of filling men's hearts. Israel itself
was not Yahweh, His ways were always His own. Israel
was chosen not for itself alone but, in the end, in
order that through her, should she be willing, be
loyal to her promises, men would have no idols but
Yahweh, particularly no political idols.
Historically, these latter are still the most common
source of deviation from the highest human norms, let
alone from Yahweh himself as their guarantee and
source.

The key issue presented by the New Testament to
the Old was whether a nation, even Israel as a
political entity, bore the context and passage of men
so that ultimate good, beatitude, for which they were
created, would be found in it. St. Augustine, as we
shall see, still stands at the heart of this
question. (See Chapter III) For he admitted that the
classic search for the good and Israel's search for
Yahweh were valid but that now, henceforth, the
relationship of men to God is not directly political.
The result is that, in finding an answer to ethically
and politically posed problems about man's highest
order, the nations, politics, were returned to
themselves, to their temporal order in which the
highest good was not primarily to be discovered, not
to be expected there. Some national contexts are
better than others, to be sure, even in St. Augustine,
who found Rome better than Carthage. That is,
political entities can be classified and judged. And
too, Plato and Aristotle also found some orders of
politics better than others. There was, then, a true,
objective basis of a rational political theory, as
Aquinas was to hold, following Aristotle himself, even
amid revelation.

The Old Testament, consequently, cannot be
considered outside the stream of classical and
scientific political theory. Not only did it form
many of the basic attitudes we have of man and the
world -- their goodness and respective destinies --
but more particularly, it taught that the nations were
responsible for the good and evil which they wrought.
While politics as such does not lead to Yahweh, still
Yahweh is concerned about what men do to each other,
for one another in the nations. Further, the Old
Testament taught that the ultimate good of men was
Yahweh, not anything they themselves could have
produced. This is why Erich Fromm's interpretation of

12

the Old Testament distorts it in the most radical and corrupting of ways. The conclusion in the Old Testament itself was that Yahweh judged the nations for their own sakes, but their own good was His Law, His Being. This, along with the existence of Aristotle's Metaphysics, was a step in the direction of making the nations to be no more than they are.

But it was also, nevertheless, an affirmation that Yahweh's justice, what is even more deeply described as his "steadfast love," is not an abstract category or classification but part of the real fabric of the relation of men and women and their children to each other. The Old Testament leaves us with Israel in subjection and dispersed, with a people whose existence is only guaranteed by the Law and the Book, by the corporate prayers said in Congregation to Yahweh. St. Paul seems to have maintained that Israel will be back, but by this time, St. Paul did not mean a political nation.(Romans, Chapters 9-11) He meant rather those who believed what the Old Testament really taught. The justification of a re-incarnation of Israel is thus one of political philosophy, not theology. And it is interesting that it has been argued mostly on this basis. The theocracy died that Yahweh might live.

Yet, when we have clarified Israel as a product of political theory from Israel as a religion, we must still recognize that there is more to reality than politics, something that Judaeo-Christian tradition knows instinctively -- and even rationally. This is something that it has insisted upon holding against modern absolutizing political theories. In this regard, the remarks of Jean Daniélou, in 1949, are perhaps more worthy of reflection today than when they were first written:

> There can be no doubt that the Jewish problem is fundamentally a theological problem. On this, we are unalterably opposed to racism, which considers it a biological problem. For us, the Jews are not at all inferior biologically, but their race is marked by a mysterious theological destiny. And that is why the Jewish race remains such a problem in the community of nations.[21]

This is why, ultimately, when we deal with politics, we do not deal with the highest of formal science or

13

knowledge open to men. This is why the struggle to
distinguish faith and reason is still at the heart of
any theoretic enterprise, especially political
philosophy.

The legacy of the Old Testament is the judgment
of the nations, the belief that none of them is chosen
unless it observe God's law for men. As Maimonides
said, correct opinion about the Law of God conditions
our judgments about politics. And if all observe the
Law of God, all are chosen. This is, ultimately, what
men have in common, the general that we learned from
the particular in the Old Testament. The Old
Testament, then, is an essential step in that limiting
and understanding of politics that does not, as
Aristotle said, make of it the highest science.

Footnotes:

1. Nothing from the Old Testament appears, for example, in the once widely used Sabine-Thorson <u>A History of Political Theory</u> (Dryden Press, 1973). The Strauss-Cropsey <u>History of Political Philosophy</u> has chapters on Maimonides and Spinoza, but nothing on the Old Testament as such, though, of course, Strauss has written widely in this area. In R. W. and A. J. Carlyle's multivolume <u>History of Medieval Political Theory in the West</u> (Edinburgh, Blackwood, 1970 Edition, V. I) has only passing references. Peter Witonski's multivolume <u>The Wisdom of Conservatism</u> (Arlington House, 1971) has nothing directly on the Old Testament. Michael Foster's <u>Masters of Political Thought</u> (London, Harrup, 1969, V. I) has nothing. James L. Wiser's excellent new <u>Political Philosophy: A History of the Search for Order</u> (Englewood Cliffs, Prentice-Hall, 1983) has nothing. Russell Kirk's <u>The Roots of American Order</u> (LaSalle, Ill., Open Court, 1974), on the other hand, has a considerable amount on the Old Testament, while Mulford Q. Sibley's Chapter, "Politics and Ethics Among the Ancient Hebrews," in his <u>Political Ideas and Ideologies</u>, (New York, Harper, 1970, Chapter I), is quite excellent.

2. Ernest Barker, <u>From Alexander to Constantine</u>, Oxford, Clarendon, 1956.

3. See Charles N. R. McCoy, <u>The Structure of Political Thought</u>, New York, McGraw-Hill, 1963, pp.99-132.

4. See Norman K. Gottwald, "The Impact of Ancient Israel on Our Social World," <u>Theology Digest</u>, Winter, 1977. See Juan Luis Segundo, <u>Liberation of Theology</u>, Maryknoll, Orbis, 1976. See also James V. Schall, <u>Liberation Theology in Latin America</u>, San Francisco, Ignatius Press, 1983; Alfredo Fierro, <u>The Militant Gospel</u>, Maryknoll, Orbis, 1977; Chapter XIII.

5. See Michael Novak, <u>The Spirit of Democratic Capitalism</u>, New York, Simon and Schuster, 1982; George Gilder, <u>Wealth and Poverty</u>, New York, Basic Books, 1982.

6. A. Wildavsky, "What's In It For Us? America's National Interest in Israel," <u>The Middle East Review</u>, Fall, 1977, p.13.

7. Erich Fromm, You Shall Be As Gods: A Radical Interpretation of the Old Testament and Its Tradition, Greenwich, Conn., Fawcett, 1966. See especially Introduction and first two chapters. See James Hitchcock, Secular Humanism, Ann Arbor, Servant, 1983.

8. See Hans Urs von Balthasar, "Christianity as Utopia," Elucidations, Translated by J. Riches, London, SPCK, 1975, pp.192-99.

9. See Leo Strauss, "Jerusalem and Athens," City College Papers, New York, #6, 1967; Matthew Arnold, Culture and Anarchy, Indianapolis, Bobbs-Merrill, 1971. See R. Sacks, "Commentaries on Genesis, Interpretation, 1982.

10. See Max Weber, The Protestant Ethic and the Spirit of Capitalism, London, Allen, 1930; Samuel Eliot Morison and H. S. Commager, Growth of the American Republic, New York, Oxford, 1969, V. I, pp.51-59; The Puritans, Edited by Perry Miller and T. H. Johnson, New York, Harper's, 1963; Edmund S. Morgan, Puritan Political Ideas, Indianapolis, Bobbs-Merrill, 1965.

11. See J. Miranda, Marx and the Bible, Maryknoll, Orbis, 1976.

12. See James V. Schall, "From Catholic 'Social Doctrine' to the 'Kingdom of God on Earth,'" Communio, Winter, 1976.

13. See Paul Demann, Judaism, New York, Hawthorne, 1961 or Bernhard W. Anderson, Understanding the Old Testament, Englewood Cliffs, N.J., Prentice-Hall, 1975, or others in bibliography for a more complete and detailed presentation of the Old Testament thought.

14. Christopher Dawson wrote: "Nowhere is this idea of divine revelation so strongly expressed or so clearly identified with the tradition of culture as in the case of Israel. For here the whole social form and historical destiny of the people had been imposed on them by the Word of Yahweh, which was not merely, as in other cases, a sacred tradition of learning, but a way of life embodied in a moral law and a sacred history which set it apart from all the other peoples of the ancient world.

From the beginning, the Jewish tradition stood

16

out in uncompromising hostility to the religious traditions of the more civilized peoples that surrounded the Jews. While the rest of the ancient world was being integrated into one great society by the influence of Hellenistic culture and education and Roman government and law, one little people obstinately refused to be assimilated. The stronger the external pressure of the world society, the more intense was the consciousness of the Jewish people to a unique destiny which set them apart from the nations." The Formation of Christendom, New York, Sheed and Ward, 1967, p.68.

15. In his 1939 Address, "The Ancient Classics in a Modern Democracy," Samuel Eliot Morison wrote: "Ohio is far from Rome; but all good roads to Ohio come from Rome, and ultimately from Greece. One road to the Buckeye State leads through Virginia, where our early statesmen read their classics in the original tongue; Virginia, where the Father of American Democracy also founded a great university where those worthy of it might receive the precious gifts of the past, and return them many-fold to America. Another road -- the one that I took -- leads from Rome to Ohio through New England, where the Puritans brought Hellenic culture with the Bible, and, in their days of poverty and struggle, provided a classical training for an aristocracy of piety and learning. And a third Roman road led to Ohio through Scotland and Princeton, where the grim Scots Covenanters, distrustful as they were of ritual and superstition, clung through the Reformation and the eighteenth century to their classical heritage, as an essential ingredient of a Christian education." New York, Oxford, 1939, p.25. See above, Footnote #10.

16. See Jacques Maritain, "The Mystery of Israel," in The Social and Political Philosophy of Jacques Maritain, Edited by J. Evans and L. Ward, New York, Scribner's, 1955, pp.195-217.

17. See James V. Schall, "The Cosmos and Christianity," in Redeeming the Time, New York, Sheed and Ward, 1968; "On Taking Possession of the Whole Universe," Christianity and Politics, Boston, St. Paul Editions, 1981.

18. Discussions of contract appear in Professor Rawls, in C. B. Macpherson. The notion of a social contract is also prominent in certain European discussions of labor contracts. See Dennis J.

17

McCarthy, <u>Old Testament Covenant</u>, Oxford, Blackwell, 1972.

19. See the discussion on promises in Hannah Arendt's <u>On Revolution</u>, New York, Viking, 1965, p.169 ff. Also a further discussion in <u>The Human Condition</u>, Garden City, Doubleday Anchor, 1959.

20. See James V. Schall, "Culture and Human Rights" <u>America</u>, January 7, 1978.

21. J. Daniélou, <u>The Salvation of the Nations</u>, Notre Dame, University of Notre Dame Press, 1962, p. 81.

<u>Readings</u>:

The literature on the Old Testament is indeed vast. Few can manage it without a proper course or guide. Both for academic, cultural, and religious reasons, a good course in this area ought to be a normal part of higher education. The following are books which will give some adequate overall view of this area:

William Foxwell Albright, <u>From the Stone Age to Christianity</u>, Garden City, Doubleday Image, 1954.

Bernhard W. Anderson, <u>Understanding the Old Testament</u>, Englewood Cliffs, N.J., Prentice-Hall, 1975.

John Bright, <u>A History of Israel</u>, Philadelphia, Fortress Press, 1981.

Martin Buber, <u>The Kingship of God</u>, London, Allen and Unwin, 1967.

Martin Hengel, <u>Judaism and Hellenism</u>, Philadelphia, Fortress Press, 1974.

Abraham Heschel, <u>The Prophets</u>, New York, Harper's, 1962.

Leonard Johnston, <u>History of Israel</u>, New York, Sheed and Ward, 1964.

John McKenzie, <u>A Two-Edged Sword</u>, Milwaukee, Bruce, 1956.

H. H. Rowley, The Re-Discovery of the Old Testament, New York, Books For Libraries (Westminster), 1969.

Seymour Siegel, "The Nation-State and Social Order in the Perspective of Judaism," in Trialogue of the Abrahamic Faiths, Edited by I. Raji al Faruqi, Papers Presented to the Islamic Studies Group of the American Academy of Religion, International Institute of Islamic Thought, 1402/1982, pp. 29-36.

Roland de Vaux, Ancient Israel: Its Life and Institutions, New York, McGraw-Hill, 1961.

Bruce Vawter, The Conscience of Israel, New York, Sheed and Ward, 1961.

Robert R. Wilson, Prophecy and Society in Ancient Israel, Philadelphia, Fortress Press, 1973.

Ernest G. Wright, The Old Testament Against Its Environment, London, SCM Press, 1960.

To consult particular passages in scripture or themes, the following reference sources are most helpful:

Theology Dictionary of the Old Testament; Interpreters' Dictionary of the Bible; Peake's Commentary on the Bible; The Jerome Biblical Commentary; Sacramentum Mundi.

Selected readings from the Old Testament more pertinent to history of political thought:

1. Genesis, Ch.1-4.

2. Deuteronomy, Ch.5-7.

3. Amos.

4. Isaiah Ch.1, 6, 40-45, 65-66.

5. Psalms, 1, 8, 74-76, 86, 89, 98, 104, 119, 139, 145, 149, 150.

6. Ezechiel, Ch.33-34.

7. Job.

8. <u>Jeremiah</u>, Ch.32-33.

CHAPTER II

THE DEATH OF CHRIST AND POLITICAL THEORY

"The just man who is thought unjust
will be scourged, racked, bound -- will have
his eyes burnt out; and, at last, after
suffering every kind of evil, he will be
impaled." -- [Glaucon, The Republic,
#361e-62a.]

"Quod scripsi, scripsi." -- "What I
have written, I have written". -- [Pontius
Pilate, Roman Procurator, John, 19:22.]

The transition from the Old Testament to the New
Testament is both a continuity and a radical
departure. The relation of Yahweh to Jesus
constitutes the first and most fundamental issue that
Christianity presents, and it is out of this that its
own uniqueness arises. The question to be discussed
above all here is not so much the validity of the
claims of Christianity but their consequences, their
effects on political theory. Thus, when the ideas of
medieval theory are analyzed, they will have little
meaning apart from the content of Christianity itself
and the kind of reasoning that it fosters and
stimulates. The faith and reason discussions of
medieval theology were not merely two separate
categories but reciprocal influences, the one on the
other.[1]

However important be the revelational traditions
of Israel, Islam, and Christianity, still, political
theory is, by all accounts, a discipline peculiar to
Western civilization, having its specific origin in
the Greek city-state, particularly in Plato's account
of the death of Socrates, with the resultant writing
of The Republic. This essential and first document of
all political theory asked whether the just man could
live in the best state. Socrates, we know, fought in
the Peloponnesian War and died by virtue of a public
trial in 399 B.C.

He died, furthermore, by his own testimony
obedient to the laws of the civil community in which

21

he chose to live his life, as he tells us in the
Crito. By this very act, of course, he condemned the
unjust use of Athenian law and stigmatized forever
those 281 hapless jurors who voted for his guilt and
death, as we read in _The Apology of Plato_. Socrates,
moreover, died calmly because he believed in the
immortality of his own soul, because he was by no
means sure that an already aging man would not be much
better off in the Isles of the Blessed, as _The
Republic_ itself intimated, though he was sure that to
do evil was wrong.

Political theory has continued to reflect on the
place of Socrates at its heart. But it has paid
relatively little attention to the second great
execution at the hands of the ancient state, that is,
Christ's crucifixion according to the procedures of
Roman Law. This latter death is and remains also one
of our essential political legacies. The Romans, whom
Bertrand de Jouvenel called the most irreligious of
people, required that the crime for which a man was
executed be placed on the cross for capital offences.
In Jesus' case, the ostensible crime was a political
one: The King of the Jews.

Pilate, the local Roman procurator, or governor,
however, tried with some persistence to avoid being
forced to this execution. He himself even washed his
hands of it all, as he himself complained in one of
the world's most symbolic acts. (_Matthew_, 27:24) And
all the available evidence shows that whatever this
Jesus meant by his claim to kingship, it did not
include the political crime of inciting to rebellion
against the Romans. The man was legally and ethically
innocent. Pilate clearly sensed this.(_John_, 18:38)
The Roman governor felt that Christ was delivered up
for spite. The trial charges against Jesus were
obviously fraudulent.

Nevertheless, the local situation was such that
Pilate was "boxed in" against his will. His desperate
ploy of offering Barabbas, who really was involved in
an "insurrection," failed also. So the Procurator
allowed the crucifixion to take place under the
command of a centurion according to the demands of
Jesus' betrayers and antagonists, who threateningly
warned Pilate that to do otherwise would make him no
friend of Caesar's.(_John_, 19:12) Pilate knew his
personal position, never strong, would be further
undermined if word got back to Rome that he failed to
suppress a petty zealot preaching domestic rebellion

in his territory. Thus, the tragic event played itself out to its bitter end, until it was "consummated," as the Man on the Cross' last words indicated. (John, 19:30)

The theoretical neglect of the execution of Jesus by subsequent and especially contemporary political theory has been curious.[2] We can look practically in vain for any adequate effort to probe its significance in modern political science journals. This is doubly strange, in a way, since the issue, under the aegis of political theology, is a very lively one among biblical scholars prodded by some strands of theology and ideology. These latter, often, are not aware of the central tradition of political theory and its key issues in relation to the death of Christ. (See Chapter XIII)

We could argue, to be sure, that the death of Jesus is irrelevant for theory, so that the reason for its neglect is obvious. Yet, that is already too facile an explanation. Is there, we may wonder, a theoretical reason for this very neglect? What, in other words, would it take to account for the trial and death of Jesus within the evolution of political theory? Can there be something permanent here which defines how one is to react to politics in any age? And does a failure to come to terms with the death of Jesus by crucifixion reveal something fundamental about the way political philosophy has developed within our tradition? The latter, it would seem, is more likely to be the case.

The problem that Plato had with the death of Socrates by hemlock was that the best man died by judgment of the best existing state. No man, of course, ever called the Roman Empire the best state, though it was better than most. To be sure, Polybius and Cicero did think the Roman Republic was the best theoretical state, a most pertinent shift away from Greek thought.[3] But the Empire, in spite of Vergil, was an imposed, often ruthless order, a necessary "peace" into which Jesus was born in the time of Augustus. Jesus himself, as a member of a subject minority population, many of whom still wanted their fleeting independence, did not deny that even Caesar had things to be rendered to him. Indeed, this granting to Caesar genuine authority -- Christians always thought in concrete, personal terms -- may well have been Jesus' most revolutionary political contribution.(Matthew, 22:21) He even paid taxes which

everyone hated. He in fact had a tax-collector as a
disciple.(Matthew, 9:9-13; 22:15-22)

Moreover, to Pontius Pilate, Jesus acknowledged
the Roman governor's authority.(John 19:10-11) Already
here, we are aware of a classical Greek reflection
about the naturalness of the polis. We sense too the
tremendous future this question of the legitimacy of
political authority is to have, largely as a direct
result of Jesus' acknowledgement that Caesar and
Pilate had in fact "authority." So the conversation of
Jesus and Pilate at the interrogation was of no mere
passing significance. Jesus' very response, "You
would have no power over me were it not given to you
from above," suggests authority and the limits of
power.

What are we to do when legitimate power is
transgressed? Peter had a sword and used it. Yet, he
was told to put it away.(Matthew, 26:52-54) So Jesus
did not deny a right to the Romans to execute
revolutionaries against the Empire. And like Socrates,
Jesus did not seek to escape His fate once He was
condemned. Indeed, Peter was even called "Satan" --
later in the Book of Revelation, the state which
claims absolute allegiance is considered satanical --
when he once tried to forbid Christ from carrying out
His judgment to die.(Matthew, 16-23; Revelation,
Chapters 12 and 13)

Thus, the death of Jesus is at the official hands
of the Romans, at the instigation of a few, though
certainly not all, prominent Jewish officials, who had
the greater guilt, as Jesus told Pilate.(John, 19:11)
Many in the mob even shouted to Pilate, "We have no
king but Caesar." But Jesus himself on the cross
whispered that even these, presumably Pilate, Caiphas,
Annas, the actual participants in the mob, did not
really know what they were doing.(Luke, 23:24) The key
word became "forgiveness." This implied acknowledging
a crime as such, not making an evil act to be good.

Hannah Arendt was later to point out in The Human
Condition that this is Jesus' real contribution to
politics. Forgiveness alone can stop the cycle of
vengeance connected with justice, that endless cycle
that was in the background of all the great Greek
tragedies from Aeschlyus to Sophocles and Euripides.
We are, in any case, left with a feeling about the
unjustness of this ancient trial, the trumped up
nature of this much meditated event. Yet, at the same

24

time, at a deeper level, we are told it was a _felix culpa_, that it somehow "needs be," even in some sense for our own well-being and destiny. It is a result, as we shall suggest later, which brings up and resolves the mystery of evil in politics and in the cosmos from a Christian point of view.[4] (See Chapter VI)

Political theory, then, has ever asked with Aristotle in the Third Book of _The Politics_ about the good citizen and the best state. Aristotle's vigorous mind was quite conscious that most men did not live under the best or even under good constitutions, each of which, good or bad, had to be classified. Yet, Aristotle found some worth, some sense of "justice" in all states but perhaps the most corrupt tyrannies, which in retrospect sound like nothing so much as that awesome 20th Century invention, the totalitarian state, the state which, like the beast in the _Book of Revelation_, (Chapter 13), demands even our worship, even our total being.

Aristotle too placed the whole ethical-political part of his theory under the active pursuit of happiness, the search for the highest activity of the highest faculty on the highest object in a complete life, as he defined in Book X of _The Ethics_. This led him to distinguish our mortal, political happiness, the kind that we can perhaps achieve in this life, from the speculative virtues which lead to a higher, more personal happiness. To this latter, we should devote all our efforts if we can. Indeed, the very polis existed for the leisure to make this possible. Aristotle was the first to recognize, in his theory of revolution and in his metaphysics, that men who do not have a right order and thought about the structure of the cosmos will be likely to turn on it and destroy the kind of polis, even the kind of reality that is capable of being lived by men on this earth. "Men start revolutionary changes for reasons connected with their private lives," he ominously told us. (1308b21-22)

Later Christian reflection on _Genesis_ and certain strands of Stoic thought were aware that something was wrong with man, though it was rather a delicate and important intellectual effort to define just what it was. Things ought to go right, yet they did not. Paul the Apostle complained about not being able to do what he would do. Thucydides, Plato, and Aristotle likewise never doubted this unsettling tendency, so

that a complete political theory as an intellectual
process had to account for the deaths of Socrates and
of Christ. That is, political theory needed to
confront both the worst and the best, even the best
possible, in politics. Even a Plato had to write The
Laws to tell us of the second best state, since it was
highly doubtful even to him that the best state could
exist among us. Cicero's De Officiis was about the
best morality while claiming to be about the second
best. (See Chapter VIII)

Yet, this perfect state, happiness, must exist
somewhere, it would seem. This consideration of the
best constituted the very structure of the human mind
reflecting on itself in its experience of the world.
In a sense, political theory and practice almost
seemed at times to tear themselves and the very world
apart in this search for the best and most noble, for
the remedy of this pristine flaw that killed a
Socrates and crucified a Christ. It seemed as if man
should be able to construct the world such that events
"could" not happen. The question remained, at what
cost could this be done?

The account of the Fall in Genesis, furthermore,
suggested to the theoretical mind that the present
unhappy state of disorder was concentrated on the pain
connected with childbirth, on physical labor,
property, and coercive government.(Genesis, 3:16-22)
These things somehow were not "meant" to be, yet they
were. Political thought from the guardians of Plato
to socialism and genetic engineering betrays an origin
here in the search for a method to remove these
"consequences" in property, genes, state structure, or
work. Thereby, theory seeks to restore man's loss or
to gain a future perfect status.[5] Professor
Macpherson, in his Democratic Theory, has even tried
to combine Aristotelian theory of the potencies of the
soul and supposit with Marx's parousial claim to full
human development as a final, political project.[6]

In any case, it seemed quite likely to a St. Paul
as well as to a St. Augustine later that the state was
primarily a remedial institution, that it was designed
to correct or control something that was already wrong
in man himself, that it would indeed eventually
disappear but not as a result of a political process
or revolution in this life. So for St. Paul, even a
Nero had some authority, as did the Tiberius under
whose reign and authority Jesus himself was ultimately
executed. St. Paul could, then, speak of the law

26

punishing our transgressions, even as God's way of punishing us. (See Romans, Chapter 13; 1 Peter, 2:13-15) He too saw all authority as coming from God, even though it could be abused and was. Christians were to stay out of law courts, settle their own controversies.(1 Corinthians, 6:1-8) The state was legitimate in certain areas because men did violate one another.(Romans, 13:4)

So Christian thought did have a place for the state, even the Empire which persecuted. Yet, it insisted on knowing what things belonged to God. No state could forbid Christians to preach what they were told. Over this, the state had no competence. "We must obey God rather than men," St. Peter affirmed in Acts, (5:27) So why could Christians do something that no previous or subsequent political thought succeeded in doing? The key is perhaps from St. Paul in his address to the Synagogue in Antioch in Pisidia:

> For those who live in Jerusalem and their ruler, because they did not recognize him nor understand the utterances of the prophets which are read every Sabbath, fulfilled these by condemning him. Though they could charge him with nothing deserving of death, yet they asked Pilate to have him killed. But God raised him from the dead .... (Acts, 13:27-29)

From this, it is clear that Jesus, the man unjustly condemned to death, was also held to be raised from the dead. This necessarily meant that the whole problematic of the unjustness of Pilate's act was transformed. There is no understanding the impact of Christianity in political theory without grasping the tremendous consequences of this result.

The passage cited above from Acts, about obeying God not men, furthermore, cannot be understood in terms of political theory without a return to the last book of The Republic of Plato wherein Socrates astonished his listeners in one of the most remarkable passages in all philosophical literature. This contained his belief in the immortality of the soul as a political question, the question of how perfect justice is to be achieved when it does not exist in any actual state.[7] The point is that political theory, as The Republic grasped, must account for particular individuals and not merely general happiness or common good.

27

This realization, then, is the ultimate significance of the particular kind of death Jesus underwent on the cross, how His death's meaning related to and differed from that of Socrates. It is this just man, Jesus, who reaches resurrection, the ultimate happiness to which the race has constantly felt itself called. The immortality of Socrates deals with the question of how rewards and punishments are dealt with when the _polis_ fails to incorporate all justice in individual cases. Resurrection accomplishes that final personal happiness which political theory initially proposes for man.

The death of Jesus, therefore, signifies that the content or context of this happiness is _not_ a political happiness nor an historical political achievement, since the just man, Christ or Socrates, was killed. It is not something general or in a vague future, for it is this Jesus Who died and is risen in the scriptures and creeds. Christianity has believed, in contrast to Plato, in the resurrection of Jesus, not merely the immortality of the soul, as with Socrates. The two, however, are not contradictory. Greek immortality became the Christian way of maintaining personal continuity until the general resurrection.

Furthermore, human life is a moral enterprise and an act of God so that this world does have significance as connecting this human race with the project of ultimate happiness as sketched out in the first book of The Ethics. But in contrast too, this happiness is not fully created by man for himself, even though he must authentically act to achieve it. God is the measure of all things, as Plato affirmed in The Laws.(716a) The political consequences of this are that the Parousia, happiness, and its attributes are not directly the result of a political process in time. Politics is thus free to be politics and not religion and metaphysics. On the other hand, as I will suggest in a later discussion, when this Christian consequence is not accepted, the political project will come to be an effort by politics to reproduce in a kind of contorted fashion the very same results found in the doctrine of the resurrection. (See Chapter X)

Is there any contemporary or abiding "consequence" then to all of this? Anyone who keeps up with contemporary political philosophy cannot but

28

be aware that a new breeze is blowing across the previously barren plains of government and political science departments, themselves too closely aligned to the scientific and behavioral methods which left the field of political thought so empty of content. As Professor Kenneth Minogue has written: "It is a striking illustration of the ups-and-downs of intellectual fashion that political theorists are now cocks of the walk."[8] And Professor Michael Nelson has found plenty with which to answer the question: "What's Wrong with Political Science?"[9] Political science as "behavior," as how governments "work," seemed to leave questions of justice unanswered. And we live in a time when justice, especially "distributive justice," is astonishingly in vogue, both in civil law and political modernization theory. This emphasis on justice is seen as the answer to the neglected problems of political theory.

All of this, of course, leads to John Rawls and his Theory of Justice.[10] In the light of what has been said of the death of Christ in political theory, a brief comment is worth making. Professor Finnis, in an excellent analysis, has noted how Rawls seems to bypass any of the earlier classical discussions of distributive justice as present in the Christian tradition.[11] Too, the popularity of Rawls especially outside political science circles, as Professor George Carey remarked, is rather perplexing.[12] On the surface and by title, Professor Rawls' book bears the same title as Plato's Republic -- "On Justice." In Rawls' ideal state of perfect justice, there is no room for a Christ or even a Socrates, nor especially for their deaths.

Indeed, there is no room for any concrete human beings at all, as Rawls' justice is even more abstract than the Platonic forms. In effect, he "created" a world as it ought to be, so that we might know what a God "ought" to have done had He wanted "perfect" justice.[13] In a subtle sense, this avoids the problem of evil and its relation to the best possible world, questions essential to medieval and all political thought. (See Chapter V) And so, Rawls' prospectus is not unlike original justice in Paradise before the Fall, a kind of might-have-been which was not.

Such speculation, to be sure, may perhaps be useful just as Christian speculations on life before the Fall were valuable. The difficulty with this, however, as the multitude of studies spawned by Rawls-type proposals suggest, is that distributive justice easily lends itself to ideological theories coming out of the intellectual left, itself strongly bearing the mark of secularized this-worldly eschatology. And this intellectual mood proposes the just state as a positive goal at the end of a historical, revolutionary process effected by exclusively human endeavor.[14] This was how Erich Fromm wanted to interpret the Old Testament. Much of liberation theology wants to interpret the New Testament in the same way. And the absolutist interpretation of the Greek humanist tradition that "man is the measure of all things" has tended in this direction since the Enlightenment, through Marxism, to secular humanism of many hues. (See Chapter I)

In this context, therefore, the execution of Christ, the precise kind of salvation He offers to men, one not "political," one not economic, nor technological, nor psychological, either in mode or achievement, needs to be understood in the context of Oscar Cullmann's remarks on how the <u>Book of Revelation</u> finally identified the state with satanism whenever the state claimed full divinity, however this be described. "It remains a most noteworthy fact that according to the Jewish, as to the early Christian outlook, the totalitarian state is precisely the classic form of the Devil's manifestation on Earth."[15] And this is why, as we shall discuss subsequently, the notion of "hell" again needs to be brought up in political theory. For without it, the worst possible state too becomes identified with ultimate perdition, a result that enables us to pretend to act "justly" and absolutely against existing human beings on the grounds that we can identify them with evil because they "cause" the ultimate evil. (See Chapter V)

Laszek Kolakowski, in a remarkable essay, has indicated the importance for political theory of retaining a consideration of evil among us in view of the political consequences of theories which propose its removal. Kolakowski emphasized the importance of the anti-Pelagian polemic in the early church to establish that evil is not absolutely inherent in the structure of the world, hence no god of evil, the position of <u>Genesis</u>. But evil is not something merely contingent, something that can ultimately be removed in Christian thought.

In Christian thought the damnation of
the devil and the concept of original sin
are the most precise forms to cover the
denial of the contingent character of evil.
I think that denial is of extreme importance
for our culture, but that we can also
discern in the Christian world a strong
temptation to abandon that position to rally
about the optimist tradition of the
Enlightenment which believes in the final
reconciliation of all that is, in a
harmonious, ultimate finality ....

The two ideas which are at the very
heart of Christian culture -- namely, that
humanity has been fundamentally saved by the
coming of Christ and that, since man has
been chased from paradise, every human being
is fundamentally condemned if we consider
him in his natural state, without the help
of grace -- ought to be considered together
to avoid a careless optimism or the despair
that can follow when we consider these two
ideas separately.

... There is nothing in the teaching of
the Church that formally excludes the
possibility that hell be empty, but nothing
which permits us to affirm that it does not
exist. The existence of the devil confirms
without ambiguity that evil constitutes a
permanent element in the world....[16]

Christ died for all, not just the elect, but the hope
of universal reconciliation as such is vain. Thus,
while it may seem presumptuous to speak of original
sin and the devil in political theory, let alone hell,
still, as Kolakowski intimated, it is precisely in
such areas that modern ideological, historical
projects are affirmed or rejected. And it is here
that the execution of Christ and the project of pure
justice are pertinent.

Justice, I think, is not an especially likeable
virtue, and, as I shall later point out, it must be
considered in a way a "terrible" virtue in all its
forms. (See Chapter VII) This is why the death of
Christ lies close to the heart of political theory,
because the best man, the Son of God Himself, was
executed by the state. This means that human justice
is not and cannot be enough. The real issue is not

31

the erection of a state in which such things could not happen, even if that were possible, but what is the meaning and destiny of the actual individual persons, no matter what the state, even the best. This, too, is why Christ is said to have died for "all," the just and the unjust, upon whom, as He once remarked, the rain equally falls, because it is the actual being and worth of each person that ultimately count. (Matthew, 5:4; Luke, 12:7)

We cannot really begin to approach the problem of real human persons, then, if we propose our justice as some project for installing right order in the future or if we conceive it as a pure idea. Probably until certain Christian Marxist-type movements came into vogue, ones coming out of the Enlightenment project of which Kolakowski spoke, no Christian, at least, ever thought justice was enough. True, the medieval Joachim of Flora tradition, which in a basic sense also was behind the Enlightenment optimism, did make the "last things" the product of a this-world evolution. But this was heretical to the medieval mind, and rightly so.[17] Besides, for Joachim, what the Spirit's Age, the "Third Age," was to bring forth was charity, not justice.

The central point is, then, the classical problem of the "common good." That is, how is the general human good and happiness for the collectivity also related to personal, individual happiness, to human uniqueness? This dilemma cannot be solved by politics if the best man is executed by the best state, or even by the average state of the Romans. The theoretical meaning of the execution of Christ, on the human side, is that ultimate happiness is achievable by any person, in any society, even in the most corrupt, but not as the result of a political action. Just as Socrates saved and condemned the Laws by obeying them, so Christ saved proper political life by freeing it from any claim to be able itself to restructure man in this life to achieve a happiness made exclusively by man, but not the one promised to him, the higher one of the Kingdom not of this world, of which Christ spoke to Pilate. The negative side of this is, likewise, rejected. That is, the optimistic ideological project to remove the consequences of original sin -- property, family, government, work -- will not remove real evil, but it will only recast it into other forms.

Aristotle had said that politics does not make

32

man to be man. Modern political theory since Machiavelli has, in a sense, been the effort to make a new kind of man, to give him his own "justice" and being. The execution of Christ puts the various theories of justice in their place, back into mere politics, the practical science that deals with real men, the mortals, in their life, their complete life. Justice is still rightly considered to be important. Christian medieval texts are full of it. But its very limits made the effort uncritically to universalize it implicitly an attack on the kind of being that man in fact was. Justice remains the most tempting virtue because, as Aristotle said, it is that moral virtue that requires others for its perfection. (1129a1-1138b12) What the crucifixion of Christ by the Roman state suggests, however, is that something more than justice is required for us even to be mostly just. It is at this point that metaphysics and grace meet political theory, even in its own order.

The classical Christian discussion of this is Aquinas' Treatise on Law, in which he asked about the reasons why divine law was needed over natural law.(I-II, 91, 4) Ironically, each of his reasons argued a position making a better political state than would otherwise have been possible. The suggestion is that political theory cannot be itself, even in its own order, without the consequences of the crucifixion of Jesus. Anyone who has followed carefully the controversy over the very nature of classical political theory as it evolved about the names of men like Leo Strauss and Eric Voegelin will realize that the thesis is at least tenable that political theory has not in fact been itself in modern times. (See Chapters VII and IX)

And so Glaucon was right about the fate of the just man. In the end, Pontius Pilate was not ultimately wrong in leaving the inscription on the cross as it was. Quod scripsi, scripsi. Jesus of Nazareth, King of the Jews -- the political inscription that restored politics to itself, by freeing it from claims to be itself a theology or a metaphysics.

Footnotes:

1. See Joseph Pieper, Scholasticism, New York, Pantheon, 1960; Etienne Gilson, Reason and Revelation in the Middle Ages, New York, Scribner's, 1938.

2. Salvador de Madariaga has suggested that each student in our modern universities, on reaching maturity, be given a copy of two books, one containing the account of the death of Socrates, the other the death of Christ. See his "Europe of the Four Karls," The Tablet, London, June 23, 1973, pp. 580-81. See also William R. Wilson, The Execution of Jesus, New York, Scribner's, 1970; Ellis Rivkin, What Crucified Jesus?, Nashville, Abingdon, 1984.

3. See Frederich D. Wilhelmsen's discussion of Cicero in his Christianity and Political Philosophy, Athens, University of Georgia Press, 1978.

4. See Hannah Arendt, The Human Condition, New York, Doubleday Anchor, 1959, pp. 236-42.

5. Igor Shafarevich, The Socialist Phenomenon, New York, Harper and Row, 1980.

6. C. B. Macpherson, Democratic Theory, New York, Oxford University Press, 1973.

7. Socrates' discourse on immortality in the Phaedo on his last day was to the same effect.

8. Kenneth Minogue, Encounter, London, August, 1977.

9. Michael Nelson, "What's Wrong with Political Science?" The Washington Monthly, September, 1977.

10. John Rawls, A Theory of Justice, Cambridge, Harvard University Press, 1971.

11. See Professor Finnis' analysis of views on justice in The Month, London, September, 1976; see John Finnis, Natural Law and Natural Right, New York, Oxford University Press, 1980.

12. See George Carey's remarks on Rawls in Modern Age, Fall, 1976.

13. Allan Bloom, in his famous interpretative

34

essay in his translation of The Republic of Plato, New York, Basic Books, 1971, has suggested that Plato himself was trying to warn us of the dangers of this very enterprise.

14. Joseph Sobran has perceptively followed out the anti-family implications of some of these propositions in his Single Issues, New York, Human Life Press, 1983.

15. Oscar Cullman, The State in the New Testament, New York, Scribner's, 1956, p. 74; Heinrich Schlier,"The State in the New Testament," The Relevance of the New Testament, New York, Herder, 1968, pp. 215-38.

16. Laszek Kolakowski, "Le diablé peut-il être sauvé?" Contrepoint, Paris, #20, 1976, pp. 130-31. See also his, Religion, New York, Oxford University Press, 1983.

17. See Bernard McGinn, Visions of the End: Apocalyptic Traditions in the Middle Ages, New York, Columbia University Press, 1979. pp. 126-41.

Readings:

The literature of and about the New Testament is likewise vast. An understanding of New Testament terms and influence is necessary to grasp the historical culture of the West. Below are listed a few studies regarding religion and politics, with some more general introductory texts, and essential New Testament texts bearing political import.

C. K. Barrett, "The New Testament Doctrine of Church and State," New Testament Essays, London, SPCK, 1972, pp. 1-19.

Oscar Cullmann, Jesus and the Revolutionaries, New York, Harper's, 1970.

Oscar Cullmann, The State in the New Testament, New York, Scribner's, 1956.

C. H. Dodd, "The Historical Problem of the Death of Jesus," More New Testament Studies, Grand Rapids, Eerdmans, 1968, pp. 84-101.

André Dumas, Political Theology and the Life of the Church, Philadelphia, Westminster, 1977.

Jacques Ellul, <u>Theological Foundations of the Law</u>, New York, Seabury, 1969.

Joseph Fitzmyer, "Paul and the Law," <u>The Advance of the Gospel</u>, New York, Crossroad, 1981, pp. 186-201.

René Laurentin, <u>Liberation, Development, Salvation</u>, Maryknoll, Orbis, 1972.

William Lillie, "The New Testament Attitude to the State," <u>Studies in New Testament Ethics</u>, Philadelphia, Westminster, 1961, pp. 82-92.

John L. McKenzie, "The Church and the State," <u>The Power and the Wisdom</u>, Milwaukee, Bruce, 1965, pp. 233-51.

Richard J. Mouw, <u>Politics and the Biblical Drama</u>, Grand Rapids, Eerdmans, 1976.

Francis Murphy, <u>Politics and the Early Christian</u>, New York, Desclee, 1967.

Reinhold Niebuhr, <u>Christianity and Power Politics</u>, New York, Scribner's, 1952.

Alan Richardson, <u>The Political Christ</u>, Philadelphia, Westminster, 1973.

James V. Schall, <u>Christianity and Politics</u>, Boston, St. Paul Edition, 1981.

A. N. Sherwin-White, <u>Roman Society and Law in the New Testament</u>, Oxford, Clarendon, 1963.

Heinrich Schlier, "The State in the New Testament," <u>The Relevance of the New Testament</u>, New York, Herder, 1968, pp. 215-38.

David Stanley, <u>Jesus in Gethsemane</u>, New York, Paulist, 1980.

General Introduction:

Joseph Bonsirven, <u>Theology of the New Testament</u>, Westminster, Md., Newman, 1963.

Hans Conzelmann, <u>An Outline of the Theology of the New Testament</u>, New York, Harper's, 1968.

Reginald Fuller, The Foundations of New Testament Christology, New York, Scribner's, 1965.

Jacques Guillet, Themes of the Bible, Notre Dame, University of Notre Dame Press, 1960.

Edwyn Hoskyns and N. Davey, The Riddle of the New Testament, London, Faber and Faber, 1931.

Walter Kasper, Jesus the Christ, New York, Paulist, 1976.

Rudolf Schnachenburg, New Testament Theology Today, New York, Herder, 1963.

Alfred Wikenhauser, New Testament Introduction, New York, Herder, 1960.

Theological Dictionary of the New Testament; Interpreters' Dictionary of the Bible; Peake's Commentary on the Bible; Jerome Biblical Commentary are useful for further study of the New Testament.

New Testament passages pertinent to politics:
1) Account of the trial and death of Jesus, especially in Matthew, Ch. 26 and 27; John, Ch. 13-19.
2) Matthew, 22, 15-22; 25:31-46; Ch. 5.
3) Romans, Ch. 2 and 13.
4) Luke, 10:25-37.
5) I Corinthians, Ch. 13 and 15.
6) Colossians, Ch. 1.
7) Philemon.
8) James.
9) I Peter, 2:13-17.
10) First Epistle of John.
11) Revelation, Ch. 13 and 21.
12) Acts, 3:11-26; 4:13-22; 4:32-37; 17:16-33; 22:22-29; 23:26-35; 27.

CHAPTER III

ST. AUGUSTINE AND CHRISTIAN POLITICAL PHILOSOPHY

But if we discard this (Cicero's) definition of a people, and, assuming another, say, that a people is an assemblage of reasonable beings bound together by a common agreement as to the objects of their love, then, in order to discover the character of any people, we have only to observe what they love. Yet whatever it loves, if only it is an assemblage of reasonable beings and not of beasts, and is bound together by an agreement as to the objects of love, it is reasonably called a people; and it will be a superior people in proportion as it is bound together by higher interests, inferior in proportion as it is bound together by lower. -- [St. Augustine, The City of God, Bk. XIX, Ch. 24.]

The revolutionary is a man with a programme or an ideology, which he seeks to realize. It is very easy to slip from eschatological hope directed to the coming Kingdom into revolutionary strategy directed to the establishment of a socialist society, without being conscious of the gulf between the divine act which alone establishes the one and the human work which builds the other. St. Augustine's repudiation of the classical 'politics of perfection' was, in effect, a repudiation of any hope of resolving the tensions inherent in fallen society through human means. -- [R. A. Markus, Saeculum: History and Society in the Theology of St. Augustine, Cambridge, At the University Press, 1970. pp. 170-71.]

The Old Testament and the Gospel accounts of the death of Christ have a life and import of their own. The Jewish tradition has a vigor and autonomy remaining independent of Christianity throughout Western history until today. The Christian tradition, which understands itself also to hold the special character of the Old Testament, looks on the world in a specific, intelligible way. Both of these traditions concentrate on man's personal dignity and worth as this is founded in a relationship to God. At the origins of the scriptural way of looking at man, however, was also a need, both political and intellectual, to confront and distinguish itself from the Greek and Roman sources of intellectual life.

Jewish and Christian thinkers, then, did this both independently with regard to their own traditions and in relation to each other, which the Islamic tradition was also to do in its turn. Western civilization, as Christopher Dawson remarked in The Making of Europe, is composed of the four streams of Greek intellectual and artistic life, Roman law and administration, the Christian Church with its Old Testament relationship, and the barbarian peoples with their own customs.[1] The drama of Jewish thought, as well as of the Eastern and Western (Greek and Latin) Christian traditions, was the degree to which they could integrate revelation and reason, experience and faith, without disloyalty to the uniqueness of scripture or to the legal and intellectual positions of the culture.[2]

Medieval political philosophy, in particular, in addition to its own unique experience caused by this tension of faith and reason, is the arena in which the classical blends in with these sources of revelation among the peoples especially of northern Europe.[3] In this sense, St. Augustine and St. Thomas Aquinas are of fundamental importance, since they stand not just as proponents of their own cultural solution, but of the universal issue of truth itself. Like the Greeks, they do not propose merely to be addressing themselves to their own times or culture, but to the human mind itself, wherever it appears.

Understanding the particular contributions of each, therefore, is one of the essential exercises of political theory as such. For the latter is that aspect of philosophy which will ultimately decide whether, in a given polity, anything but politics will be permitted space and freedom. That there be something other than a "political" definition of truth, ironically, requires, in practice, a polity and a justification for it, which do not presume that a polity is itself alone capable of defining truth.

Some four hundred years stand between the death

of Socrates and the death of Christ (399 B.C.-29 A.D.), while it was another four hundred years from the death of Christ to the death of St. Augustine (430 A.D.). It was about eight hundred years from the death of St. Augustine to the death of St. Thomas Aquinas (1274 A.D.) and less than three hundred more years to the death of Machiavelli, the founder of modern political theory, (1527 A.D.), that theory whose intelligibility can only be grasped in relation to classical and medieval reflections and positions.[4] Time, of course, is an intellectual problem of the greatest perplexity, as St. Augustine himself recounted for us in his Confessions (Book XI), probably itself the most unique book in the ancient world. Nevertheless, it does not tell us how differing traditions are to be related or even if they can be. This is the work of experience and reflection.

In his book on The Modernity of St. Augustine, Jean Guitton pointed out the interrelationship of Greek, Jewish, and Christian thought on the cause of evil and its classification, a subject in one form or another always at the heart of political responsibility. "The tendency of the Greeks was to look on sin as something that happened inevitably ...." Guitton wrote.

It was in Israel that the mind of man discovered the nature of evil. In this history we see man becoming conscious of history through sin, repentance, vocation and return. This happened at first in a collective fashion, the individual feeling himself guilty or called merely in so far as he was a part of the whole people; but the work of the prophets individualized this communal feeling. Ultimately there came a time when certain privileged souls among the Jews became convinced that in their own particular lives, obscure though these were, they re-enacted the whole history of the people ....

Yet before St. Augustine the history of personal sin ... found no literary expression. We may say that St. Augustine is the first man in the West to have attained, in a personal way, the experience the Jewish people had reached, in a collective way.[5]

This Greek awareness of inevitable disorder was to be seen in the light of the Old and New Testaments, wherein evil was located not in matter or nature or fate, but in the will.

How Greek philosophical categories fuse and emerge in the context of the Old and New Testaments to form that civilization in which political philosophy and science were born is the context of medieval thought.[6] The Platonic guardians were designed to remove from the polis those evils of greed and envy which caused so much disruption, but at the cost of the natural institution of the family. The reflections of St. Augustine on his personal choices, however, were designed to ground envy, greed, and the other vices not in natural institutions but in the human heart, which was open to us by acute self-reflection.[7] This inner depth of human personality became for St. Augustine the basis of all social life and organization.

In considering the meaning and influence of classical and Christian thought, the Christian social tradition must include both St. Augustine and Aquinas, just as, classical Greek thought must include Plato and Aristotle, or German thought Kant and Hegel. Often, the reason for this inclusion has been considered to be purely historical. That is, both St. Augustine and St. Thomas were the most famous and significant Christian thinkers during a long period of human history.

Yet, Christianity has always spoken of a "perennial" philosophy, not just an historical or culturally conditioned one. History, in Christian thought, while not to be identified with the eternal, as St. Augustine so well recounted, still had metaphysical overtones. The contingent is also real being. God did create the world, as Genesis taught. This meant that something of the spirit and content of St. Augustine and Aquinas were present in every age after each had written. Christian thought did not conceive itself to grow by losing what had been handed down to it, even from the Greeks. On the contrary, it felt itself to grow by preserving the content of what it has known to be true in any age. Indeed, it might even be observed that what it learned to be in error, the very history of its own heresies, is as fruitful as what is true. Paradoxically, as both Plato and Aristotle had taught, the knowledge of error is itself

42

good, something to be known truly, that is, as error.

During the past century, however, in spite of considerable interest in St. Augustine, Aquinas appeared to have won the day as the main source of modern Christian intellectual inspiration. For many, St. Augustine came to be considered no more significant than a Gregory the Great or a Bonaventure, or even a Bossuet. In fact, St. Augustine quite often came to be seen as lurking at the heart of almost every major heresy in the modern era, beginning with the Reformation, Jansenism, and perhaps even Hegelianism.[8] The ideologies of the 20th Century, moreover, so far seemed to have favored Aquinas, even though in fairness to Aquinas himself, he never wrote as if St. Augustine did not exist.[9]

Indeed, Aquinas may have been St. Augustine's most sympathetic and precise commentator in many ways. As modern thought has become more and more "political", St. Augustine has begun to regain attention from secular scholars concerned with the origins of political realism. The distance from St. Augustine to Machiavelli and Hobbes has not seemed so great in this regard to a good many, granted the great difference between them that must in truth be maintained.[10] But, especially in the light of events of the 20th Century, the century in which totalitarianism seemed often to flourish, this has not seemed to be an argument in favor of St. Augustine.

The argument for the superiority of Aquinas, in any case, as we shall indicate in later chapters, deserves profound reflection.[11] (See Chapter VI-XI) But this has been subject to considerable scrutiny both through the events of recent years and through the exhaustion of those ideologies based upon the secularized optimism of the Enlightenment.[12] The doomsday schools of ecology have challenged the optimism of modern science, as have the totalitarian experiences of this century confronted democratic political institutions and theory.[13]

Paradoxically, the more optimistic ideologies, particularly ones that promise a better world through political reorganization, have often been what seem to fascinate particularly Christian religious social thought. Many thinkers have indeed wondered if Christianity will retain that essential core of beliefs and practices that defined its unique contribution to mankind, especially its clear

43

tradition that ultimate happiness was not a project of this world.[14] This is, moreover, the very issue posed to Christianity by classical political theory.[15]

In this regard, Barrington Moore's reflections on The Causes of Human Misery and Upon Certain Proposals to Eliminate Them are indicative of a rather new sensibility beyond the dominant theologies which have more and more seemed to have consumed their own intellectual capital. Moore betrays a realism that has its ultimate roots in St. Augustine. "Why is it that revolutionaries sooner or later adopt and sometimes intensify the cruelties of the regime against which they fight?" Moore asked.

> Why is it that revolutionaries begin with comraderie and end with fraticide? Why do revolutionaries start by proclaiming the brotherhood of man, the end of lies, deceit, and secrecy, and culminate in tyranny whose victims are overwhelmingly the little people for whom the revolution was proclaimed as the advent of a happier life? ... In my estimation, the essence of the answer rests on this fundamental contradiction between the effectiveness of immoral political methods and the necessity for morality in any social order ... Mankind can expect to oscillate between the cruelties of law and order and the cruelties of changing it for as long as it leaves this globe fit for human habitation.[16]

Anyone mindful of St. Augustine will be able to see here the abiding wisdom of not locating the City of God in any political order of this world.

Thus, ever since at least Reinhold Niebuhr's Moral Man and Immoral Society in 1932, we have been aware that an Augustinian-based political realism had a significant role in the modern world. In his perceptive essay on "Augustine's Political Realism," written in 1953, Niebuhr reflected:

> This modern generation with its confidence in a world without mystery, and without meaning beyond simple intelligibility, will not be beguiled from its unbelief by a reminder that its emancipation from God has betrayed it into

44

precisely those idolatries, the worship of
false gods, the dedication to finite values
as if they were ultimate, of which St.
Augustine spoke. But it must be recorded
nevertheless as a significant fact of modern
history. While it is an offense to regard
communism as the inevitable end-product of
secularism, as some Christians would have us
believe, it is only fair to point out that
the vast evils of modern communism come
ironically to a generation which thought it
would be easy to invest all the spiritual
capital of man, who mysteriously transcends
the historical process, in some value or end
within that process; and communism is merely
the most pathetic and cruel of the
idolatrous illusions of this generation.[17]

In this context perhaps, one of the great intellectual
questions of this era is why this Augustinian
tradition did not become the actual basis of the
development theories that have given most of the
specifically ethical content to contemporary political
thought, without producing the modernization.[18]

The essential issue is especially over the
relation of Christianity to political life and
thought. Christians have spent much of the the modern
era trying to overcome the charge that they hindered
first science and technology, then social development
by their beliefs in original sin and in the
transcendent personal location of beatitude. The
"liberal" Christian mind in the modern era has usually
tried to accommodate itself to the latest scientific
and political developments, almost as if these were
the primary norms of value.[19] Since Thomism in
particular has acknowledged the validity of human
knowledge and the naturalness of the state, this
seemed to argue that the proper tactic for
Christianity was that of accommodation to modern
thought wherever possible, almost as itself a final
norm.

Whatever the admitted value of this latter
approach, and it is very great if properly understood,
the fact remains that it has been hard to exorcise St.
Augustine, especially when it seems evident that
so-called "modern" thought itself was not really
philosophically neutral in the face of a religious
vision of man and God.[20] Official Catholic thought
in the modern era has been extremely sensitive to the

45

content of the various ideologies and philosophical positions that have appeared since the French Revolution, indeed since the Reformation.[21] Catholicism, for better or worse, has recognized that ideas have consequences in the world, and these cannot be neglected even in their incipient and apparently indifferent forms.

When Aquinas wrote, in the beginning of De Ente et de Essentia, that a small error in the beginning will lead to a great error in the distance, he did no more than reaffirm the great Greek and Christian sensitivity to the power of thought and spirit. Christianity's attention to ideas, to be sure, has often been considered to be a kind of "authoritarianism" at odds with the modern temper. Yet, in retrospect, an argument can be made that sensitivity to the intellectual content and spirit of modern philosophical and theological movements was based upon a real sense of threat against and deviation from the kind of man that Christianity presupposed and fostered.[22] Many of the positions condemned in one way or another by the Church have come subsequently to be condemned by later secular thinking itself.[23]

St. Augustine, in this context, holds a special place. Many have remarked, as I have indicated, that St. Augustine lies at the origin of almost every subsequent heresy in some way or another. And this can probably be acknowledged, if we also recognize that St. Augustine is also at the origin of every subsequent orthodoxy.[24] Hannah Arendt, in her Beyond Past and Present, called St. Augustine the greatest of the Christian political philosophers, while Eric Voegelin in his New Science of Politics did not hesitate to place St. Augustine at the very heart of any substantial refutation of the "gnosticism" that has formed "modernity."[25]

Professor Herbert Deane's Political and Social Ideas of St. Augustine seems in many ways to be the most perceptive work to clarify the meaning of modern thought. He does this through the medium of Christian thinking.[26] Meanwhile, the essays of Sir Ernest Barker, Christopher Dawson, Reinhold Niebuhr, Charles N. R. McCoy, Ernest Fortin, and Etienne Gilson on St. Augustine remain fundamental in understanding not only St. Augustine, but perhaps even more so in grasping the nature of contemporary politics.[27] The question of why St. Augustine is not well known may in fact

46

reveal something about the nature and limits of contemporary Christian political philosophy.

Perhaps the most interesting consideration of this subject is Professor (now Senator) John East's "The Political Relevance of St. Augustine." East addressed himself to this neglect, particularly Catholic neglect of St. Augustine. Noting that the supposedly "tough-minded" tradition of Aquinas, perpetuated by world-government-oriented theorists like Maritain, Adler, and Hutchins, has gained ascendancy, East believed that the real problem was the ability of the Catholic Church to retain, with the aid of classical Protestantism, the more realistic approach of St. Augustine.

East's remarks are worth reflection:

Today the Roman Catholic Church may be in a unique historical position to move effectively in the direction of a genuinely believing ecumenism by standing firm against the corrosive effects of modern liberalism, Christian and non-Christian. As dominant Protestant leadership moves leftward to accommodate itself to the world of the nonbelieving, it is losing its believing membership at an accelerated rate. If the Catholic Church should insist on following this course, the believing faithful are left relatively leaderless and isolated.

To build a bona fide ecumenism, the Church will need to rely more upon the Augustinian perspective, and less on the Thomistic. St. Augustine is basic in the Catholic and Protestant traditions of Christianity, and he would have no peers as a point of departure in building a philosophical unity of all Christian believers. It is curious that Thomists should find universalism in Aquinas and provincialism or particularism in St. Augustine. The facts seem otherwise, for if you are talking about Christian universalism, it is St. Augustine who has the Universalist appeal, while Aquinas has become the unique property of the Catholic Church and liberal ecumenists.[28]

Ultimately, as John East argued, St. Augustine is

anti-Utopian and rejected the notion that environment rather than freedom causes our problems. The state is only a limited power which cannot cure all or even most of our ills and problems. St. Augustine could always conceive things as potentially worse than they are. St. Augustine, in other words, came to describe the way men act in politics so that, while retaining the value of the good, unlike Machiavelli, he could still include the "possibility" of what is not good as an essential element in politics -- something Aquinas followed in his theory of law. St. Augustine, then, could lay claim to the notion of a universal society, while recognizing the real and not to be ignored limits of actual states.[29]

What is the importance of St. Augustine in modern social thought? St. Augustine provides certain basic correctives that are necessary if the kind of "development" possible to man and professed by modern politicans and thinkers in fact is to take place. To put it another way, the major causes of continued underdevelopment are the ideologies that promise a this-worldly, perfect human society. St. Augustine's sense of the possible, the awareness of the real condition of men, prevents the kind of absolutism that has often gained dominance over ethical development theory, usually in the name of correcting real evils. It is important not to confuse rhetoric or ideals for actual performance.

St. Augustine is, in this context, especially worthy of recall because undoubtedly the next major accusation to be leveled against contemporary Christian social thought will be analogous to the Hochhuth-originated controversy over Pius XII, only this time it will be a "social" charge.[30] That is, Christians in particular, because of the way they regarded the issue of modernization and development, will be seen as a major contributing factor to the new "Leviathan". Christians will be accused of neglecting that Augustinian element in their own tradition that would have made them more aware of the limits of the state.

This seems more than ironic since there was a time when the Christian religion seemed to be the major bulwark against the totalitarian forces of our time. Liberal thought, of course, always held Christianity to be a contributor to totalitarianism by its insistence on authority, truth, and natural law. But modern liberalism has shown itself incapable of any sustained resistance to the newer ideologies which have insisted, mostly correctly, that the "pluralism" of values, their formal unknowability, has made the totalitarian option both "rational" and indeed the most effective path to proclaimed liberal values in development.[31] This, together with the ease by which the "right to life" has become essentially an avenue to attack and destroy life itself in the ecological schools and in the courts, has left man in his traditional sense almost without an intellectual defender in the modern world. This is why a key question remains Christianity's ability to remain itself.[32]

Both the strength of and objection to Christianity have been its ability to insist on man's formal vocation to this world while retaining its sense of original sin and its consequences. All of this has been within the personal vocation of each human person to transcend all social and natural orders to receive the gift of eternal life, the Trinitarian life of God, which is how Christianity came to define beatitude. In a sense, the hammering out of formal doctrine in the early Church in Christology, grace, and Trinitarian theology is still as it was for St. Augustine, the main line of defence of the "human" in this world.[33] This is why all social philosophies in modern times -- wherein, more often than not, "religious" speculation is found today -- must eventually arrive at a point of disagreement with classical dogma as found especially in the great Creeds and in classical political philosophy.

Eric Voegelin was not wrong, I think, to call the modern era "gnostic" for this reason. In shifting the locus of beatitude from transcendence to millennial perfectionism in this world, it had to deny the unique nature and mission of Christ. On the other hand, the Christian insistence on an absolute difference between good and evil, in its belief that original sin does not mean that nature itself is evil, has enabled Christian social thought to preserve a moral value in a world wherein evil can in fact be recognized in its origin in the will. This position prevents it from seeking evil radically in nature or society, or even in God. This central tradition has been essential to the understanding of modern thought and its own notions of what is to be hoped for. The mark of St. Augustine is present in all of this kind of Christian analysis.

49

The great social question during the next century will not be development and underdevelopment. The lines for development are already established and known. If nations fail to develop, it is largely because of their choices, as David Apter said in his The Politics of Modernization, a theme reiterated by Professor Beckermann in his Two Cheers for the Affluent Society.[34] Professor P. T. Bauer put it well:

> The belief that the prosperity of particular individuals, groups or countries accounts for the poverty of material backwardness of others is almost always invalid ... Material progress depends primarily on the development of suitable human qualities, attitudes and social institutions, and not on the inflow of external amounts of money ... The policies of the recipient countries have on the whole served to retard or obstruct possible advance.[35]

These choices that retard development are usually based on a faulty notion of the institutions and ideas that can do the task at hand. These faulty choices are almost invariably rooted in contemporary ideologies, with their roots in a this-worldly cause for removing the consequences of original sin, consequences seen classically in property, labor, government, or even sex itself. But again, that most humans do have difficulty in seeing and realizing their own good is itself a part of the heritage that Christianity has called original sin. This is the mystery of why we are not perfect in the first place, a mystery that is as much a problem of the beginning as of the end of historical processes.

The great social question, then, lies elsewhere in the capacity of the Christian religion to retain its central "supernatural" mission in the light both of the "optimistic" Marxists and the "pessimistic" ecologists. Peter Berger, in his A Rumor of Angels, put his finger on the basic question: "The supernatural elements of the religious traditions are more or less completely liquidated, and the traditional language is transferred from other-worldly to this-worldly referents."[36] This is the reason why St. Augustine becomes more and more central to the next century, to the effort, that is, to retain the primacy of the kind of finite beings we are, without

50

lapsing into a this-worldly eudaemonism that implicitly denies any supernatural destiny to men. This too is why, in a way, it is important to retain even the idea of the "supernatural" no matter how much it has come under attack in various contemporary ideologies, especially those which refuse to accept any limits to man in this world, which consequently wish to repropose beatitude as a political enterprise.

St. Augustine, then, ought to be remembered at the present time. He is the link between Christianity and the ancient world, between ancient and medieval worlds, the one figure who remains vividly alive and personal in any century in which he is read, as his Confessions still attest. Not only is he the father, along with Thucydides, of any "realistic" political theory, but he is the most dramatic witness to the limits of politics. These are the limits that arise directly from the Christian answer to the classical dilemma of political thought. This is the issue which Plato first broached in The Republic, of why personal immortality in the end is a political question.

Modern ideologies have tried to secure a "corporate" immortality in the form of some future this-worldly good, one that offers really no hope to existing men under any given, imperfect, even barbarous political order. This is why the classical discussion of the actual forms of rule is not alien to theology, to the question of the ultimate form of happiness for men. What is expected of any valid religion is an ability to keep before the nations the primacy of God not merely in the worst societies, but also in the best. The secularized Enlightenment tradition of modern times has constantly promised the best government in the world, usually called some form of "democracy" because it is good. (See Chapter VIII) But with the actual states that we have in fact produced in the 20th Century, we again see that political societies will not live up to their promises. And even when they approximate a just social order, they do not yet confront the final question of man's ultimate happiness, the question about which political theory began in the first place.

This means that we need to find a reason for the kind of men we are, men whose future and hope do not essentially lie in or against the political and scientific utopias and deformities of our time. In this context, it is St. Augustine who makes considerable political sense, not just because he does not locate beatitude in this world -- a belief Aquinas clearly shared with him -- but also because he has a sense of clarity about what we might in fact accomplish. In other words, only by lowering our expectations for politics that can we preserve genuine beatitude, together with a sense of real improvement for men. St. Augustine was not a pessimist. He expected that the worst could and often did happen. But he was also a man who believed that the only solid basis for any limited improvement was this clear recognition about the worst. Without it, paradoxically, the worst was indeed likely to happen, and this because of that very freedom which he saw at the basis of human choice. (See Chapter IX)

St. Augustine, to be understood in his full import, needs to be seen against the background of Greek political thought and the scriptural view of the world. In classical Greek and Roman thought, politics occurred in the context of human happiness and human good. The nature of this happiness was considered to be proportioned to the given capacities and qualities of the being to which happiness was attributed. In making each being for what it was, in giving it consequently certain faculties and activities, nature was said to be making nothing in vain. Rather, it was indicating to intelligence, even when that intelligence appeared in the cosmos, as it did with man, what happiness meant for this or that being. This varied according to the different complexities found in each type of being. In this sense, there was a happiness unique to each kind of being found in nature, be it a human or a horse, as <u>The Republic</u> of Plato intimated.

Politics and ethics, moreover, were activities of a special sort of creature, not all. They dealt in some sense with that sort of happiness specifically proper to humans insofar as they were humans. Human beings thus lived in this world, for their normal period of time, to old age ideally, as Cicero told us, unless by an act of courage, they could complete their self-definition sooner. In human beings a sort of happiness was also experienced that was somehow more than human. The relationships between these two kinds of happiness defined the classical distinction between contemplation and action.

On examination, the content of this particularly

52

human happiness had to do with the proper functioning of the various sensory and intellectual powers given in man as man, as part of his very being. The defining faculty in man was his mind. To this were ordered the other powers man, in a sense, shared with plants and animals. This mind in a body made man distinct in the cosmos. This enabled him to guide himself to his own unique end and also to understand, through it, all reality, both within and without himself. This rational power allowed man to put the stamp of individual intelligence on each of the peculiarly human acts coming out of him by which he acted in the world by art, technique, and ethics. This power of intelligence could be abused because it could be directed to many purposes, not all of which conformed with man's own being. Nor was man freed from the need of discovering rules, discipline, and order in his effort to exercise his faculties properly on their objects.

The Greeks did not hold that most men used their moral and intellectual faculties properly, even though the possibility of using them properly was always open them. The Greeks did not, as we have seen, seem to see this as a personal "fault" in the same sense as the revelational tradition did. The degree to which men did or did not guide themselves adequately and the differing ways they could deviate from the norm were in fact the substance of classifying different human ethical characters and political regimes, as Plato indicated in Books VIII and IX of The Republic. The account of the worst regime and those that were less good was a basic part of political theory. (See Chapter IX)

In this sense, Plato and St. Augustine, however different they might seem at first sight, are very close. Neither expected most men, for the most part, to achieve a high level of virtue. The cyclical decline of politics in The Republic accounted for the consequences of a lack of virtue. What St. Augustine, as a believer in the revelational tradition, wanted to know concerned the destiny of each actual man and woman who lived in deviant states, the only kind that really existed. St. Augustine did not hold that the answer to this question was primarily or theoretically political, even though politics does manifest the problem of ideals not achieved. In one sense, the imposition of ideals on practical political life is the central issue of political theory, the major one to which St. Augustine addressed himself.

The description of man in the non-revelational tradition came to St. Augustine in his Roman education primarily in its Neo-Platonic and Stoic forms. This meant that the experience of change was a sign of deviation, while immutability was central to the discovery of reality and truth. The forms of Plato, by which all things exist unchangeably in their purity and according to which they are classified in their differences, are embraced also by St. Augustine, though he located them ultimately in the mind of God.

St. Augustine understood, however, that the Platonic concept of change, the idea that matter or body was not an essential aspect of man, ran counter both to the Old Testament idea of creation and the Christian doctrines of incarnation and resurrection.[37] Neither of these doctrines, while implicitly acknowledging the finite notion of man as such, suggested that matter was in any sense an "evil." The Platonic notion that to escape evil one has to escape matter also, thus, was necessarily rejected by St. Augustine, who posed another, now classical, theory that evil was not itself a substance, but a lack of what ought to exist in a good subject or substance.[38]

"Evil" in this sense was not simply nothing, nor was it another god, but the powerful absence of what ought to be. (See Chapter VI) At the human, moral level, the level of those acts proper to man, this lack was a result of choice. This is what links the Old Testament doctrine of the Fall with the Platonic realization of deviation from the good, without blaming matter for the same deviation. "And I inquired what iniquity was," St. Augustine wrote in his Confessions, "and ascertained it was not to be a substance, but a perversion of the will, bent aside from Thee, O God, the Supreme Substance, towards the lower things ...."(VII,16) Thus, St. Augustine was able to accept the goodness of what is not God, even the "lower things," without changing God or causing Him to be considered the cause of evil or of being evil Himself. The possibility of evil is intrinsic to what is not God, to what is not immutable. This possibility, paradoxically, indicates the real autonomy of what is not God and grounds its higher dignity.

Thus, what the human being chooses has an ultimate significance, which it would lack otherwise without this freedom, even though it can be abused. This abuse, in fact, is part of the experienced history of mankind which concerned St. Augustine so much in his City of God. The actual choice of something less than one might or ought, however, is, for St. Augustine, a choice against these immutable norms whose locus is in the mind of God. This is what gives the whole dramatical relationships between man and what he does in the cosmos a firm basis in reality. This explains the dialogue effect of St. Augustine's particular style, which sees all things not in terms of abstract laws, but personal words.

Will and conscience, then, enable St. Augustine to relate each personal human act to an individual's own destiny, his own way to define himself. The history of these personal choices defines the "city" to which a person is ultimately to belong. Ernest Fortin has explained the Augustinian thesis well in this regard:

> It was left to St. Augustine, under the influence of both Stoicism and Sacred Scripture, to elaborate a theory of conscience.... Man's moral life is invested with an objective autonomy that it did not have for any of St. Augustine's pagan predecessors.... Conscience as St. Augustine understands it ... basically assumes ... that man's life as a whole is governed by rational principles that are naturally known and universally valid even in the most extreme circumstances....

> The crucial political implication is that human life acquires a universality that it did not have and could not have as long as the polis and its regime represented for most men a total way of life. Civil society is displaced as the locus of virtue and the object of man's deepest and most noble attachments.... It ceases to be ... the sole horizon lending meaning and substance to the highest undertaken by its citizens. The love of one's own is no longer concentrated within its borders, and ... citizenship itself loses its most fundamental significance.... The gods of civil religion, which St. Augustine with characteristic reserve refrains from attacking directly, are deprived of their

ultimate political justification and are
replaced by the cult of the one true God,
the author and supreme good of all
things.[39]

The reason why "The City of God," as St. Augustine
conceived it, is neither a church nor a polity is
because of the problem presented by human choices, for
good or evil. Since the two are not the same, St.
Augustine recognized an ultimate incompatibility
between them. This is why there are, for St.
Augustine, precisely two cities.(Book XI, Chapter I)

How the Augustinian answer to the death of the
just man in the best state of its time, then, is
resolved, turns out to be an essential step in the
definition of what is political philosophy itself.
"The City of God is stranger to every nation and every
state, and recruits its citizens from every quarter,"
Etienne Gilson wrote.

It is indifferent to diversities of
language, habits and customs, and attacks
nothing, destroys nothing which is good and
useful; on the contrary, among nations of
widely differing character, it strives to
consolidate whatever each places at the
service of the earthly peace, provided only
that there is no opposition to the
establishment of God's peace. Thus, without
being able to achieve it here below, it
prepares the way for that perfect social
life ... where absolute order will reign
through the union of many wills in one
common happiness, namely the eternal life in
the bosom of God.[40]

This meant that the philosophical enterprise which
Plato entered upon, in which the Philosopher-King
could see the real good of each person in the Good
itself, is indeed a necessary one. St. Augustine did
not disagree with this in Plato. Nor did he disagree
with him in the endeavor to discover what is
unchangeable, the reality to which all things tend in
all they do.

However, the historical challenge to St.
Augustine by the pagans of his time led him to account
for the rise and fall of Rome, an actual state to
which he belonged. For St. Augustine, in The City of
God, Rome was not the worst of regimes. Indeed, it

was a far sight better than most, even though St.
Augustine did not share Cicero's enthusiasm for the
Roman Republic as the best of states. But that
Christianity caused the decline of Rome, rather than
preserve all that was good in it, was something St.
Augustine would not tolerate. "Meanwhile, I will
briefly, and to the best of my ability, explain what I
meant to say about these ungrateful men who
blasphemously impute to Christ the calamities which
they deservedly suffer in consequence of their own
wicked ways ...."(Book I, Chapter 3; Vol. II, p. 7)
He agreed with the Greeks and with Cicero that there
are political consequences for human activity,
especially immoral activity. He held that if a
religious people live well, the state, whatever its
classification as to form, will be better. But he did
not maintain that any empire, even Rome, was capable
of settling the restless heart of man, which he
discovered for all men in himself.

Political entities, then, were at best, for St.
Augustine, remedial institutions designed mostly to
prevent the worst, rather than establish the good, let
alone the best.[41]

> According to the definitions in which
> Cicero himself ... briefly propounded what a
> republic is, and what a people is, and
> according to many testimonies ... Rome was
> never a republic because true justice had
> never a place in it. But accepting the more
> feasible definition of a republic, I grant
> there was a republic of a certain kind, and
> certainly much better administered by the
> more ancient Romans than by their more
> modern representatives. But the fact is,
> true justice has no existence save in that
> republic whose foundation and ruler is
> Christ, if at least any choose to call this
> a republic; and indeed we cannot deny it is
> the people's weal.(Book II, Chapter 21, Vol.
> II, p. 46)

This is, in many ways, the most remarkable passage in
Christian political philosophy as it reflected on the
Greek experience in its own light. This related
Christian thinking to the polis and distinguished
itself most sharply from any enterprise that would
seek absolute justice or good by political means.
Though keeping the drive for justice and good alive as
the ultimate desire and destiny of man, St. Augustine

denied it can be applied in its full sense to any political entity, even to the best around. He located the highest in a realm that is real, but not political.

St. Augustine's political thought, then, is the great endeavor to reconcile classical Platonic political philosophy to Christianity, in a way that did justice to the real experience of political history and the doctrines of the Judeao-Christian revelation, especially the doctrines of creation, the Fall, freedom, salvation, will, incarnation, and resurrection, without denying the validity of what the classics discovered. St. Augustine's _City of God_, in its full understanding, is the Christian answer to the dilemma of classical political theory. This consisted in the questions, initially brought up by politics, namely, what is the final location of human happiness and in what does it consist? That is, does final happiness imply a perfect, worldly political state?

And if this latter is not the case, how does political philosophy relate to those actual persons in history who do not live in a perfect society, even if they are good in themselves? In not locating human happiness in an actual polity, or in one that will be actual in some definite generation or place, down the ages, St. Augustine provided a Christian solution to that perplexity, ever present in _The Republic_, wherein the question arose about the existence of this same _Republic_ constructed outside the mind.

Socrates always insisted that he did not know whether his "Republic" could exist outside its constructed intelligibility based on the real intellectual requirements of justice. But he did know that its very intellectual construction was a necessary endeavor for each human mind which wanted to know what justice is, what ultimate good is. The mind, to be mind, had to think about this rigorously. The rereading of _The Republic_ in this sense remains the foundation of all subsequent political philosophy and the context of questions that may be more than political. However, the philosophic polity could not be put into this world without overturning what was normally meant by politics, something Aristotle understood.

Must Socrates, then, always be killed by pursuing truth in any existing polity whose constitution was formed to foster interests less than the highest? Or

58

was the execution of Christ the basis for answering
the question which really concerned Socrates, namely,
how always to act rightly and always contemplate the
Good? In this sense, The Republic and The City of God
are the same book, both attest to questions that must
be asked about the highest things.

The answers of Socrates and Plato, however,
differed existentially, since St. Augustine included
the whole human person in final happiness, not just
the soul, while he rejected any thought that existing
polities could embody this happiness. This lowers the
importance of existing polities, no doubt, but
conversely, allows us to see them for what they are.
St. Augustine's political realism is, thus, the
consequence of rightly locating questions posed first
in The Republic, without jeopardizing the actual
existential desire of each person to achieve a
complete happiness for himself as he is. By seeing
Plato as the best of the ancients, St. Augustine
associated himself directly with that ongoing
enterprise which sees in revelation the correct way to
proceed in questions already posed by the
philosophers, particularly the political
philosophers.

"Plato determined the final good to be to live
according to virtue," St. Augustine wrote,

> ... and affirmed that he only can
> attain to virtue who knows and imitates God
> - which knowledge and imitation are the only
> cause of blessedness. Therefore, he did not
> doubt that to philosophize is to love God,
> whose nature is incorporeal. Whence it
> certainly follows that the student of
> wisdom, that is, the philosopher, will then
> become blessed when he shall have begun to
> enjoy God. ... The true and highest good,
> according to Plato, is God, and therefore he
> would call him a philosopher who loves God;
> for philosophy is directed to the obtaining
> of the blessed life, and he who loves God is
> blessed in the enjoyment of God.(Book VIII,
> Chapter 8, Vol. II, p. 110)

St. Augustine clearly held that Plato's good was God,
that the philosopher's goal was to contemplate and
enjoy God. He held that nothing less would satisfy
mankind, least of all St. Augustine, himself one of
its members. Plato held that in only two polities,

the best and a democracy, could the philosopher exist without being killed, and even in the latter, as in the case of Athens, this was dangerous.

For St. Augustine, the death of Christ at the hands of the Roman state cut the Platonic link between the polis and the good permanently. Thenceforth, any man in any polity was related to God directly in a relationship that was not political, though it was social. This is the most radical reason why political societies are limited. They cannot deliver what is not theirs to give. And when they seek to, as they often do, they become the "City of Man", to use St. Augustine's words, wherein man's own definition of the good becomes the form of the polity. St. Augustine's political philosophy constitutes the radical reason why this sort of eventuality, however historically possible, is not theoretically valid. In this sense, he continued and perfected the project of classical political philosophy.

Footnotes:

1. Christopher Dawson, The Making of Europe, New York, Sheed and Ward, 1950.

2. Charles Norris Cochrane, Christianity and Classical Culture, New York, Oxford University Press, 1944.

3. Ralph Lerner and M. Mahdi, Medieval Political Theory, New York, Free Press, 1963.

4. See Charles N. R. McCoy, The Structure of Political Thought, New York, McGraw-Hill, 1963, Chapter VI; Leo Strauss, Thoughts on Machiavelli, Glencoe, Free Press, 1959.

5. Jean Guitton, The Modernity of St. Augustine, Baltimore, Helicon, 1959, pp. 12-14.

6. See Etienne Gilson, Reason and Revelation in the Middle Ages, New York, Scribner's, 1938; Stanley Jaki, The Road of Science and the Ways of God, Chicago, University of Chicago Press, 1978; Josef Pieper, Scholasticism, New York, Pantheon, 1960; A. C. Crombie, Medieval and Early Modern Science, Garden City, Doubleday, 1959.

7. See Etienne Gilson, "The Future of Augustinian Metaphysics," Monument to St. Augustine, London, Sheed and Ward, 1930.

8. See Henri de Lubac, Augustinianism and Modern Theology, New York, Herder, 1969.

9. R. A. Markus, "Augustine and the Aristotelian Revolution of the Thirteenth Century," Saeculum: History and Society in the Theology of St. Augustine, Cambridge, At the University Press, 1970, pp. 211-30.

10. Herbert Deane, Political and Social Ideas of St. Augustine, New York, Columbia University Press, 1956.

11. Etienne Gilson, The Philosophy of St. Thomas Aquinas, Cambridge, 1937.

12. See J. Talmon, The Rise of Totalitarian Democracy, Boston, Beacon, 1952.

13. See A. Solzhenitsyn's Gulag trilogy; B.-H.

61

Levy, Barbarism With a Human Face, New York, Harper's, 1979; James V. Schall, "Apocalypse as a Secular Enterprise," Scottish Journal of Theology, #4, 1976, pp. 357-73.

14. See E. O. Norman, Christianity and the World Order, New York, Oxford, 1979.

15. See Joseph Cropsey, "The United States as a Regime," Political Philosophy and the Issues of Politics, Chicago, University of Chicago Press, 1977.

16. Barrington Moore, The Causes of Human Misery and Upon Certain Proposals to Eliminate Them, Boston, Beacon, 1975, pp. 36-39.

17. Reinhold Niebuhr, "Augustine's Political Realism," in Perspectives on Political Philosophy, Downton, Editor, New York, Holt, 1971, pp. 255-56. See also James L. Wiser, Political Philosophy: A History of the Search for Order, Englewood Cliffs, Prentice-Hall, 1983, Chapter IV on Augustine.

18. See James V. Schall, "Conservatism and Development," Cultures et Developpement, Louvain, #2, 1977, pp.315-34; "Christianity and the 'Cures' of Poverty," Christianity and Politics, Boston, St. Paul Editions, 1981.

19. Emmet John Hughes, The Catholic Church and Liberal Society, Notre Dame, University of Notre Dame Press, 1961.

20. Eric Voegelin, The New Science of Politics, Chicago, University of Chicago Press, 1952; Leo Strauss, Natural Right and History, Chicago, University of Chicago Press, 1951.

21. E. E. Y. Hales, The Catholic Church in the Modern World, Garden City, Doubleday Image, 1958.

22. See James V. Schall, The Distinctiveness of Christianity, San Francisco, Ignatius Press, 1983.

23. See E. F. Schumacher, Small Is Beautiful, New York, Harper, 1974, Chapter V; Battista Mondin, L'Eresia del Nostro Secolo, Torino, Borla, 1971.

24. John O'Meara, Charter of Christendom: The Significance of the 'City of God', New York, Macmillan, 1961.

25. Hannah Arendt, _Beyond Past and Future_, New York, Viking, 1968; Voegelin, _ibid_.

26. Deane, _ibid_.

27. See Readings to this Chapter.

28. John East, "The Political Revelance of St. Augustine," _Modern Age_, Spring, 1972, pp. 170-71.

29. Etienne Gilson, "St. Augustine and the Problem of Universal Society," Introduction to the Fathers of the Church Edition of _The City of God_, New York, 1960, V. VI, pp.xi-xcviii.

30. Rolf Hochhuth, _The Deputy_, New York, Grove, 1964.

31. This was the import, I think, of Christian Bay's "Politics and Pseudo-politics: A Critical Evaluation of Some Behavioral Literature," _Apolitical Politics_, McCoy, Editor, New York, Cowell, 1967.

32. See James V. Schall, "Catholicism and Intelligence," in _The Distinctiveness of Christianity_, _ibid_.; _Christianity and Life_, San Francisco, Ignatius Press, 1981.

33. J. N. D. Kelly, _Early Christian Creeds_, New York, McKay, 1972.

34. David Apter, _The Politics of Modernization_, Chicago, University of Chicago Press, 1965; Wilfred Beckermann, _Two Cheers for the Affluent Society_, New York, St. Martin's Press, 1975; Michael Novak, _The Spirit of Democratic Capitalism_, New York, Simon and Schuster, 1982; George Gilder, _Wealth and Poverty_, New York, Basic, 1980.

35. P. T. Bauer, "Foreign Aid: An Instrument for Progress?" Occasional Paper, N.9, London, The Institute for Economic Affairs, 1966, pp. 54,58; also Bauer's _Equality, the Third World, and Economic Delusion_, Cambridge, Harvard University Press, 1981; _Reason and Rhetoric_, Cambridge, Harvard University Press, 1984.

36. Peter Berger, _A Rumor of Angels_, New York, Doubleday, 1970, p. 20.

37. Henri Marrou, <u>The Resurrection and St.</u> <u>Augustine's Theology of Human Values</u>, Philadelphia, Villanova University Press, 1966; Paul Henri, <u>St.</u> <u>Augustine on Personality</u>, New York, Macmillan, 1960.

38. See <u>The City of God</u>, Book XI, Ch.22, in <u>The</u> <u>Basic Works of St. Augustine</u>, W. J. Oates, Editor, New York, Random House, 1948, V. II, pp. 163-64; <u>The</u> <u>Confessions</u>, Book VII, Ch. 5-7, 16, V.I, pp. 94-99, 104.

39. Ernest Fortin, "The Political Implications of St. Augustine's Theory of Conscience," <u>Augustinian</u> <u>Studies</u>, V.I, 1970, pp. 142-44.

40. Etienne Gilson, <u>The Christian Philosophy of</u> <u>St. Augustine</u>, New York, Random House, 1960, p. 182.

41. See Deane, <u>ibid</u>., Ch. IV.

<u>Readings</u>:

There are many editions of individual works of St. Augustine especially of <u>The Confessions</u> and <u>The City of God</u>. The best introduction to St. Augustine is always his own <u>Confessions</u>. <u>The Basic Writings of St. Augustine</u>, Edited by W. J. Oates, New York, Random House, 1948, 2 Vols., remains the most useful collection. The Fathers of the Church and Loeb have his complete works in English editions. The best introduction to St. Augustine's political works is probably found in Herbert Deane or Henry Paolucci, cited below.

Essays and Books on St. Augustine's Political Thought:

Ernest Barker, "St. Augustine's Theory of Society," <u>Perspectives on Political Philosophy</u>, New York, Holt, 1971, which is the Introduction to Everyman's Edition of <u>The City of God</u>, New York, Dutton, 1945.

Norman Baynes, "The Political Ideas of St. Augustine's <u>De Civitate Dei</u>," in <u>Byzantine Studies and Other Essays</u>, London, Athlone, 1955.

Vernon Bourke, "The Political Philosophy of St. Augustine," Proceedings of the 7th Annual Meeting of the American Catholic Philosophical Association, St. Louis, 1931, pp. 45-55.

Anton-Hermann Chroust, "The Philosophy of Law of St. Augustine," Philosophical Review, March, 1944, pp. 195-202.

Christopher Dawson, "St. Augustine and His Age," Monument to St. Augustine, Edited by M. C. D'Arcy, London, Sheed and Ward, 1930, reprinted as St. Augustine, New York, Meridian, 1957.

Herbert Deane, Political and Social Ideas of St. Augustine, New York, Columbia University Press, 1956.

John East, "The Political Relevance of St.Augustine," Modern Age, Spring, 1972, pp. 167-81.

J. N. Figgis, Political Aspects of St. Augustine's 'City of God', London, Longmans, 1921.

Ernest Fortin, Political Idealism and Christianity in the Thought of St. Augustine, Philadelphia, Villanova University Press, 1972.

Ernest Fortin, "The Political Implication of St. Augustine's Theory of Conscience," Augustinian Studies, V. I, 1970, pp. 133-53.

Etienne Gilson, "St. Augustine and the Problem of World Society," Introduction to the Fathers' of the Church Edition of The City of God, New York, 1960, V. VI, pp. xi-xcviii.

R. A. Markus, Saeculum: History and Society in the Thought of St.Augustine, Cambridge, At the University Press, 1970.

Reinhold Niebuhr, "Augustine's Political Realism," Perspectives in Political Philosophy, Downton, Editor, New York, Holt, 1971.

Henry Paolucci, Editor, The Political Writings of St. Augustine, Chicago, Gateway, 1962.

Mulford Q. Sibley, "Augustine and the Politics of the Two Cities," Political Ideas and Ideologies, New York, Harper, 1970, pp. 170-94.

James L. Wiser, Political Philosophy: A History of the Search for Order, Englewood Cliffs, Prentice-Hall, 1983, Chapter 4.

Other Pertinent Books on St. Augustine:

A. II. Armstrong, St. Augustine and Christian Platonism, Philadelphia, Villanova University Press, 1967.

Vernon Bourke, Augustine's View of Reality, Philadelphia, Villanova University Press, 1964.

Etienne Gilson, The Christian Philosophy of St. Augustine, New York, Random House, 1960.

Jean Guitton, The Modernity of St. Augustine, Baltimore, Helicon, 1959.

Paul Henri, St. Augustine on Personality, New York, Macmillan, 1960.

Henri Marrou, The Resurrection and St. Augustine's Theology of Human Values, Philadelphia, Villanova University Press, 1966.

Monument to St. Augustine, Edited by M. C. D'Arcy, London, Sheed and Ward, 1930, also published as St. Augustine, New York, Meridian, 1957.

John O'Meara, Charter of Christendom: The Significance of the City of God, New York, Macmillan, 1961.

Josef Ratzinger, Volk und Haus Gottes in Augustin's Lehre von der Kirche, München, Karl Zink, 1954.

CHAPTER IV

CHRISTIAN GUARDIANS

"And the only life which looks down
upon the life of political ambition is that
of true philosophy. Do you know of any
other?"

"Indeed, I do not," he said.

-- [Plato, The Republic, #521b.]

Looking backward to Plato and forward to our own
time, always a possibility if truth remains one and
intelligible to a mankind united to itself in time,
even if all do not live in one time, the particular
manner in which Plato's philosophy came to be
understood by the revelational tradition coming out of
the Old and New Testaments is worth some reflection.
This is not merely because of the relationship of the
death of Socrates to the death of Christ, though this
relationship remains at the basis of the matter.

This relationship can also be considered because
of the way revelational ideas seemed to "save"
proposals which, however "rational", seemed, on
examination, distorted and outlandish. Nothing
perhaps exemplifies this more than the way the
Christian monastic tradition, with its order of the
day, its vows, its purpose, was related to Plato's
guardians. This was, moreover, not just an accidental
relationship, but one which went to the very
philosophic heart of human life itself seeking to
define its meaning and how to accomplish what is
noblest in it.

From the monasteries of Vivarium, Monte Cassino,
and Fulda, to Cluny and Citeaux, the medieval
Christian world was filled with monks and nuns, who
stood in a special legal and religious relationship
both to the Church and to the feudal order.[1] St.
Augustine himself wrote a rule for the monks, which in
some form is still operative within the Catholic
Church today. Luther was, in his early years, an
Augustinian monk, and his thought, in some sense,

67

brings to a theoretical end that peculiar medieval intellectual enterprise which sought to reconcile faith and reason, the enterprise Josef Pieper called "scholasticism."[2] (See Chapter XII) The very nature of modern political theory from Machiavelli, moreover, is premised on an elevation of politics to cover the consequences of this shift away from the cultural unity of faith and reason.

On no other single issue, perhaps, can the peculiarly rich relationship between human reason and revelation be seen than that of Christian monasticism. Here, revelation is addressed to reason, though not exhausted by it. Thus revelation is capable of inciting a completeness in reason that it would otherwise lack. The context of this relationship derives from classical political philosophy and from scripture itself in a way that forces any open philosopher to consider their similarities and differences.

Undoubtedly, Plato's guardians in Book V of The Republic, who had no families, property, or duty other than to the good of all on which they identified their happiness, seemed strangely similar to the institution of the Twelve Apostles, though these twelve had families. Both the Gospels and Plato, nevertheless, provided for a category of ruler whose personal good was to be identified with the communal good or purpose, which itself was directed to some highest end. That the Church was not exactly the polis seemed less significant because of the ambiguous locus of the Platonic republic itself.[3] (See Chapter III)

Yet, it was not so much the hierarchy of the Church in its bishops that seemed the best parallel to Plato but the non-hierarchical monastic communities that arose within the Christian Church and which were so central to the development of the Middle Ages and its culture. Christopher Dawson suggested that the whole classical political tradition found its home in the monastic communities of the Middle Ages, rather than in the feudal order itself.[4] It was from this source in monasticism that the classical political tradition was passed into modern political philosophy. The passages in The Acts of the Apostles about the early Christians holding all possessions in common struck a chord when they began to know Plato's communality of property.(Acts, 4:32-7).

Those who made themselves "eunuchs" for the

Kingdom of Heaven, moreover, seemed to offer a more proper response than Plato's confused communality of wives and children.(Matthew, 19:10-12) Finally, when the rich young man asked the Lord what yet was lacking to him, he was told to go, sell what he had, give it to the poor, and to follow Jesus.(Luke, 19:18-30) The scripture says that the young man "went away sad, because he had many possessions." Needless to say, when Christian philosophers reflected on such passages in the light of Plato's guardians, they were, like certain passages in the Republic itself, "amazed." Like St. Augustine, they were struck about how close certain elements in Plato were to revelation. Was this merely an accident? Or was there some sort of "intelligence" that somehow was able to explain how all these things ought to be ordered and related?

This particular theme of the Christian guardians is worth pursuing at this point. It serves to suggest, in an initial fashion at least, how revelation and classical political philosophy worked on each other and why such ideas about family, property, and civil society keep recurring in political thought and experience in various forms up to the present. Igor Shafarevich has argued to the abiding relations of these ideas in socialism, how the death of man seems to be involved in them.[5] The history of Christian heresies almost invariably suggests the danger of these ideas when they appear outside the limits of Christian orthodoxy as it reflects upon and corrects classical insights.[6] But the relationship is mutual, since the scriptural revelation never implied that man could not find out many things by his own reason and was, indeed, obliged and incited to do so.

Undoubtedly, the most outlandish and oft-cited passages from Plato have to do with his proposals for the communality of wives, children and property for his guardians in the Fifth Book of The Republic. Indeed, the proposal caused considerable astonishment to Socrates's friends, Adeimantos and Polymarchus, themselves. And when Socrates had previously suggested that his discourse about the delicate subject of "friends having all things in common" should have a limit, Glaucon replied that "the whole of life is the only limit which wise men assign to the hearing of such discourses." (#450b)

Historically, as we now realize, not even many centuries of lifetimes have sufficed to resolve the implications of the proposals of Socrates with their overtones of eugenic planning, their rigid asceticism, and their hope that economic reorganization will cure human ills. Christianity, with its rich young man who was told to sell what he had and give it to the poor, was nowhere as radical as Plato seemed to be on the same subject, though both seemed to be driving at the same point, that some ultimate sacrifice was necessary should we hope to attain the highest things.

Yet, Christianity has had a love-hate relationship with Plato, even with his guardians. Somehow, even when Plato seemed most wrong, he seemed at the same time almost right. The Christian principle that grace cures nature has nowhere worked more remarkably that with Plato who may well have been the greatest thinker our kind has yet produced. Thus, on the one hand, Plato seems like a providential precursor, a kind of intellectual John the Baptist, preparing the way for the coming of the Lord. Whereas John had said, "Repent, the Kingdom of God is at hand", Plato advised, "My counsel is that we hold fast ever to the heavenly way and follow after justice and virtue always, considering that the soul is immortal and able to endure every sort of good and every sort of evil. Thus shall we live dear to one another and to the Gods .... "(#621d)

Furthermore, Socrates sighs in The Republic, when asked of the perfect state if it might come about on earth, that, except perhaps by a "divine call," no statesman could ever hope to achieve good in any existing society. The only time the Socratic "voice" is silent is when Socrates goes to the trial of his death. And Plato sadly prophesied that when the truly good man does appear on earth, he will be thought unjust, will be "scourged, racked, bound -- will have his eyes burned out; and, at last, after suffering every kind of evil, he will be impaled". (#361e-62a) No Christian, of course, could read such lines in retrospect without a sense of awe. And surely no one was more devoted to the good, more concerned to abolish evil, than this same Plato.

Yet, Plato is also accused, because of his charm, of almost corrupting Christianity. His immortality was not the doctrine of the resurrection; his ideals were not the kind of concrete actions in which virtue existed, evidently. His body-soul dichotomy has been chastized again and again. Professor Kreyche in his essay, "Christianity and the Person," attributed our failure to understand what properly a person is to Plato. He wrote:

> Part of the fault for past overstress on 'souls' often to the detriment of persons, was due to Christianity's long-standing flirtation with Greek philosophy, especially that of Plato. We recall that St. Augustine leaned heavily on Platonic ideas and expressions and so gave an impetus to a one-sided view of man. For Plato, man was a 'soul using a body'. Man did not have a soul so much as he was a soul 'imprisoned in a body as an oyster in a shell'.[7]

Plato's description of that "wild beast" which is within us harboring every conceivable form of folly and vice would seem to suggest that Plato had a very pessimistic view of actual human beings. He seemed to go even beyond the classic doctrine of original sin to imply that human nature itself was somehow at fault. (#571c-d)

On the other hand, Plato seemed to expect that, given the right training and the right use of dialectics, we could actually arrive at a direct vision of the good. He seemed to pass from pessimism to optimism without bothering to ask about the real condition of most men. And even when he tried to account for the way most men are, he ended up in The Laws mostly closer to his constant ideals. Also he seemed almost Gnostic or Pelagian in setting forth an ideal of self-achievement in the very highest things, though he did bear hints that some kind of divine help was needed.

Plato, of course, must be first judged by what he really held and this in his own context. We must first begin by being loyal to him. But we should be loyal to him as he was to the poets -- "loving Homer, as I do ...." -- rejecting only what is not in conformity with the truth. (#391a) Plato is not responsible for parts of him taken out of his context, though it must be admitted as an historical fact that no one is more easy to take things from than Plato. Professor Karl Popper accused Plato of being at the origin of fascism, a most dubious and unfair charge against that ancient philosopher, whose castigations of tyranny are still perhaps the most eloquent in political philosophy. (#573ff.)

Nonetheless, Plato did inaugurate many ideas the human mind evidently cannot let go of because somehow they seem to be true even when they seem false. The most noteworthy of these ideas is undoubtedly Plato's proposal that there be philosophic guardians in the ideal state who really know the just and the good. That they might do this, Plato proposed that the guardians have a special kind of practical life so that they might not deviate from their first devotion to the common good of others who depended upon a real vision of the good.

Quite logically, and even rigidly, Plato then followed the consequences of this conclusion. This meant that there was to be no distinction of male and female. All that was normally thought to be joined to this basic relationship was removed. Eros was completely replaced by justice in an intellectual act that probably reveals best their radical differences. Wives and children were to be in common. Property, the institution that enabled the life of man in the household to come to be and continue, was eliminated. An ideal of poverty and asceticism was put in the place of the normal erotic and familial spirit. Plato's guardians received practically nothing, not even honor, for they were to rule because if they did not, some one less qualified would.

Plato held, moreover, that uncontrolled desires, especially those for wealth and of passion, would destroy any polis. Thus, he naturally sought to remove any such temptations from his guardians. He therefore became the father of a thought that has reappeared in every era subsequent to his -- namely, that if we would have men to be truly good, we must rearrange, limit, even abolish their marital and property structures. The training of the guardians sounds, not without reason, like nothing so much as the rule of the Christian religious orders.

This is heady doctrine, to be sure, and much more attractive than Aristotle's sane criticism of it would seem to indicate. Plato only applied this eccentric and exalted discipline to a few, and it awaited more modern times for an attempt to apply its rigors to all, as various socialist-inspired ideas tried to do. The idea that what is wrong with the public order is due to property and family structures, however, is perhaps the most abiding and attractive of political heresies. This theory gained double plausibility when joined with the description in the <u>Book of Genesis</u> of the consequences of the Fall such that communality of material goods and primitive family relationships were seen to be the pure condition of mankind. Again Plato seemed like a prophet.

This is why, no doubt, it is extremely difficult for the human mind to accept Aristotle's perceptive caveat concerning this redistributionist mentality:

> Such legislation (wives/property) may have a specious appearance of benevolence; men readily listen to it, and are easily induced to believe that in some wonderful manner everybody will become everybody's friend, especially when someone is heard denouncing the evils now existing in states -- suits about contracts, convictions for perjury, flatteries of rich men and the like -- which are said to arise out of the possession of private property. These evils, however, are due to a very different cause -- the wickedness of human nature. Indeed, we see that there is much more quarrelling among those who have all things in common .... (1253b15-25).

The question arose historically, then, how was Plato to be saved from this insightful perception of his great pupil, and this especially since Aristotle was no less devoted to the contemplative truth and good than Plato?

I do not want to argue this question here primarily in terms of subsequent political philosophy. Yet, and this will be my point, the Christian version of the Platonic guardians is currently at the heart of a social movement to implant a modernized edition of the property-wives controversy into the whole world. In so doing, of course, we risk losing both Plato and Aristotle. Indeed, we risk losing Christianity itself. Religious and monkish controversies are perhaps at first sight insignificant. On the other hand, there is a view of Christianity which would make them the really significant ones in the world, since what happens in the heart of the monk foreshadows what will happen in the world. Plato's own fear was undoubtedly a real one -- "And may we not say, Adeimantos, that the most gifted minds, when they are ill-educated, become pre-eminently bad?" (#491e) Thus, confusions or corruptions in the guardians, of whatever style they be designated, have vast ramifications in the political and spiritual orders.

But what does it mean to speak of "Christian guardians"? Plato, as I have suggested, was almost right on everything he did. Aristotle's corrections taught us to realize this, as did St. Augustine's. That we humans look for a city in which the true justice and the true goodness rule for our own sake, that this good is the source of all our good -- such is not a wrong vision. Indeed, it is a right one. Whether such a vision is a "political" one, however, is the crucial issue which Christianity, along with Aristotle, put to Plato. Or perhaps it would be more correct to say that it is the issue that Plato put to himself in Book X of The Republic, wherein the great astonishment over the belief in immortality is brought up.

Yet, it only arises after we decide what justice is and whether we ought to love it for its own sake. Indeed, the question of rewards and punishments only arises when we are assured we ought to love the good no matter what rewards or punishments we may receive. The final myth of The Republic was designed to prove not so much that we will be punished or rewarded in the after-life, but that we must choose "virtue" in this life or else our after-life will be as disastrous and as disordered as this one. Plato told us, in other words, that the life we are given is the one wherein we must initially choose correctly.

The implications of this position are profound. The intellectual guardians have a special obligation to the good in the first place. Anyone who reads Plato's proposals for communality of wives, children, and property, his eugenic proposals, is quite normally shocked by their evident inhumaneness. These ideas, however, are powerful ones, as I have suggested, so that the human race has not let them go easily, least of all that part of the human race that calls itself Christian. Plato was correct in The Laws in insisting that " ... sight, hearing, sensation, life itself, are superlatively evil, if one could persist for ever without dying in the enjoyment of these so-called goods unaccompanied by justice and virtue at large." (#661b)

If the path to this vision means the sacrifice of personal happiness that Plato required for the common

74

good, there are many who will accept it. The Christian tradition, interestingly enough, did not reject Plato out of hand but rather discovered a way through its own light in which what he argued could be accepted. Though their origins are not exclusively Platonic, the Christian guardians did seek to transform the Platonic vision in such a way that it could be lived without the terrible implications of the community of wives, children, and property.

How was this to be accomplished? There were two steps, the first made possible largely by St. Augustine. Since the necessity for the guardians arose because human society needed some group devoted to the highest good as its proper goal -- a goal no longer political in origin but contemplative -- this became the main vocation of the monk, the life devoted first to God. In the division of societal labor, itself a Platonic thought, the religious was to do that exclusive task that transcended all the others, to keep the idea of the Lord and devotion to Him alive within society. Secondly, he needed to be free of those goods and ambitions that might interfere with his full devotion to the good, to God. All were to benefit from this, all were to have their place and charism. But the setting-aside of some to this exalted end in a special fashion divided them from both the home and the polis.

Consequently, the Platonic proposal whose purpose was to prevent eros or greed from interfering with his guardians' life of knowing the good and ruling society in accordance with it was neatly solved by the religious vows of chastity and poverty. These bore a remarkably sane similarity to the spirit of Plato's original purpose and avoided all its obvious, indeed inhuman difficulties. Nor it was now necessary to worry about marital and filial problems, to speculate about eugenics. Property was in common but the rule was to guarantee that the mine and thine were regulated within the monastery. Moreover, the distinction of a proper political life from a contemplative one, and also of a proper family one, enabled the polis to have its legitimate place but yet not absolutely the highest one. Neatly, the city, the family, and the contemplative life were saved by a Christian insight that protected all three.

The breakdown of the solution of Christian guardians has taken two steps. The first step was the Reformation, in which, as Max Weber pointed out, the distinction between the secular and the religious "vocation" was eliminated. Even Plato had insisted that the guardians ought to live a different life from the one normal to most people. Furthermore, there had always been a current in Christianity which held that monkish life was either impossible or dangerous. The traditional Church, on the other hand, held that it was possible and indeed dangerous, but that it was not for all. The special service to the Lord was, thus, to be by rule, in some sense, set apart. Consequently, Catholic Christianity had realized the danger to the normal life of most people in comparing them with the monk, who was devoted to the contemplative life.

Holiness, it had to be recognized, however, contained a wide variety of possibilities which ought neither to be reduced to a common level nor forbidden in its diversity. The "City of God," furthermore, was not the city of the world. The mystical and metaphysical aspects of Plato were indeed worthy and necessary ones. But their fulfilment was ultimately pretty much where Plato himself placed them, in the life of immortality. This end was transformed in Christianity by the doctrines of the resurrection and sharing in the Trinitarian life of God as the ultimate and permanent destiny of man. Compared to this, no earthly city was at all complete -- again a feeling we get from Plato.

The Christian solution is undergoing a second transformation in our own times. The "City of God", as an aspect and object of contemplation and of life from death, has been gradually transformed for many monks into a worldly task. The purpose of religion, especially of religious life, came more or less to be seen as aid in transforming the world into the perfect or better society. The intellectual tension and faith in classical Christianity have not been holding, something sceptics from the Enlightenment never thought they could do in any case. A vast and growing intellectual effort to transform the classic Christian doctrines into functional images and goals for a worldly purpose and city, this, often under the impetus of monks and religious, has now been largely completed.

Currently, the basic drama within Christianity is over whether this new doctrinal formulation can gain the seats of ecclesiastical power; that is, whether the older doctrines will be evaporated of their

contemplative, transcendent content. To suggest that
Christian monasticism has given up its historical
justification of contemplative worship leading to
prayer, resurrection, and eternal life for a political
role in the world would, perhaps, be too much. The
older Jesuit axiom of contemplation-in-action,
however, came to be used as a tool to justify largely
this-worldly activities as religious. Today, people
are hard pressed to find preached in their churches or
to read in the religious media anything that is not
sociological, economic, or religious-political. When
they wonder, they are then told that this is what
faith is about.

Thus, the classic Christian idea of things of
Caesar and of God has come to be practically
interpreted, to be reunited in an effort, supposedly,
to produce a new international order or what have you,
one thus that results from transformed property and
institutional structures, the modern guise of the
Platonic formula. Religious zeal is seen primarily in
work, not prayer, work within the world, for the
world. Contemplation approaches action to the degree
that it disappears as a real function of monastic
life. The poverty and celibacy of religious life are
to witness, when they are still held, not to God but
to worldly example. At the further extremes, to which
so many ideas currently lead, the institutions
supporting classic religious life become levelled.
Plato's rigid feminine egalitarianism demands entrance
into convent and monastery. Children themselves have
become mostly obsolete, if not evil. Population, not
wickedness, has become the great scourge.

When we seek to define the goal of this kind of
spirit, we must go back again to Plato himself, to a
remarkable, prophetic passage from The Laws:

> If there is now on earth, or ever
> should be, such a society -- a community in
> women-folk, in children, in all possessions
> whatsoever, if all means have been taken to
> eliminate everything we mean by the word
> 'ownership' from life, if all possible means
> have been taken to make even what nature has
> made our own in some sense common property,
> I mean, our eyes, ears, and hands seen to
> see, hear, and act in common service, if,
> moreover, we all approve and condemn in
> perfect unison and derive pleasure and pain
> from the same sources -- in a word, when the

institutions of a society make it utterly
one, that is a criterion of their excellence
than which no truer or better will ever be
found. If there is anywhere such a city,
with a number of gods, or sons of gods, for
its inhabitants, they will dwell there in
all joyousness of life. (#739c-e)

I cite this remarkable passage at some length since it
is almost certainly the ultimate source of Marx's
famous passage in his Economic and Philosophic
Manuscripts of 1844, wherein he wanted his atheist
humanism, his version of the perfect earthly city, to
self-create even man, even what he sees and does.

Marx's words are instructive in this context:

The suppression of private property is
therefore complete emancipation of all human
qualities and senses. It is this
emancipation because these qualities and
senses have become human, from the
subjective as well as the objective point of
view. The eye has become a human eye when
its object has become a human social object,
created by man and destined for him. The
senses have therefore become directly
theoreticians in practice.[8]

What I wish to suggest in citing these passages is
that the classic Platonic object of the guardians, the
contemplative vision of the good, has by a series of
ironic, historical twists come to be identified with a
practical political project to conform to the ideal
now seen not as an ultimate form, nor as a
supernatural life given of God, but as the
construction of an earthly city wherein Socrates would
not have been killed. What is new recently is that
this idea and project (essentially belonging to the
Enlightenment) has appeared most obviously in the
religious orders.

Christian guardians, thus, are now seen not as
separate from economic and political society to
preserve and worship a higher good, but rather as
"doers" making the good. The spiritual seeing,
hearing, and feeling have their objects in the public
order wherein property organization and removal of
sinful structures -- by this very reorganization and
contrary to Aristotle -- will produce the kind of
world the Lord presumably wants here below.

Underneath it all, this is the intellectual spirit of our times. This is an era still fascinated by part of the Platonic vision, one now reaching the extreme that not even Socrates suspected would come to be.

In Book VI of The Republic, Socrates said that what remains is this: "The question how the study of philosophy may be so ordered as not to be the ruin of the state: All great attempts are attended with risk ...."(#497d) This remains true. Nowhere is the risk greater than in pursuing the visions of Plato. Near the end of The City of God, St. Augustine wrote: "Some Christians, who have a liking for Plato on account of his magnificent style and the truths which he now and then uttered, say that he even held an opinion similar to our own regarding the resurrection of the dead."(Book XXII, Chapter 28)

In conclusion, I suspect, those ancient Christians who were enamored with Plato's style were closer to his truth than our modern Christian guardians, tempted to assure us, contrary to Socrates' feeling and inspiration, that the ideal kingdom is about to become an existing one.

"In heaven," I replied, "there is laid up a pattern of it, methinks, which he who desires may behold, and beholding may set his own house in order. But whether such an one exists, or ever will exist in fact, is not matter; for he will live after the manner of that city, having nothing to do with any other." (#592b)

In searching for the completion of Plato's vision in the resurrection rather than in the transformation of this world as the Christian truth, I suspect the Christians cited by St. Augustine had much the better insight into the real Platonic mystery.

At a certain point in The Republic (#505a), Plato ceased talking about justice and began to talk about the good. Recently, among what I have been calling Christian guardians, discourse about the good, especially under its form of mercy and charity, has practically ceased, to be subsumed into a discourse about justice. Ultimately, however, Christian guardians exist to tell us in all existing states that we have here no lasting city. When in their actions and speech they fail to do this, they betray not only the Christianizers of Plato, but indeed Plato

himself. We still must look for the only life that
looks down on political ambition, a life not only of
true philosophy, but also one of true gift, one not
made, but given to our own eyes and ears.

Footnotes:

1. See Christopher Dawson, The Making of Europe, New York, Sheed and Ward, 1945; Religion and the Rise of Western Culture, New York, Sheed and Ward, 1950; Christopher Derrick, The Rule of Peace, St. Bede's Press, 1979; Ernest Barker, The Dominican Order and Convocation, Oxford, Clarendon, 1913.

2. Josef Pieper, Scholasticism, New York, Pantheon, 1960; James V. Schall, "Luther and Political Philosophy: The Rise of Autonomous Man," Faith and Reason, Summer, 1982, pp. 7-31.

3. See James V. Schall, "Monastery and Home," in The Distinctiveness of Christianity, San Francisco, Ignatius Press, 1983, Chapter XIII, pp. 200-17.

4. Dawson, Religion, ibid., pp. 45-72.

5. Igor Shafarevich, The Socialist Phenomenon, New York, Harper, 1980.

6. See Michael Walzer, The Revolution of the Saints, Cambridge, Harvard University Press, 1965. See G. K. Chesterton, Heretics, New York, John Lane, 1905.

7. Robert Kreyche, Christianity and the Person, London, Catholic Truth Society, ND, p. 4.

8. Karl Marx, "Economic and Philosophical Manuscripts of 1844," Marx's Concept of Man, Bottomore, Editor, New York, Ungar, 1961, p. 132.

81

CHAPTER V

ON THE NEGLECT OF HELL IN POLITICAL THEORY

Man, as by good or ill deserts, in the
exercise of his free choice, he becomes
liable to rewarding or punishing justice.
-- [Dante, to Can Grande della Scala,
Commenting on his Divine Comedy.]

The most significant consequence of the
secularization of the modern age may well be
the elimination from public life, along with
religion, of the only political element in
traditional religion, the fear of hell. --
[Hannah Arendt, Between Past and Future,
Viking, 1968, p. 133.]

If the value of medieval political theory is for
us that it retains and deepens our appreciation of the
events and meaning of the Old and New Testaments, of
the death of Jesus as well as the death of Socrates,
of the powerful reflection of St. Augustine, how this
might relate to the intellectual position of the
Greeks, it would indeed already be enough to justify
its continuing study. But beyond this, there are
other sorts of reflections that Christian and medieval
theory brings up, ones based more on points of
doctrine or philosophy, but points that remain
fundamental to the structure of the human mind
itself. The question of "Christian Guardians," as we
have seen, is one of these. Questions of the best and
worst forms of rule, of the meaning of evil, of how we
are to look at law and destiny, likewise, cannot be
avoided in any complete political philosophy, however
curious at first sight they may sound.

These are, moreover, issues that were of
particular concern to Christian medieval thought,
issues that somehow reappear in obscure and
secularized forms when they are not confronted
directly as major elements in political theory. The
first, and perhaps the most perplexing of these, is
undoubtedly the question of hell, of ultimate
damnation, a question, as I will suggest, that finds
its legitimate place in political theory as an aspect

83

of the classical question of the worst form of government. Often, the contemporary problem of nuclear war is confused with this question of hell.[1] (See Chapter IX) The relation of these questions to that of the worst state as it appears in classical political thought is, indeed, a fundamental one.

Professor J. W. Allen once remarked about the man who forms the intellectual transition to Machiavelli and modern theory, that for Marsilius of Padua, "The function of the priest, in fact, is to supplement the action of the police and the judge by the fear of hell."[2] Even Marsilius seemed uneasy with this curious thesis, but his whole political thought was an effort to add to Aristotle's causes of revolution, the one cause that the author of The Politics could not have foreseen, the Christian clergy. Since Marsilius had reduced the spiritual power already to pure interiority, this left the priests with nothing to "do" except perhaps make mischief and civil unrest. And yet, in recalling this hesitation, that perhaps police and judges did need something more than themselves and bare reason to preserve the very public order itself, Marsilius unconsciously placed himself within an aspect of political reflection going back at least to Plato and forward to certain neglected aspects of contemporary thought.

The very idea of "judges and police," moreover, recalls the Stoic and Christian notions of the origin of coercive government in The Fall. The modern theoretical effort to gain for politics complete autonomy from "the priestly causes of revolution," from the claim that not all things belong to Caesar, on the other hand, has resulted in an attempt to identify "hell" with a worldly political movement or event -- a Hitler, a holocaust, a nuclear war, a class structured society, a tyranny. In this sense, "hell" has come to be identified with the question known since the Greeks as the worst form of government. "Hell on Earth," the need for some absolute rejection of the good, has become a viable political polarity against which to define and practically justify political movements and thoughts, ones which purport to avoid this ultimate, politically defined evil. (See Chapters VI and IX)

This idea, to be sure, seemed stable enough in a culture based on known natural law and values such that the evils to be described were commonly agreed upon. Here, the locus of ultimate punishment was

dogmatically taken out of the hands of civil power,
taken indeed out of this world itself. With the
introduction of Joachim of Flora's Ages of History,
with the presence of Hegelian methodology in its
various forms, however, the distressing possibility
that the worst could become the best came to be posed
at the heart of practical politics because of the
nature of a certain kind of abstract metaphysics, the
kind that proves better than any other the value and
need of classical metaphysics.

The intellectual history of political theory, of
course, recalls with uneasy equanimity the last days
of Socrates, when the best state condemned the best
man, the long discourse on the immortality of the
soul. (See Chapter II) This is the classic context,
even yet, to ponder the relation of human politics to
human happiness. The argument in The Republic that
the tyrant was really the only wise man is still
difficult to refute. The end of The Republic,
moreover, presented a different issue. Socrates, in a
passage of much power, had raised the still startling
issue of immortality at the heart of political
discourse. By this time, in The Republic, he raised
it not in the face of death by the state but rather in
the inability of the public order to rest if justice
was not rewarded and injustice punished. Only then
did the question of absolute punishment come up.(Book
X) This was already one very large step beyond the
Sophoclean notion that vengeance can only be stopped
in the polis. And so it seemed clear that since no
existing order less than the one formed by the
philosopher-king as a direct result of his clear
knowledge of the Good could guarantee this, the idea
of future rewards and punishments was necessary for
the good of the existing political order itself as
well as for the theoretically inadequate idea of
justice.

Hell is not an exclusively Christian concept, of
course, but its history and necessity arise out of
justice questions. However, Homer and Vergil
themselves remind us of the places below. We have
only to recall the relation of Augustus Caesar to
Vergil to suspect there might be for political thought
some subtle connection between the underworld and
political justice. Nonetheless, the long theoretical
refinement of what "hell" might mean has given it in
our eyes distinctly Christian overtones as it has been
explicitated over the centuries. Here, perhaps, it is
well to cite The Oxford Dictionary of the Christian

Churches to recall the theological point of the idea
of hell, a point that conditions Western political
reflections:

> ... In the New Testament, Hell ... is
> an ultimate state or destiny into which
> souls pass only by God's final and
> irrevocable judgment ... According to
> traditional scholastic theology, souls
> experience in Hell both the poena damni,
> i.e., the exclusion from God's presence and
> loss of all contact with him, and a certain
> poena sensus, denoted in the Bible by fire,
> which is usually interpreted as an external
> agent tormenting them.

> Modern theology tends rather to stress
> the fact that Hell is but the logical
> consequences of ultimate adherence to the
> soul's own will, and rejection of the will
> of God, which (since God cannot take away
> free will) necessarily separates the soul
> from God, and hence from all possibility of
> happiness. This exclusion from Heaven (in
> which the unrepentant person would from his
> very character be both unable and unwilling
> to share) is held to be contrary neither to
> God's justice nor His love, since He will
> not force response to the good from any
> creature against his will.[3]

From this -- the point of evil will be taken up in the
following chapter -- it is evident that "hell" is a
doctrine about the ultimate reality and possibility of
human freedom, as well as a recognition that,
logically, evil must be punished and good rewarded.
To relativize the distinction of good and evil, then,
to deny any final reckoning, necessarily lessens any
possible or final importance to mankind. Hell is not
so much a doctrine about God as about man and the
importance of his actions both within and transcending
the polis.

The effect of these ideas is nowhere more clear
than in St. Augustine. And St. Augustine is in the
direct line of both Plato and the New Testament. He
himself is a political philosopher of the greatest
moment, so it is well to recall that the ultimate
"City of God" and hell are irreversibly connected in
his thought. St. Augustine, in the City of God still
wanted to know about the "fire" of hell, about its

eternity, its permanence.(Book XXI, Chapters 9-15)
Yet, the essential point -- and this is again the
characteristic Christian emphasis -- is that the
question of hell is the question of the nature of the
free will, not directly of cosmological place or
material substance, though not necessarily excluding
some material manifestation either.

From this point of view, St. Augustine's great
contribution to political theory falls precisely
within the Platonic tradition of properly political
thought. (See Chapter III) Can we, namely, expect
that a rearranging of the civil order will give us all
our proper places within the true good? Can politics,
in other words, yield the kind of happiness to which
we seem ultimately called? This is the issue that
will lie at the heart of all political theory proper
and wrench the very minds and states of men. In
defining the City of God and the city of man so that
they be not identified with Church or Empire, St.
Augustine was careful to deny to actual politics the
burden of guaranteeing man's ultimate good or
punishing his ultimate evil. Much peculiarly "modern"
political theory will be a valiant, if vain, effort to
retain this impossible burden for itself.[4] And yet,
St. Augustine himself, paradoxically, did not deny
that there was such an ultimate good and happiness,
nor did he deny it was open to man. What he denied,
following St. Paul, was that it was the product of a
political construction or reconstruction, which
depended on mainly human genius, will, or merit.

St. Augustine, placed the center of the whole
discussion clearly on will. What unites and divides
is the very will, not law nor polity. This is why St.
Augustine, in a momentous act, as we saw, denied
justice to be the constitutive element in any existing
state. Instead, he replaced justice with a common
"love", a will, a recognition that man can in fact
choose a politics that is not just and often he does.
St. Augustine, therefore, was not concerned with the
ultimate status of the city of man because it kept men
in order in the state. Rather, he was concerned to
confront the Platonic and Aristotelian questions about
the ultimate locus of human happiness and its relation
to political life.

Hell, in this sense, was a metaphysical and
religious issue, flowing out of the choice of one's
own form of justice. So St. Augustine held, that it
is a choice, a love, that has built the two cities.

87

With this profound insight, St. Augustine became, along with Thucydides, the founder of "political realism." According to this notion, more or less unjust societies had to deal with more or less unjust men and such will be the abiding condition of men in all generations wherein there continue to be men.

Aquinas, in his Treatise on Law, likewise was concerned with the legitimate place of politics.(I-II, 90-97) Aristotle was for him the main guide, though Aquinas ought never to be read without also realizing that he is St. Augustine's greatest follower. This meant that the political order does address itself to a certain kind of happiness, to the question that came to be known since Plato's Laws, as the second-best state. (See Chapter VIII) Thus, politics has a legitimate area. There are things that do belong to Caesar. But politics does not exhaust the meaning of man nor his happiness even though he be the "social and political animal," to repeat again Aquinas's translation of Aristotle.

In his famous question about the philosophic "necessity" of the divine law, of revelation, therefore, Aquinas argued clearly that civil law could not directly of its own force reach the internal forum of conscience, that it could not punish all wrongs nor reward all rights.(I-II, 91, 4) Consequently, without some revelation of divine justice and mercy, men would not be able to accept the "rightness" of the whole cosmic order nor of their own political systems, which could never be themselves direct responses to transcending issues.[5](I, 21, 4; 65)

Again, the issue of hell, of our ultimate punishment, arose in a political context, this time in Aquinas' question about whether all evils had to be punished by civil law. But this time it served to restrict the civil order so it would not claim absolute power over all mind and action. Nor could the civil order uphold the philosophic sense of justice that logically demanded the punishment of all politically undetected wrongs.(I-II, 96, 2) Such "wrongs" were conceived in Aquinas to be acts against the kind of rational, free being, whose explanation for what he is lies ultimately with God, not in men. This is precisely why there is a hierarchy of laws, so that the law of freedom cannot be set against the law of God that made man to be man in the first place, as Aristotle said.

Aquinas, moreover, in the <u>Contra Gentiles</u>, wherein he treated of the ultimate consequences of serious fault, again argued on a political analogy. He held, on the Augustinian-Christian premise that it is free will that makes the eternal punishment justifiable, that a "free" creature, with no possibility of choosing God or refusing His world, would be an intrinsic contradiction. Hell is part of the necessary consequences of being human in the first place.

Aquinas thus argued:

> Natural equity would seem to argue that one would be deprived of that precise good against which he acted. Because of his act then, he renders himself unworthy of that good. Thus it is that according to civil justice, anyone who acts against the commonwealth is deprived of that same commonwealth either by death or by exile. Nor is the issue how long the crime took, but what it is against when it did take place.

> The same comparison is valid if the whole present life is referred to the earthly estate, and of all eternity to the Society of the Blessed which achieves the ultimate end eternally. So whoever sins against this ultimate end and against charity, through which in the first place exists the Society of the Blessed and those tending towards it, ought to be punished eternally even though they seemed to act for a brief moment of time. (III, CXLIV)

From this consideration, then, the purpose of eternal punishment was to allow freedom the consequences of its metaphysical choice, its own seriousness. This is taken against the kind of "good" which classical political philosophy somehow proposed searching for from its beginning in Plato and Aristotle. Hell, thereby, frees politics from an impossible worldly burden inasmuch as it backs up a contingent, imperfect civil order in such a way that this same political order is not forced to see its task that of exercising absolute justice and punishment by its own efforts.

So long as hell was conceived as a purely "religious" problem, no doubt, it was largely ignored

89

by political theory. A reading of the last book of The Leviathan, however, will readily show that even the most rigorous materialistic philosopher acknowledged its need to be accounted for, if only to prevent his own political construct from itself becoming a "hell," which indeed it appeared to be. The tendency of liberal theory in modern times, in any case, has been systematically to deny that anything done by man within society, or even in his own personal life, could be so horrendous as to deserve such a consequence known from theology as hell. This indeed did seem "liberal."

But whether the elimination of the absoluteness connected with hell results in a "liberal consequence" remains to be discussed. From the Enlightenment, we supposedly learned that this doctrine of hell was one that so shackled men that they did not strive to eliminate the social ills they could remove. They assumed hell would ultimately correct all unpunished wrongs. But if hell is "demythologized," so to speak, then it logically follows that evil and destructive social orders, the classical forms of bad rule, need not be seen cyclically as with Thucydides, nor as an absolutely stable sign of what is wrong, as with the Christians. Rather, they could be seen programatically in order that "evil" and its consequences in human life become objects for political elimination.

This was the project of Rousseau, when he, prophetically, decided to identify the source of evil in the state and civilization not in the Fall as in classic Christianity and in its consequences -- in labor, birth in pain, and coercive government, as St. Augustine and Aquinas saw it -- but in the property and governmental relationships themselves. Aristotle had previously hinted that the human condition itself had a tendency to rebel against its proper limits, its seeming bondage as the lowest of the spiritual beings, because the highest good was properly contemplative.(982b:25-32)

Therefore, human nature was not directly the product of man's own political making, his own "action". Aristotle thus set the stage for a political theory refusing to accept Aristotle's own limits. This meant, as it historically worked itself out, that the goal of politics could be conceived as an effort to produce a full and proper happiness for man, one proper to him because formed and chosen for him not by "nature" but by himself. The "optimism" of

Enlightenment thought and that flowing from it, even until today, is based upon the rejection of any metaphysical limits to this project.

The other side of reducing the proposal for ultimate happiness to a political project, however, was already revealed in the French Revolution, wherein the terror seemed to be the logical consequence of optimistic theory. Burke, from his post in England, was not wrong in suspecting that something was radically dangerous about the perfectionist project. His words linger still to echo the thesis that even kings and queens remain human against the first signs of utopian ideologies in the modern world, philosophies that invariably reduce actual human beings, no matter how bad, to types and figures:

> This king, to say no more of him, and this queen, and their infant children, (who once would have been the pride and hope of a great and generous people) were then forced to abandon the sanctuary of the most splendid palace in the world, which they left swimming in blood, polluted by massacre, and strewed with scattered limbs and mutilated carcases. Thence, they were conducted into the capital of their kingdom. Two had been selected from the unprovoked, unresisted, promiscuous slaughter, which was made of the gentlemen of birth and family who composed the king's body guard. These two gentlemen, with all the parade of an execution of justice, were cruelly and publicly dragged to the block, and beheaded in the great court of the palace. Their heads were stuck upon spears, and led the procession; whilst the royal captives who followed in the train were slowly moved along, amidst the horrid yells, and shrilling screams, and frantic dances, and infamous contumelies, and all the unutterable abominations of the furies of hell, in the abused shape of the vilest of women.[6]

And ever since this time, especially since the post-World War I era, there has been an underground tendency that recognized that an acutal this-worldly "hell" was on the other side of the perfectionist endeavors. All the "anti-utopians" of the 20's to 50's of this century began to warn us solemnly of

91

1984, now here, the Darkness at Noon, the Brave New World.[7] And Dostoyevsky had already foreseen that the old theory of tyranny would have to be replaced by a devil incarnate, a hell on earth, which made men believe that bread was really their goal. Notes from the Underground were rapidly becoming the realities of our political choices.[8]

Hell has not been abolished, therefore, as theologically untenable but rather it has reappeared in secular guise. No longer is evil seen as a resultant from the choices of responsible, fallen human persons in their historical ambiguities, but evil has been incarnate, something classical Christianity never attributed to it. Classes, nations, beliefs are the "causes" of evil and must be rejected in toto since, we are told, there can be no compromise with it in its visible form. The Hegelian dialectic not only broke the absolute dichotomy of good and evil, the one symbolized in the very account of creation in Genesis, but it also showed how evil in the world could be "overcome." From the classic point of view, this had the effect of assigning evil to groups and movements so that the personalist evolution of Western thought was reversed.[9] (See Chapter XI) Individuals could be eliminated -- beginning with the king as Burke saw and ending with just anyone as our current revolutionaries and terrorists teach us. They bore the sign of visible evil on their foreheads. And their lives literally became a hell since no human traditions governed their existence and limited what could be accomplished against them.

At this point, the problem of hell enters modern political thought. For the effort to establish an absolute happiness by political means is a heresy still very prevalent in various Third World political and religious trends, trends almost always revealing Enlightenment origins. Its consequence is the need to eliminate the causes of evil as such, so that its embodiment does not lie in a human will but in a group or class with no reference to individual choice or moral status.[10] This is why modern revolutionary violence pays relatively little attention to personal guilt, but justifies itself in terms of variously disguised forms of "collective guilt," various "social sins." No one is "innocent" who falls under the ideological definition of the cause of evil. Again the old theological issue of original sin becomes re-enacted in a perverse manner within a political context. And in a perfectionist political theory, be

92

it noted, when ultimate happiness is promised to arrive with the movement down the ages, the elimination from this life through terror of any opposition is equivalent to hell, to the absolute destruction of what supposedly opposes the good.

The belief that evil can be removed by political action, thus, turns out to be the cause for the secularization of hell as a political instrument to justify the good life. The good life arrives when the evil classes or movements or types are eliminated. Eric Voegelin touched upon this in The New Science of Politics:

> The death of the spirit is the price of progress. Nietzsche revealed this mystery of the western apocalypse when he announced God was dead and that He had been murdered. This Gnostic murder is constantly committed by the men who sacrifice God to civilization. The more fervently all human energies are thrown into the great enterprise of salvation through world-immanent action, the farther the human beings who engage in this enterprise move away from the life of the spirit. And since the life of the spirit is the source of order in man and society, the very success of a Gnostic civilization is the cause of its decline.[11]

The life of the spirit, thus, comes to be challenged by the life of politics seen as a means to salvation. This salvific claim was consistently denied to politics in the classical Christian tradition, as well as in Aristotle.

What this consideration suggests, therefore, is an issue rarely faced any more in the heart of political theory but nevertheless one continually present in often undetected forms: namely, is "the modern project" for a completely rational politics possible without a revelation to save reason? This was, of course, the Thomistic implication, that it was not in practice possible. And it would be deceptive, even on empirical grounds, to maintain that this is still not the question. Leo Strauss, with his usual perception, put his finger on the exact issue:

> The natural law which is knowable to the unassisted human mind and which

93

prescribes chiefly actions in the strict sense is related to, or founded upon, the natural end of man; that end is twofold: moral perfection and intellectual perfection; intellectual perfection is higher in dignity than moral perfection; but intellectual perfection or wisdom, as unassisted human reason knows it, does not require moral virtue. Thomas solves this difficulty by virtually contending that, according to natural reason, the natural end of man is insufficient, or points beyond itself or, more precisely, that the end of man cannot consist in philosophic investigation, to say nothing of political activitiy. Thus natural reason itself creates a presumption in favor of the divine law which completes or perfects the natural law. At any rate, the ultimate consequences of the Thomistic view of natural law is that natural law is practically inseparable not only from natural theology -- i.e., from a natural theology which is, in fact, based on belief in biblical revelation -- but even from revealed theology. Modern natural law was partly a reaction to this absorption of natural law by theology.[12]

Now, of course, St. Thomas is somewhat more nuanced than Strauss suggested. But St. Thomas did hold that revelation is necessary for most men to know and keep most of the natural law, while one of the reasons for this same revelation was precisely the inability of civil law to punish all violations.(I-II, 91, 4) This clearly suggests that modern theory insofar as it explicitly rejects the idea of reason's limits, so that it claims the possibility of constructing rationally the good life, cannot be reconciled with classical Christianity. This is why medieval and modern natural law theories are fundamentally at variance.[13] And this too is the precise origin of the reappearance of hell as a political doctrine and practice, however it be called.

How is this to be understood? Hannah Arendt has argued that Christianity, when it became established, faced the same problem in the public order as did Plato in The Republic. She argued further that even the French and American revolutionary founders were concerned to emphasize the public function of hell.

94

In the context of Leo Strauss' reservations, Hannah Arendt's reflections are of uncommon significance:

> For the obvious reason why the men of the revolution of all people should be so strangely out of tune in this respect with the general climate of their age was that precisely because of the new separation of church and state they found themselves in the old Platonic predicament. When they warned against the elimination of the fear of hell from public life because this would pave the way to "make murder itself as indifferent as shooting plover, and the extermination of the Robilla nation as innocent as the swallowing of mites on a morsel of cheese (John Adams)," their words may sound with an almost prophetic ring in our ears; yet they were clearly spoken not out of any dogmatic faith in the "avenging God" but out of a mistrust in the nature of man.[14]

This latter, of course, is a remarkable line, since it locates the political necessity for the doctrine of hell exactly where Aquinas located the need for revelation with respect to reason, with the idea that reason was <u>not</u> sufficient to account for and punish all violations of justice.

Naturally, if pure reason closed off from any revelation -- the modern project -- ends up creating a kind of political hell, then it would follow, evidently, that political theory must reassess Strauss' restriction about the kind of reason that would save us. John Hallowell was one of the few contemporary theorists to grant the necessary conclusion. In his <u>Main Currents in Modern Political Thought</u>, he wrote:

> ... The basic insights of the Christian faith provide the best insights we have into the nature of man and of the crisis in which we find ourselves. That crisis is the culmination of modern man's progressive attempt to deny the existence of a transcendent or spiritual reality and of his progressive failure to find meaning in some wholly immanent conception of reality. Modern man's worship of the Class, the Race, or the State has only further alienated him

from reality, plunged him deeper into despair and impelled him further along the road to destruction and annihilation. Only through a return to faith in God, as God revealed Himself to man in Jesus Christ, can modern man and his society find redemption from the tyranny of evil.[15]

Professor Hallowell, then, considered that the alternative to an actual tyranny of evil, a hell, was not an exclusively "rational" project, even though, as least in Thomistic metaphysics, rationality need not be opposed to revelation no matter how much the latter aids the former. That it was so opposed was the central mistake in Professor Strauss' analysis of the relation of natural law to revelation. The systematic thinking out, the political activist's endeavor to root out those Christian supplements to pure reason, has left us with the kind of man motivated by no corrective influence. The penalty for thinking in a purely rational manner has been exactly that, pure reason.

Jacques Ellul's study The Betrayal of the West, is clearly an effort to trace this consequence. Its essence is to describe the victory of the modern political project, the founding of all right, history, and nature on man himself presupposed only to himself. Classical Christian metaphysics, as Jacques Maritain once wrote:

> ... is a philosophy of being; more than that, a philosophy of the superabundance of being ... Christian philosophy, better than the Greek, has seen that it is natural that immanent activity should superabound, since it is superexisting. Purely transitory activity is transitory ... Immanent activity is 'generous,' because, striving to be achieved in love, it strives to achieve the good of other men, disinterestedly, gratuitously, as a gift. Christian theology is a theology of divine generosity....[16]

And it is the disappearance of this universality, this "superabundance," that is most gravely affecting the present civilization.

Ellul himself put it quite well:

> It is in our day that Jesus is, in the

fullest and most radical sense, being rejected by everything -- I mean literally everything -- and in every area of man's endeavors: his thinking, his willing, his undertakings, his building of his world, his consumption. It is in our day that Jesus is being, in the fullest and most radical sense, humiliated: simply left aside as possessing no interest or significance in comparison with what man discovers for himself and bestows upon himself....

.... God's silence means that the world that wanted to be left alone is now indeed alone.... [17]

Again, it is this faith, which is thought to have been unnecessary to reason, together with what is still feared from human nature, that combine to make the classical Christian solution almost empirical. However much it may have been abandoned now by its own adherents, the consequences of any experienced alternative make it "reasonable" to look again at revelation.

To speak of the absence -- absence of something somehow felt to be "due" -- of what Christian belief has argued must be added to us if we would be whole, if we would achieve happiness as empirical, is, to be sure, paradoxical. Yet, in a real sense, if we consider that much of the duty and function of the modern state is to bureaucratize and organize, to make public, as it were, all the human concerns with poverty and sickness and weakness that Christianity brought initially into the world, a theme R. H. Tawney used to touch upon, then we can see the significance of the remarkable essay of Professor Gaylin, "In the Beginning -- Helpless and Dependent," in which he almost literally re-opens the whole question of the inadequacy of justice in private and public lives of men and nations.[18] (See Chapter XII) And Professor Glasser has suggested the empirical basis for the belief that natural reason, in the terms it has been understood in the modern era, is totally inadequate to substitute for personal benevolence. The only Christian addenda to this would be to wonder about the rather heroic effort of Professor Gaylin and his colleagues to discover a purely natural charity.

Professor Glasser wrote:

Liberal society, which is to say, caring society, came mostly to believe that the only difficulty with social services was that there weren't enough to go around; the public sector, they argued, was being starved in the midst of private affluence. If the quality of public education, public housing, child care, medical care, and welfare was not what it should be, it was primarily because of inadequate resources. What was needed, according to the liberals, was more not less State intervention....

The record of public charity is an unmitigated record of punishment, degradation, humiliation, intrusion, and incarceration ... The power of 'loveability' which normally saves the child from disaster has no precise social analogue....

Dependence upon the institutions of caring establishes -- for millions of people -- a condition of fragility against encroachments of power, and benevolence is the mask that hides it....

The state was all too willing to allocate substantial resources to the children if they were removed from their parents. But the state was not willing to provide equivalent services -- probably at less cost -- directly to the family in its own home.[19]

Benevolence, that secular rendition for Christian charity, cannot somehow retain its value apart from its original inspiration.

Ellul himself argued that the contemporary heresy is the belief that what men lack is clothing, food, shelter, and that this is the definition of religion, that of helping the brother.[20] And yet, this can be a complete, enclosed humanism out of which there is no escape, a perfect definition of hell. Here, all relationships are defined exclusively in terms of justice, in which no one is related to any one else except by legitimate obligation.[21] And from another tradition, as we suggested, this is the real implication of the widely read thesis of John Rawls' A Theory of Justice.[22] Men, consequently, end up alone -- again the classic definition of hell, the existence

98

of a world totally of our own norms and makings. This is a world of no relationships except those of justice, a justice we even make ourselves.[23]

Perhaps the best analysis of this result in its Christian implications is, again, Leszak Kolakowski's essay on saving the devil.[24] The question Kolakowski addressed himself to was the significance of the Christian doctrine of evil and hell, epitomized by the figure of Satan. To do this, he placed himself squarely before the modern political enterprise which set itself up as a project to eliminate evil. Evil was again defined variously through the Rousseauian tradition as property, labor, pain, and coercive government which need to be eliminated. Is evil, in other words, contingent? Is hell an illusion? To put it in other terms, what happens if these doctrines are relativized, as they have been in modern thought? Can we reconcile evil, as Kolakowski held many contemporary Christian thinkers try to do?

The fact is, in this tradition, that man is saved only in Christ in the Christian view so that he cannot ultimately save himself. Evil is not to be reconciled to the good but kept separate. Satan does not become Christ, the two value systems are not fused but ever to be kept apart. Man cannot then save himself, but he can refuse salvation. This is why, undoubtedly, in the classic medieval philosophic tradition, freedom could be affirmed without likewise holding that man created his own salvation.

Kolakowski, thus, pointed out that the changed belief of many Christians in precisely these dogmatic areas has political consequences. He suggested that the concepts of original sin and the existence of the devil have almost disappeared even in Christian circles. In fact, "the faith in the unlimited perfectability of natural man, in that Parousia that man himself prepares for progressively, is prevailing among Christians."[25] Yet, the ideological concepts of a man-made paradise and a society in which all capacities are fulfilled -- the classic radical dream -- would undermine both the idea of love (and this is also the position of Professor Gaylin) and creativity for which they are said to aim.

The conclusion is remarkable: "Complete satisfaction is equivalent to death and partial satisfaction implies suffering. Thus, the whole ideological project is itself a failure. Human corruptibility is not contingent...."[26] Few people would work for progress if they really knew the cost to be paid. And at a more fundamental level, the promise of a terrestrial paradise, to return man to his innocence, attacks the very right we have to remain the individuals we are, a central theme to which we shall turn in the next chapter.[27] Every good work can become corrupt so that some doubt is healthy against the prevalent Promethean principle. Kolakowski's view, then, is directly related to the remark of Strauss as to that of Hallowell about the need for what the Christians call "grace" even to be fully natural -- a theme also often stressed in Chesterton's Orthodoxy.

Kolakowski, then, continued:

Our natural forces are able to find no sure support against evil: all that which we are able to do is to practice the art of placing in balance the contrary dangers. It is precisely this which the Christian tradition affirms when it maintains that certain effects of original sin are ineluctable and that there can only be salvation through grace.[27]

The reality of grace and devil, the idea that mankind is free, yet not able by its own exclusive efforts to achieve its highest happiness, that being is ultimately gift-oriented, that evil is definite and permanent, that hell is stability for the belief that not all is compromiseable, these serve to refashion our thinking on political theory. This era is caught between a relativism that grants all and a belief that only the right shall and should prevail. But the tyrannies of the 20th Century were moral evils clearly acting against the human good which is not an abstraction, which perhaps is not even known fully by reason alone.

Hell, consequently, does have a proper function in political theory. Whenever it is neglected, like original sin, it merely returns under another form. The tradition of Aquinas is that all evil will be punished, that all human evils are precisely chosen. But it need not be the function of politics to correct all the evil choices. This remains a central proposition. The effort to create a perfect, self-conceived society on earth invariably seems to result in a kind of incarnate jail. And yet, it seems

100

such an attractive idea, for it does witness to the questions Aquinas asked in the first part of the Prima Secundae of his <u>Summa Theologica</u>, to the human search for absolute happiness. When modern political theory decided to base its initial proposition, contrary to the classics, on moral indifference to good and evil, with Machiavelli and before him with Marsilius' reduction of all morality to interiority, it set off on a project that was metaphysically impossible. The limits of pure reason, the paradox that man usually cannot know his own good or happiness -- the impact of Aquinas' argument for a divine law -- seems to be an affront to modern theory.

Nevertheless, again and again, the political consequences of the denial of the existence and definition of evil and permanent punishment cannot be ignored. Hell is not a neutral or mythical element in the political context. The essence of this means that good cannot "evolve" from evil, even though out of evil, God can draw good, as Paul of Tarsus taught.(<u>Romans</u>, 5:20; 8:28) All of this makes the political enterprise distinctly different from its manner of presenting itself in modern thought. In the modern era, evil and hell have become objects and movements to be overcome rather than mysteries lying deeply in the heart of human choice, where St. Augustine properly placed them. Political theory, in other words, is conditioned by our metaphysics and our theology, as the very structure of the <u>Summa Theologica</u> suggested to us.

What we believe about hell, therefore, remains the touchstone of what we believe about politics. The mystery of evil, to which we must now turn, of hell, its consequence, is neglected at a very high cost. The value of medieval theory was that it never ignored this. And Plato was not wrong at the beginning of political thought to suspect that immortality, that final punishment and reward, all grew out of the way men must begin their reflections on politics. What finally made it all fit together was when men learned that there were in fact things that did not belong to Caesar. And the first of these is precisely hell, the doctrine of eternal punishment.

101

Footnotes:

1. See James V. Schall, "Religion, War and Political Theory," Catholicism-in-Crisis, January, 1983.

2. J. W. Allen, "Marsilius of Padua," Social and Political Ideas of Medieval Thinkers, F. Hearnshaw, Editor, New York, Barnes and Noble, 1923, p. 180.

3. "Hell," The Oxford Dictionary of the Christian Churches, Cross, Editor, Oxford University Press, 1958, p. 620.

4. See James V. Schall, "Cartesianism and Political Theory," The Review of Politics, April, 1962; "The Significance of Post-Aristotelian Thought in Political Theory," Cithara, November, 1963; "The Recovery of Metaphysics," Divinitas, v. 23, #2, 1979, pp. 200-17.

5. See James V. Schall, "On the Non-Existence of Christian Political Theory," Christianity and Politics, Boston, St. Paul Editions, 1981, Chapter I, pp. 16-41.

6. Edmund Burke, Reflections on the Revolution in France, Chicago, Gateway, 1955, pp. 105-106.

7. See the discussion on the anti-utopians in Edward McNall Burns, Ideas in Conflict, New York, Norton, 1956.

8. See F. Dostoyevsky, Notes From the Underground, New York, Dutton, 1960.

9. Maurice de Wulf in his Philosophy and Civilization in the Middle Ages, New York, Dover, 1953, argued brilliantly that the whole tenor and trend of the medieval experience was to proceed from abstractions of every kind to personhood, to the concrete, existing individual.

10. Burke's observation is worth recalling here: "History consists, for the greater part, of the miseries brought upon the world by pride, ambition, avarice, revenge, lust, sedition, hypocrisy, ungoverned zeal, and all the train of disorderly appetites, which shake the public.... These vices are the causes of those storms. Religion, morals, laws, prerogatives, privileges, liberties, rights of men,

are the _pretexts_." _Ibid_., p. 201.

11. Eric Voegelin, The New Science of Politics, Chicago, University of Chicago Press, 1954, p. 131.

12. Leo Strauss, Natural Right and History, Chicago, University of Chicago Press, 1953, pp. 163-64.

13. This is essentially the thesis of Charles N. R. McCoy about the difference between modern and medieval natural law. See his The Structure of Political Thought, New York, Rand-McNally, 1963. See also, James V. Schall, "Generalization and Concrete Activity in Natural Law Theory," Archiv fur Rechts- und Sozialphilosophie, Mai, 1959; "Medieval Natural Theory," Modern Age, Forthcoming; "On the Christian Statement of the Natural Law," Christianity and Politics, ibid., Ch. VIII, pp. 213-42. See also John Finnis, Natural Law and Natural Right, New York, Oxford, 1980; A. P. d'Entreves, Natural Law, London, Hutchinson, 1951; Henry Veatch, "The Natural Law," Literature of Liberty, October-December, 1978; Heinrich Rommen, The Natural Law, St. Louis, Herder, 1947; E. B. F. Midgley, The Natural Law Tradition and the Theory of International Relations, London, Elek, 1975.

14. Hannah Arendt, Between Past and Future, New York, Viking, 1968, pp. 133-34.

15. John Hallowell, Main Currents in Modern Political Thought, New York, Holt, 1950, p. 651. See A. Pegis, Christian Philosophy and Intellectual Freedom, Milwaukee, Bruce, 1955; Alasdair MacIntyre, After Virtue, Notre Dame, University of Notre Dame Press, 1981.

16. Jacques Maritain, Scholasticism and Politics, Garden City, New York, Doubleday Image, 1960, p. 174. See also, F. Wilhelmsen, "The Christian Understanding of Being," The Intercollegiate Review, Winter-Spring, 1978, pp. 87-93; Brian Benestad, "Rights, Virtue, and the Common Good," Catholicism-in-Crisis, December, 1983, pp. 28-32, and James V. Schall, "Metaphysics, Theology, and Political Theory," Political Science Reviewer, Fall, 1981, pp. 2-25; "The Supernatural Destiny of Man," Modern Age, Summer, 1982, pp. 411-15.

17. Jacques Ellul, The Betrayal of the West, New

York, Seabury, 1978, pp. 78-79.

18. See Professor Gaylin's essay in "Doing Good:" The Limits of Benevolence, New York, Pantheon, 1978.

19. Ira Glasser, "Prisoners of Benevolence," in "Doing Good," ibid., pp. 107-123, 158. See Joseph Sobran, Single Issues, New York, Human Life Press, 1983; Iredell Jenkins, Social Order and the Limits of Law, Princeton, Princeton University Press, 1980.

20. Ellul, ibid., pp. 184-85.

21. "In a recent discussion between scientists and theologians at an interdisciplinary conference on the 'nature of man,' (which could have been a replay of the Scopes Trial), half of the group insisted on seeing Homo Sapiens as one (albeit the highest) in a continuous line in the animal kingdom, while the other half of the group insisted on the uniqueness and special quality that separates the human being from all other creatures. Only this time the theologians, in defence of the rights of animals and nature, defined man as merely another animal variant; the scientists -- while not quite speaking of 'man in God's image' -- implied as much with their equivalent terminology."

"Coming from the traditions of science and medicine, I stand for man. Homo sapiens to me represents an incredible gap in 'the great chain of life'; a discontinuity that is not measurable in the traditional incremental changes from the lowest species to the highest. We are a splendid and peculiar discontinuity -- sui generis. And the irony in our development is that part of the uniqueness that makes us transcendent rests in the miserable, extended, helpless state in which we are born and remain for so long -- untoward in the extreme and unparalleled in the animal kingdom." Gaylin, ibid., pp. 3-4. See James Hitchcock, Secular Humanism, Ann Arbor, Servant, 1983.

22. See John Rawls, A Theory of Justice, Harvard University Press, 1971.

23. See James V. Schall, "On Hatred" and "On Loneliness and Silence," in The Praise of 'Sons of Bitches:' On the Worship of God by Fallen Men, Slough, England, St. Paul Publications, 1978.

104

24. L. Kolakowski, "Le diablé peut-il être sauvé?" _Contrepoint_, Paris, #20, 1976. See Kolakowski's _Religion_, New York, Oxford, 1983.

25. _Ibid._, p. 133.

26. _Ibid._, p. 136.

27. _Ibid._, p. 137.

28. _Ibid._, p. 138.

CHAPTER VI

ON THE SCIENTIFIC ERADICATION OF EVIL

The Fall is a view of life. It is not only the only enlightened but the only encouraging view of life. It holds, as against the only real alternative philosophies, those of the Buddha or the Pessimist or the Promethean, that we have misused a good world, and not merely been entrapped into a bad one. It refers evil back to a wrong use of the will, and thus declares that it can eventually be righted by the right use of the will. Every other creed except that one is some form of surrender to <u>fate</u>. -- [G.K. Chesterton, <u>The Thing</u>, 1930.]

While fate (fatum) declines evil in the third person ("Society is at fault"), the Christian affirmation of sin places himself in the first person ("I have sinned before God and before men. I am responsible even in <u>this</u> society.") While fate alienates to the measure in which its denunciation gives consistency to an anonymous power, the Christian avowal of sin frees the individual by placing him in an act of responsibility. It does not place responsibility for evil on some universe (natural or social), a veritable alibi for calling one's own self innocent. Rather it affirms our solidarity in the actual creation of a universe where men do exploit one other men ... but each one (does so) within his own collective solidarities. Only that affirmation frees us from a despairing Manicheanism, which just results in contributing to the extension of evil and its regime. Evil only exists if we believe in its actuality more than in the actuality of a Good to be willed. -- [Paul Valadier, "Actualité du Mal," <u>Christus</u>, Paris, October, 1975.]

If the first of the great negative metaphysical

and religious themes that comes out of classical and Christian thought is that of hell, the second is clearly connected with it, that of evil. These stand in contrast to, and must be considered in relation to, the themes of the best form of rule and the best possible form of rule. Hell, as we have suggested, is a theme that has proper roots in political theory from Plato, in the problem of the nature of justice itself. However, the possibility of hell, connected as it is with the reality of freedom, is the other side of the more basic question of why is there evil in the first place.

Hell is a recognition of the permanence of evil by definition and by consequence. In a way, hell is easier to come to terms with than its "cause" as it were, with the idea that any evil, with real consequences, can or ought to occur in the first place. Once we grant that evil is possible, that it is chosen, then the existence of a hell only logically follows. Thus, to understand the substance of the medieval reflection and its modern consequences on the nature of man in the universe, we must return to the scriptural and philosophical origins of the problem of evil to see how it relates to properly political philosophy.

We hold, with Aristotle, that men are social and political animals. But if because of the problem of evil, unlike the Greek philosopher, we deny the existence of a God or First Cause, it will eventually occur to us as "atheists," against and in part because of a Christian mentality and tradition, that evil can be removed by social means, since its existence, like man's, is, as Marx also held, a social one. This means that the project of society, its organizational requirements, will be the proper location for identifying and removing the causes of evil. And we will eventually, in this line of thought, come to consider that such a project is not only possible, but even rather easy.[1] Needless to say, as Paul Hazard often recounted, this is the mentality of the Enlightenment.[2] Furthermore, to recall Waldemar Gurian's comment, in the 20th Century, "heresy" has occurred not primarily in dogma but in social ethics.[3] It seems no accident too that more and more, descriptions of "possible" nuclear war sound like the classical descriptions of hell, that evil is described, even by Christians, not as "sin" but as physical annihilation. (See Chapter IX)

And what would be the most subtle and pernicious "dogmatic" heresy from a Christian background that might be found in these social ethics? Would it not be precisely a reformulation of Christian thinking on the nature and essence of evil so that its removal could be considered not only possible but especially possible by man himself? And would not this occur in that area in which even Aristotle held is peculiarly man's, in politics?[4]

The reason this line of thought became possible is that ontology, wherein the classic discussion of evil resided, on the surface, at least, has yielded to a theory of action. The primacy of _esse_ to _agere_, being to action, is reversed such that the "Pure Act" that traditionally defined God has come to mean "praxis" or "agere," now taken to mean the historical, corporate human whole in its various relational webs of human interchanges.[5] However "logical" this may be -- and it is logical, granted the premises -- its force, to be properly grasped, must take us back intellectually to two relevant traditions concerning the existence and meaning of evil in the world, one scriptural, the other metaphysical.

The liberal-Enlightenment thesis was that evil is essentially an historical, political product. In fact, evil has a twofold root, one in the notion from, evidently Socrates, that evil is ignorance, the other in a secularized Christian idea of the divine economy within a salvation history. In a sense, both of these approaches were united when the modern notion of scientific knowledge came to be looked upon as an instrument to achieve a secularized, ideal human goal in which evil no longer would exist. Thus, this project takes its origin in opposition to the Augustinian solution to the Platonic problem of the locus of the good and the relation of the political order to this very good.

In classical Greek thought, however, especially in Aristotle, the existence of particularly moral evil was accounted for in ethics and politics: in ethics in the discussion of the vices, in politics in the discussion of the corrupt forms of rule. And within this discussion, furthermore, there was room for a consideration of lesser and greater goods, lesser and greater evils. Even an admitted good, consequently, had something unsettling about it if it was less than the best, as most goods were. Christianity handled this same problem under the rubric of the precepts and

109

the counsels. (See Chapter IV)

The intellectual nature of Greek political science, moreover, required that the mind account for the whole moral range, from absolute good to absolute evil, with everything in between. The cyclic order of this relationship, of this concept of history as seen best perhaps in Thucydides, yielded intelligibility in that the connected sequence of the vices and the virtues, the good and the bad forms of government, accounted for all there was in the social order, all the kinds of being possible to man, so that the mind could rest in its comprehension. And while this sort of analysis in one sense did satisfy the intellect, still the nature of desire seemed to demand that men strive in and produce only the best form of rule or only the highest form of virtue. (See Chapter VIII)

Aristotle had already noted the tendency in man to revolt against his ontological status as the least of the spiritual beings, the fact that his highest good belonged to those things that were properly divine and could not be otherwise. Man's unique status in the universe, on the other hand, what belonged to him and to no one else, i.e., politics, was not in fact the highest thing there was. Already here, we have intimations of an "original" fault, one not merely "promethean," whereby men steal the secrets of jealous gods, but more pretentious, wherein there are no more divine "secrets" to steal, only human ones to make.

The question of whether men could define and remove any encountered evil, consequently, arose inevitably in the history of thought. And if they could not remove evil, the reason why they could not became even more crucial. This is the essential meaning of both Plato and St. Augustine. Socrates knew in The Republic that the good man could only ultimately live in a city modeled after the good against all existing societies. Whether such a city might exist or not, he was not at all sure.

By the time of St. Augustine, however, and a new concept of history, Christianity had set the stage for a separation of politics and metaphysics, closer perhaps to Aristotle than Plato. Also, it acknowledged that our ultimate happiness did exist in the good, now seen to be the Trinitarian God. But this happiness, while properly ours, was not a personal or corporate human construction and achievement, certainly not to

110

be gained by primarily political means. In fact, its fullness could not be attained in this life, so that politics was given an important but secondary role. (See Chapter X) Politics accounted for and controlled the human evils that did exist and would continue to recur within the world, but this only within certain very narrow limits.

Much of modern intellectual history has been, in various degrees, an attempt to escape from the implications of this Christian dispensation. This latter affirmed man's dignity and destiny to be assuredly real and attainable but not fully in this life nor by any other than by graced means. Even the Thomist tradition, which more clearly accepted the positive and natural value of the world, did not hesitate to retain the basic Augustinian thesis about the locus of beatitude. But if evil did appear as Christians admitted through their doctrine of original sin and free will, then a secularized version of Christianity might conceivably be able to think evil potentially out of existence by reexamining salvation history to find within it the causes of evil in the world, to find it elsewhere than in Christian orthodoxy.[6]

When this is done, however, it becomes startlingly clear that the Platonic and Old Testament accounts of the origins of evil, as well as some Stoic ones, have rather much in common. All of these traditions held that there was a kind of intimate parallel between what goes on within man and how this same man forms his public order. Perhaps, it would be possible to construct the public order -- or else our psychological make-up or our environment -- so that the visible evils and deformities within the world and man would be eradicated.

The dynamism of this theory, it seems, which ultimately undergrids both modern socialism and ecology, comes indirectly from Plato's idea that the individual is the state writ small, that a rearrangement of property and family would enable the good to be achieved, such that every one did what was just.[7] In the Christian reflection of the Old Testament, certain institutions like the division of property, coercive government, birth in pain, labor in sweat, as we have seen, were not "due" to human nature, even death itself belonged to this category.(Wisdom, 1:13) Rather they were due to the Fall. They ought not to exist, but once they did, they

111

became necessary as a corrective to greater evils.

Beginning with Joachim of Flora, however, in the late Middle Ages, there has always been a Christian underground enthusiastically at work trying to eradicate these results of original sin in this world.[8] This viewpoint would hold, in its pure formulation, that the radical evil we encounter is rooted in society, that social reforms precede personal ones, that evil is essentially contingent.[9] (See Chapter V) This mental attitude makes the very central Christian belief that evil exists first in personal will appear "conservative." A caution or doubt that such projects would make the world really better are "reactionary," as they have been designated generally in radical political theory.

On the other hand, the equally central Christian teaching about free will and the quasi-permanence of evil in this world firmly insists on the "totalitarian" tendencies in such optimistic theories. These tendencies have in fact recurred regularly when these ideas and enthusiasms were put into practice.[10] Again and again, those imbued with the most noble ideals for the complete elimination of evil end up being its most dangerous propagators for the actual common men who do live in this world.

The remarks of Solzhenitsyn to the Harvard students are pertinent here:

> The Middle Ages had come to a natural end by exhaustion, becoming an intolerable despotic repression of man's physical nature in favor of the spiritual one. Then, however, we turned our backs upon the Spirit and embraced all that is material with excessive and unwarranted zeal. This new way of thinking, which had imposed on us its guidance, did not admit the existence of intrinsic evil in man, nor did it see any higher task than the attainment of happiness on earth. It based modern Western civilization on the dangerous trend toward worshipping man and his material needs. Everything beyond physical wellbeing and accumulation of material goods, all human requirements and characteristics of a subtler and higher nature, were left outside the range of attention of the state and the social system, as if human life did not have

112

any higher meaning. That provided access for evil, of which in our days there is a free and constant flow. But freedom does not in the least solve all the problems of human life, and it even adds a number of new ones.[11]

We are not wrong to discover in all of this a spiritual and theological problem of the first rank.

To understand this point more clearly, perhaps, it is well to state the Christian ideas about evil once again as they are pertinent to political theory. The very first, and most enigmatic, of course, is that evil does exist in some way and now is a permanent reality in the cosmos. Even the classic Christian idea that evil is primarily a "negation" does not subtract from this firm affirmation about the "reality" of evil. This must be the meaning of the Christian teaching about the devil, as well as its reflection on the "trial" nature of this (or angelic) life.[12] A world without any actual moral evil is at least conceivable in Christian thought as the direct result of the teaching about the Fall, a teaching that emphasizes the "choice" aspect of every existing moral evil and the possibility of its forgiveness.

On the other hand, in the actual world in which we live, with choices already made, evil cannot be totally removed. The claim to do so is itself one of the basic human temptations. "This is how it will be at the end of time: the angels will appear and separate the wicked from the just, to throw them into the blazing furnace where there will be weeping and gnashing of teeth."(Matthew, 8: 49-50) The consequence of this view is that evil is not so much an "object" to be eradicated but a choice to be made or rejected. Scripture teaches that evil and good will grow up together in the same fields, in the same world till the end. This kind of analysis, of course, radically determines how we look on evil for, in this latter scriptural view, it is always presented as a possibility even in the best of hearts for as long as they abide. This is where the real "spiritual combat," as the old mystics used to call it, really resides.

Christianity believes that real evil exists in the world alongside real goodness, without necessarily reifying either as some kind of a vague abstraction. However, in firmly rejecting any Manichean view, any

113

view that there is a specific, separate "god" of evil, co-eternal with the Creator, a god responsible for the existence of matter, Christianity did not intend to eliminate any place in its system for the force of evil. But because there was no specific "god" of evil, this did not mean, from another point of view, that namely of free will, that there could be no beings who choose evil as a permanent or temporary condition. Evil could, of course, be comprehended, as we noted within the Platonic-Augustinian tradition, as the absence of a due good. But evil could never be mere "illusion," as with certain Oriental views.

The locus of evil, then, is not primarily in finitude. Beings less than God are precisely "good." The force of evil is to be discovered, in a Christian view, in the power of the will within all rational creatures.[13] This means that real evil need not exist. Perhaps a cosmos without it is conceivable. When evil does appear, however, it is chosen. This is what gives the true dramatic, both tragic and comic, noble and ordinary qualities to existence. And to this corresponds the gradation of good and evil in the objective order. Since evil is chosen, then, it can likewise be "unchosen," except to the degree free choice can permanently fix itself in its own selected world, a world discussed under the scriptural rubric of hell, as we have seen. (See Chapter V)

If all this be so, the possibility of evil lies before every free will in its every act and habit. This is basically the impulse behind all medieval ethical reflection. Even the considerations which tend to reduce freedom, such as passion or ignorance, are designed to leave us with a real freedom. Thus, evil must appear as something intrinsically mutable since freedom cannot be determined from the outside. The will always remains open to the potential attraction of the authentically good. Likewise, the good equally is mutable for this same reason. The first point to clarify, then, must be the decision of whether the faculty of will constitutes good and evil for men. Or is it the task of the will to discover, realize, and opt, in connection with our minds, evil or its opposite? Does the human will "make" evil or is its possibility already existing through some natural or supernatural standard or value?

Probably the best Christian presentation of this issue, the one that most clearly sums up this long history of reflection, is found in John Henry Newman's famous and oddly titled sermon, "Obedience Without Love, as Instanced in the Character of Balaam."(April 2, 1837) Newman, the scholar in the last century probably most attuned to Christian history and ideas, was concerned to distinguish between the appearance of good and real good itself. He was likewise concerned to uncover the mask of good that appears before the world, the "moral" that is not at the same time religious. In a sense, this is a reflection of the problem Leo Strauss had with the relation of natural law and revelation, or the Chestertonian suspicion that once revelation is occurred, natural reason is no longer merely neutral. Balaam in the Old Testament, Newman said, was not "content with ascertaining God's will, but he attempted to change it."[14] This is the key, even in "religious exertions" wherein we aim "to attain anyhow a certain definite end, religious indeed, but of man's own choosing...."[15]

From this follows, then, Newman's classic and abidingly valid principle which still governs any Christian reflection on evil:

> Men do not take for the object towards which they act, God's will, but certain maxims, rules or measures, right perhaps as far as they go, but defective because they admit of being subjected to certain other ultimate ends which are not religious. Men are just, honest, upright, trustworthy; but all this not from the love and fear of God, but from a mere feeling of obligation to do so, and in subjection to certain worldly objects. And thus they are what is popularly called moral, without being religious.[16]

Newman persistently held that moral laws and rules were not abstractions, but they dealt with a personal God's relation to living human persons, a relationship that founds all "spiritual exercises," all spiritual life in the Christian tradition. And yet, this relationship did depend on God's norms which indicate who He is and what we are. Personal "authenticity," consistency to one's own standards, then, is not the norm of good but the ultimate danger and deflection from it.[17]

Newman's reasoning is pertinent and conclusive:

> ... We see how little we can depend, in

judging of right and wrong, on the apparent
excellence and high character of
individuals. There is a right and a wrong
in matters of conduct, in spite of the
world; but it is the world's aim to take our
minds off from the indelible distinctions of
things, and fix our thoughts upon man ...
But if Scripture is to be our guide, it is
quite plain that the most conscientious,
religious, high-principled, honourable men
... may be on the side of evil ... For in
the world's judgment, even when most
refined, a person is conscientious and
consistent, who acts upon his standard,
whatever that is, not he only who aims at
taking the highest standard....[18]

These are, of course, words of the highest Christian
wisdom. Cited in the context of a discussion of evil,
they serve to remind us that the Christian view of
evil is not permeated by some Manichean view of the
inevitable, unyielding force of an abstract, necessary
fate -- be it capitalism, or matter, or tyranny, or
phobia -- but by our free will choices over the
"indelible distinctions of things," whereby we can
strive to substitute our standards for God's.

Evil is not to be identified with any worldly
system, with any matter as such. Rather, it arises
from myriads of human wills freely choosing and
rejecting standards of God as given to us in nature
and grace. These are the standards which, when
chosen, serve to define best what we are and want,
what best our destiny. The metaphysical problem of
the "existence" of evil as such, then, is not opposed
to but supportive of this Christian analysis. The
question might be posed: Ought God to have chosen
another world? Belloc's witticism -- "How odd of God
to choose the Jews" -- might well be to the point
here. Philosophically, we have long wondered whether
God as Absolute Good created the best possible world.
On the assumption that the existence of various evils
creates insolvable problems to this thesis, it was
concluded either that God was less than absolutely
good (and thus not God) or that He did not create the
best of all possible worlds (hence a rather
parsimonious sort of deity).

Still another possibility, of course, might be
that God did indeed create the best world possible.
But within this best world, considerable evil, though

none strictly necessary, might possibly exist. Otherwise, there could be no world at all outside God, who, by virtue of the rejection of Manicheanism, could not Himself be a god of precisely _evil_. In this sense, again, Newman's powerful words at the end of the same Sermon on Balaam ring true. They serve to underscore what we deal with in Christianity when it is suggested, against all odds, that evil must be located not in God, nor in the world, nor in the laws God places in our being to separate finally good from evil, but in our own choices. Man has it in his power to select basically his own standards because they are his against God's as found in reason and revelation.

The great English Cardinal warned:

> Lastly, I will say this in addition, -- God gives us warnings now and then, but does not repeat them. Balaam's sin consisted in not acting upon what was told him _once and for all_. In like manner, you, my brethern, now hear what you may never hear again, though with your outward ears you hear it a hundred times ... True, this may be so, and it may arise, as you think, from the doctrine I have been setting before you not being true and scriptural but it _may_ also arise from your having heard God's voice and not obeyed it. It may be that you have become blind, not the doctrine been disproved.[19]

In other words, the existence and furtherance of evil are to be searched in the human will, within a universe whose very structure is to bear evil's possibility. The dire results of evil are able to be communicated to those who also have ears and minds to listen to its message. This is why St. Augustine spoke both of a City of God _and_ a city of man.

The ontology of this possibility, as it were, has been recently argued by Professor Robert Pargetter. Summing up recent philosophical discussions, he wrote:

> ... Along with the failure of the (religious) apologists to justify the existence of evil, the supposed logical inconsistency between God and evil has been more successfully challenged by a simple logical point. Following (N.) Pike and (A.) Plantinga, it has been pointed out that God

117

could have a reason for the world being as
it is, and hence there is no logical
contradiction in both acknowledging the
existence of evil, pain and suffering in the
world and asserting that an all-knowing,
all-powerful and totally good God
exists.[20]

Professor Pargetter went on to deal with the objection
that, however much particular evils might be allowed
on this premise, still it would seem that the amount
of evil could best be explained on the hypothesis that
God did not exist. Since we neither know all the
reasons why God might create a world in which evil
exists, however, nor do we know his actual reasons, we
cannot reject His existence because all or some evils
do exist.[21]

There is logically no reason, then, why the
non-existence of God might explain evil better than
His existence, nor is there any proved reason why the
best possible world may not include the possibility of
evil. Pargetter simply concludes that, "the claim
that the existence of evil is strong evidence against
the existence of God has not been justified...."[22]
Medieval theory, of course, generally held that both
God and evil must be accounted for. The evidence
pointed to both. The rational enterprise in this
regard was not to eliminate the one or the other. In
any case, Pargetter's conclusion has enormous
consequences for social theory, since it calls into
question any Enlightenment-based thesis for the
eradication of all evil by social means.

Thus, if it is intellectually conceivable that
the best world may include the possibility of evil, we
ought again to concentrate, as Newman did, on where it
is that such a possibility might occur. And that is
in the possibility of a free choice which decides
whether or not "good" will be chosen and which, if
not, will define a "lack" of a good that ought to be
placed in the world. If this be so, then, the drama
of creation will mostly lie where St. Augustine said
it did.[23] (See Chapter III) From a philosophical
point of view, moreover, this position is argued in a
remarkable essay by Professor David White. The
argument against an omnipotent and wholly good God on
the basis of the existence of evil in the world does
not seem at all conclusive.

White suggested that the issue may be best

formulated in this fashion:

> Is the evil (of, if you like, the pain
> and suffering) in the world sufficient
> grounds for believing that the universe is
> not good in the highest practicable degree?
> If it is, then it is sufficient grounds for
> denying the existence of God. I shall argue,
> on the contrary, that the evil in the world
> does not give us even the least degree of
> evidence, let alone sufficient evidence,
> against this claim that the universe is good
> in the highest degree practicable.[24]

Professor White went on to suggest how no proposal
offered for the elimination of some particular evil
would really make the world better. In fact, the
removal of any known evil or certainly type of evil
would most probably make the world worse, both in
particular instances and in general.[25]

A theist, to be sure, is trying to account mainly
not for evil, whose existence seems obvious, but for a
reason why it exists. Certain virtues, clearly,
require the existence of evil that their opposite
virtue might exist. The test of a free faith that God
exists, thus, requires that coerced certainty be not
present. Evil then is not evidence against a good
God, who may have a logical reason for its existence
in the best world. White argued that there is no
evidence for the actual existence of unnecessary
evil. We are really free, and this is a greater good
than the exclusion of every possible and probable
evil.[26] God could perhaps create only people who
would not have sinned. But that would mean that
almost none of the people who have in fact existed
would have lived. This is a dubious alternative.
Furthermore, the "holocaust" type claim, that there
are no future happinesses that some sufferings would
justify, seems to entail that the kind of world in
which redemption through suffering was possible itself
was impossible.

Yet, it is by no means clear that anyone, in the
long run, would prefer non-existence to existence plus
suffering, wherein the existence of evil or suffering
was itself what made his existence and the happiness
that followed from it possible. The intellectual
meaning of the medieval Christian reflection on
martyrdom occurs at this point. The existence of the
actual evil that does exist in the world, in other

words, is necessary that the best possible world be realizable. That is, a world in which free, creative choice of real human persons exists so that many virtues and all free members of the Kingdom of God might come to be and continue to be, this in spite of evil.

The "sociological" conclusions to be drawn from such considerations, it seems, are clear: there is no political, psychological, economic, or social program whose effectuation will eliminate every evil within the world. All such totalist plans only serve to make the world worse. This is why the world was not created according to such plans in the first place. The "temporal" purpose of creation, thus, serves its ultimate one -- that of associating other free creatures, no matter in what family or society or age they historically might exist, with the divine Trinitarian glory.[27] The existence of corporate evil demanding a complete "restructuring" of society to eliminate it, itself long the radical dream, appears, in this context, hopeless of achievement. Further, it implies a depersonalization of a Manichean nature that looks on evil as a corporate force and not as the result of human personal free choices.

Several years ago, in this regard, Professor R. C. Zaehner of Oxford wrote a short essay in _Encounter_ on "The Wickedness of Evil: On Manson, Murder, and Mysticism." This essay is pertinent to this discussion since it well reflects the issues at stake in the history of evil in society. "'Evil' and even more Bonhoeffer's term 'the wickedness of evil' have a very old-fashioned ring nowadays..." Zaehner wrote, reflecting on the theories of the then infamous Charles Manson, whose exploits seemed almost the epitome at the time of what we instinctively call 'evil.'

> For both 'evil' and especially 'sin' have come to be regarded as Judaeo-Christian taboos designed to exclude from our experience a whole range of liberating activities which (it is alleged) lie at the heart of the mystical religions of the East. Morality, on the whole, seems out, while ecstasy is very much in.[28]

While the climate of opinion has perhaps changed since these lines were first written, they still suggest that there is a classical philosophical problem

120

involved, that of the effort to transcend the absolute distinction of good and evil. This was, ironically, the choice presented to man in _Genesis_, the constitutive knowledge of good and evil.(_Genesis_, 3:22) Zaehner saw in Manson a reflection of this desire to experience all, including evil. This was the source of the opposition to its being defined as ultimately wrong. This is a thesis also seen in recent Western philosophy from Nietzsche.

Professor Zaehner interpreted Manson, a kind of obvious symbol of evil, as being rather a witness of a mystical encounter that achieved its reality by transcending good and evil. This tended to obviate any encounter with a creator god, a factor that perhaps explained the attraction of Buddhism, which denies the creator.[29] The effort to reconcile good and evil, so that we do not have to "choose" between them to reach God, so that they are unified in some exalted "one" to be equally experienced and equally to be preferred, an idea from at least Hegel, is clearly the means to reject the notion of evil in Christian thought. Professor Zaehner himself pictured God as a cause of genocide in the Old Testament, as a God we would easily reject on humanist grounds, for evil evidently comes from Him. Yet, this same God rejects the evil men do when they do the same. This constitutes a charge of unfairness or inconsistency against God. But man wanted this mystical power.

Zaehner's conclusion is worth recording, as it serves to recall what is at stake when the eradication of evil becomes a theory of the deity:

> For many, Charles Manson personifies what Bonhoeffer called the 'wickedness of evil.' Perhaps: but on his own premises, he was anything but illogical. He had won his flash of enlightenment the hard way, and he had learnt that in Hindu mysticism and in Zen the enlightened man who had realized himself in the Absolute was beyond good and evil....
>
> Interpret this as you will. Say with Lucretius ... "So many evils has religion inspired." Or take the Zoroastrian way out and insist that evil is, and must be, a principle independent of and absolutely hostile to God. Alternatively, if you believe in God at all, you must accept the

Jewish paradox in some form and simply admit that the 'wickedness of evil' must somehow proceed from the very heart of God and that what God excuses in himself he hates in us. There is no solution to the mystery unless we can understand these hauntingly cryptic words of the Hindu poet Kabai:

'God is a Thug: and Thuggery's what he has brought to the world. Yet how can I live without him? ...

... Says Kabai: What of it? I'm pleased with the Thug as he is: For once I recognized the Thug, the Thuggery vanished away.'[30]

Whether such words, no matter how cryptic, are understandable, of course, and whether they solve the question at hand are problematical. This is not so much the rejection of evil, as the Christian tradition would insist on, but its approval because of whom it proceeds from, another version of beyond good and evil.

From its beginning, Christianity has recognized that one way to "account" for evil was to make God its "cause." Another way was to eliminate God. Still a third was to fuse the two into mutually possible and related experiences, both of which would be necessary. All of these were to be rejected, mainly because of the sufferings and death of Christ. These allowed no compromise with evil. They did allow that suffering was possible even for the God-made-man. (See Chapter II)

Evil thus is not something that can be "eradicated" because its existence depends upon personal will. This will can always see evil as a temptation to accept. This condition exists at the cost of there being no truly rational creatures at all less than God. This has certain definite and concrete implications in the social order, since it becomes clear that evil is not reckoned to be a project that can be wholly eliminated by human means. This will lead directly, as we shall see in the following chapter, to the Thomist idea of the limits of law in the face of public evils.

The first of these consequences, it would appear, is that real evil done to human persons should be

122

absolutely accounted for before men. This is a theme Solzhenitsyn is ever insisting upon, an insight that probably lies behind the Christian idea of the Sacrament of Penance.[31] An obscure slave who froze to death in Siberia in 1925, for example, should not be forgotten, nor the names of those responsible for his being there, who struck the first and last blow.

The second consequence is that forgiveness is ever possible even for the worst crime since, as Hannah Arendt used to insist, only forgiveness can stop an order of justice and retribution from constantly destroying or disturbing society itself.[32] The lack and practice of a theory of forgiveness are often signs of absolutism. Yet, forgiveness is not a theory of "beyond good and evil," which would be indifferent to aberration, but rather an admission and definition of actual evil as it exists among persons.

Finally, since evil can occasion good -- the patience of the sufferer, the humility of the proud -- no social order or situation is hopeless. Nor is any well-governed society completely secure. The condemnation of evil is not also a condemnation of existence itself. From the worst social orders can come the best men and women. From the best can come the morally and religiously worst. Social philosophy can never replace or substitute for a theory of grace and free reponsibility for real acts within any given order, even the worst.

Christianity, consequently, however much it defined, identified, and rejected evil in any of its willed forms, has been instinctively uncomfortable with grandiose theoretical schemes to eliminate it. This is why it deals first and last with movements of grace and desire in each individual human heart. This is why authentic, classic spirituality is ever more important than politics and cannot be substituted for it. This is paradoxical, to be sure.

Few of the ideological programs to eliminate evil, however, really come up with a better world. Indeed, they almost always come up with a worse one, one in which one or other essential human value -- freedom, creativity, variety, grace, even life itself -- is sacrificed. Ultimate happiness is not to be found in this life, even though it is ultimately to be found or better given. This is what frees us from the ideologies of this world that seek to remove evil or explain it away at the cost of the most vital things we have been given.

Evil is not to be explained away or "removed" in Western Christian tradition. Rather it is to be chosen or rejected, an activity that constitutes the heart and hence the destiny of each member of this actual human species that individually lives on this earth. (See Chapter XI) This is why scripture, which lies at the heart of the Christian view, constantly speaks of calling and casting out, of "come blessed of my Father" and "weeping and gnashing of teeth." For it respects the reality of evil in the one place it is in most dire need of respect, in human choice. Evil, thus, to repeat with Chesterton, refers to a wrong use of the world by the will, not to a bad cosmos.

Hope exists in the universe, then, because evil can be corrected by a right use of the same will, the one each individual human person possesses. This use can be corrected by wisdom and absolved by forgiveness. Its effects can be controlled by promise. This is indeed the one approach that is not governed by _fatum_, by a belief that something beyond us necessarily explains and gives evil its existence and power. This is, finally, why Christianity is historically both the most realistic and most hopeful of religions. For it does not doubt the reality of evil, because it locates it before the will, that one power that can be otherwise, even before evil.

Footnotes:

1. In this connection, it is worth citing Professor Kenneth Minogue's remarks on the liberal optimism of John Kenneth Galbraith: "Professor Galbraith believes that social and political problems are essentially simple; I believe them to be essentially complex. The point can be illustrated from the last few pages of (Galbraith's) The Age of Uncertainty where, in a mood of mellow conclusion, we are told that 'Few social problems, if any, are difficult of solution. The difficulty, all but invariably, is in confronting them. We know what needs to be done; for reasons of inertia, pecuniary interest, passion or ignorance, we do not wish to say no ... The greatest support to evasion comes from complexity'"....

"In my criticism of Professor Galbraith I ... (suggested) that this kind of theoretical simplicity constituted a peculiar political danger. It is the simplicity of despotism ... Professor Galbraith is, then, an exponent of what might be called despotic simplicities, those likely to appeal to people who have a lot of force at their command and are quite prepared to use it.... (Galbraith's style tends) ... to give support to that special and dangerous form of human impatience which believes everything would be lovely if only people weren't so damned stupid." K. Minogue, "The Galbraithian Fallacy," Encounter, April, 1978, pp. 88-89.

2. See Paul Hazard, The European Mind, Yale, 1953; European Thought in the 18th Century, Chicago, World, 1967. See also Stanley Jaki, The Road of Science and the Ways to God, Chicago, University of Chicago Press, 1978.

3. See W. Gurian, Bolshevism, Notre Dame, University of Notre Dame Press, 1962.

4. See James V. Schall, "Some Remarks on the Current Problematic of Theoretic Atheism," The Homiletic and Pastoral Review, October, 1972; "Atheism and Politics," Christianity and Politics, Boston, St. Paul Editions, 1981, Ch. IV, pp. 94-117.

5. Dante Germino's Political Philosophy and the Open Society, Baton Rouge, Louisiana State University Press, 1983, seeks to avoid this particular alternative, though perhaps at the cost of losing the

125

distinction between St. Augustine's "Two Cities."

6. See Carl Becker's The Heavenly City of the 18th Century Philosophers, Yale, 1948. See also James V. Schall, "On the Non-Existence of Christian Political Philosophy," Worldview, April, 1976.

7. See James V. Schall, "Revolution and Development in the Christian Social Perspective," Studies, Dublin, Summer, 1974.

8. See F. Heer, The Intellectual History of Europe, London, Weidenfeld and Nicolson, 1953.

9. See L. Kolakowski, "Le diablé peut-il être sauvé?" Contrepoint, Paris, #20, 1976.

10. For the religious side of this evolution, see R. Knox, Enthusiasm, Oxford, 1953.

11. A. Solzhenitsyn, "A World Split Apart," The Harvard Address, National Review, July 7, 1978, p. 841; also in Solzhenitsyn at Harvard, Washington, Ethics and Public Policy Center, 1980; also his "Men Have Forgotten God," National Review, July 22, 1983, pp. 872-76.

12. See the Congregation on the Doctrine of Faith, "Christian Faith and Demonology," The Pope Speaks, #3-4, 1975, pp. 209-33.

13. See James V. Schall, "Ethics and International Relations," World Justice, Louvain, July, 1965; also in Christianity and Politics, ibid, Chapter III, pp. 65-93.

14. John Henry Newman, "Obedience Without Love, as Instanced in the Character of Balaam," Sermon found in L. Barmann, Editor, Newman at St. Mary's, Westminster, The Newman Press, 1962, p. 183.

15. Ibid., p. 183.

16. Ibid., p. 184.

17. See James V. Schall, "On the Most Dangerous Virtue," in The Praise of 'Sons of Bitches': On the Worship of God by Fallen Men, Slough, England, St. Paul Publications, 1978.

18. Newman, p. 186.

19. *Ibid*., p. 188.

20. R. Pargetter, "Evil As Evidence Against the Existence of God," *Mind*, #2, 1976, p. 242.

21. *Ibid*., p. 244.

22. *Ibid*., p. 244-45.

23. This is why for St. Augustine, men are united and divided not on the basis of nation or background or talent, but on the basis of what they choose.

24. D. White, "The Problem of Evil," *Second Order*, An African Journal of Philosophy, Nigeria, January, 1975, p. 15.

25. *Ibid*., pp. 15-16.

26. *Ibid*., p. 20.

27. See John H. Wright, "The Eternal Plan of Divine Providence," *Theological Studies*, March, 1966.

28. R. C. Zaehner, "The Wickedness of Evil: On Manson, Murder, and Mysticism," *Encounter*, April, 1974, p. 50.

29. *Ibid*., p. 51.

30. *Ibid*., p. 58.

31. See the discussion of this in James V. Schall, *Redeeming the Time*, New York, Sheed and Ward, 1968, Chapter VI, pp. 175-212.

32. See Hannah Arendt's discussion of forgiveness and promise in *The Human Condition*, Chicago, University of Chicago Press, 1959.

CHAPTER VII

THE LIMITS OF LAW

Each actor in that drama (Watergate) is a product of the American school system, taught in a value free society. As a result they have no values, and we are incensed. -- [Bruno Bettelheim, Stanford University, July, 1974.]

Our modern social confusion, intellectually considered, is the consequence of confounding the sphere of private morality with the sphere of public activity. This is the enormous error of the humanitarians. When the religious impulse is contracted to mere "brotherhood of man," fratricide is not far distant. -- [Russell Kirk, The Conservative Mind, 1953.]

The consideration of hell and evil that we have been pursuing leads us not to expect a perfect order in this world. Yet if the Judaeo-Christian theory of happiness be valid, that it be attainable ultimately, but not by political means, where does this leave actual politics? This leads us directly into the classical considerations of the limits of law and the second-best state. These are theoretical issues of the most vital concern in classical theory. They become even more central once we are able to separate the idealist and perfectionist theories from those that continue to deal with actual men in the kind of world wherein good and evil co-exist, wherein choice, persuasion, even coercion become the factors in the moral quality of life.

The theoretical background for such considerations, of course, will go back to The Laws of Plato and to Cicero's Second Best State. However, the medieval political tradition with its wrestling about the relation of grace and reason, with its better awareness of the moral basis of society, the value and meaning of habit and custom, has become the immediate background to modern theory. What needs yet to be argued is that the philosophical basis of specifically

129

modern political theory was not superior to that of the medievals in practice. Indeed, what is most valuable in modern theory comes rather from what was preserved from the medieval and classical heritage.

Anyone familiar with today's university circles cannot but be struck by the influx of particularly idealistic students during recent years into the medical and legal faculties at a time when what we probably need most on a world scale are technicians, farmers, information specialists, agronomists, scientists, astronauts, truckers, shippers, engineers, and entrepreneurs, these latter above all.[1] In a sense we have often decided that protecting and taking care of ourselves are more important than expanding our world. There is a kind of loss of spirit and confidence in our social and political experience, which masks as a pursuit of health and justice.

This, evidently, has meant that medicine with its new influx of personnel will have further to over-specialize to employ the newcomers, if the supply of new doctors is not severely controlled by the medical profession itself. We shall, also, witness a growing proletariat of underemployed and underemployable lawyers -- ever a cause of civil and political unrest in any society. In The Republic, Plato already noted that an oversupply of doctors and lawyers was an infallible sign of a sick society.(#405a) More and more fields, the educational one not the least of them, are being turned into the adversary relationship typical of the court room. No gentler spirit is prevalent. When law and medicine have become so popular, we must suspect that in some social ethos, they are believed to provide the answers for needs a significant portion of the community believe lacking to them. These needs are, presumably, health and justice, if, that is, we suppress the temptation to believe that here we have merely a phenomenon of utility, something the costs of medicine and legal service at least make arguable.

To state categorically that health and justice are in no wise the results of techniques and methods applied by practitioners, whose main viewpoint and justification are to correct what is wrong with a person or a state, would, of course, be a mistake. But health and justice have roots that mostly lie outside the professions that concern themselves with civil or corporal malfunctionings. The approach of both the lawyer and the doctor is primarily remedial,

130

both act mainly when something has gone wrong. This is true in spite of all the talk of "preventive medicine" and "preventive justice." Each profession surely must know what is right and normal before it can interfere for the benefit of the patient or the victim. In this, the doctor, traditionally, had an advantage since good health is more easily defined and recognized than good law and public prosperity. The well-being of civil societies contains the very norms or standards that, as we saw in the previous chapter, can be freely chosen or rejected.

The good and normal functioning of man and society is not primarily the result of the workings of the doctor or the lawyer. Consequently, when we witness a significant rush into these fields in some sense disproportionate to the problems at hand, something confirmed by the cost of these professions, we must conclude that the symbols of law and medicine have come to be identified with a mission to set aright something felt to be disordered in man, something capable of remedial correction. Perhaps it is not as bad as the temptation in a field like psychiatry to judge everyone sick except the psychiatrist. But still there is not a little of this rather elitist position in the medical and legal fields.[2]

Further, the rise of "cosmetic" medicine and dentistry is not unconnected with the Greek notion of the perfect and beautiful human form, the one that bore the "species" as the repository for the good man, the one who need not have any occasion to envy his fellows. The modern biological endeavor to "produce" this good and perfect man by science has certain curious connections with Aquinas' analysis of the ultimate state of mankind. (See Chapter X) Likewise, the noble public defender, the "poor" man's lawyer, seeks to create the healthy citizen who has no rights being violated, no benefits not coming to him. Thus, he has no reason to rebel against society because society's laws and practices presumably approach the perfect. That such a theory may eliminate the very possibility of society itself serves to caution the extreme application of the theory.

Health and justice refer to the normal functioning of a man and society insofar as man is a worldly being.[3] Both deal with what an older, medieval tradition called man's "temporal" sphere. Both similarly recognize that man and society

131

naturally tend to their own destruction. It is "good" that men get old, normal for societies to follow a cyclic pattern, as the great Greeks held. Thus death and corruption must be anticipated and reckoned with. Just as men die, so states change from one form of rule to another. One kind of evil begets another, while men do not seem to be able to stem the effects of their self-interest enough even to allow the better states to last.

In a sense, law and medicine rise in importance to the degree that continuation in physical life and the achievements of rewards due in this life (often conceived negatively as preventing injustice) become the principal objects of human hope. When this life becomes all there is, bad health and injustice become intolerable, if not maddening and destructive. This principle of survival at any cost also lies behind much of the anti-war movements.[4] (See Chapter IX) And this is why the status of the ultimate good and happiness relates directly to ordinary politics. (See Chapters II and III)

Thus, the movement to kill deformed children at or before their birth on "humanitarian" grounds has gained great persuasive force in recent years because little or no value can be seen in a life that is less than "perfect" in this world. The laboratory conception of Louise Brown in England, her subsequent "normal" birth, portend the idea that perfect physical shape is the arena of science. The births of normal men and women have something wrong with them. The ideal of health, thus, becomes tyrannical with regard to the unhealthy. Life yields to perfect life as the criterion of value and morality. This is almost the very opposite of Christian and medieval theory which found the least, the weakest, and sickest to be the locus of special beatitude.

Therefore, those who argue a poor or deformed life is not worth living have the most difficulty in esteeming the absolute value of human life on grounds other than abundance and prosperity.[5] The transcendent worth of human life is a value which Christian, Old Testament, and medieval thought worked most to establish. Human life's value was not subject to human judgment for its constitution. The elimination of this value substitutes the perfect human form or the totally "developed" society as the criterion by which we judge human worth in the concrete. The particular, personal human condition in

132

its sacred uniqueness loses its awe and mystery.

We live in a vale of tears, the Augustinian tradition has told us. We are told that the poor and the vicious will, to some degree, always be with us, as the New Testament seems to have clearly held. In this context, we must begin to look elsewhere, beyond health and justice, for comprehension about the meaning and purpose of human life as it manifests itself on earth. The preservation and development of the "good life" on earth may not be the central value about which our very being revolves. This is the conclusion we have reached from our discussion of evil. (Chapter V) Men and women should be relatively healthy and just, of course. But there is a fine line, no longer so clear, between a view of the world that believes men ought to <u>reduce</u> ill-health and injustice and one which suspects they should be <u>eradicated</u>. There is even a much greater difference among the various means by which these ends are to be accomplished.

The fact of our era is that such views for the control of so-called "imperfect" life in the name of "perfect" life are growing in power and prominence. And such views are metaphysical. They have to do with a refusal to admit the kind of world men live in. This refusal, clearly, can take theological shape as a charge against the God who made men so subject to sin and death in an imperfect, enigmatic world. Thus, it ought not surprise us if the bio-medical and legal sciences become the ideological contexts of our time. The relation of law to the formation of human life is already a crisis question. In its pre-natal stage, what is allowed to live is determined almost solely by civil law. It is indeed at this point that the most fundamental of the ancient heresies, those of Gnosticism and Pelagianism, reappear as active forces in the modern world. Their prospect and program would seek to eliminate by human means those signs of worldly insufficiency which, since Plato, we associate with death and injustice.[6]

Thus, law and medicine bear the signs of "vocation" in the sense that Max Weber used this word of Luther.[7] That is, the notion of service came to be associated not with contemplation, as with the monks, but with a man's task or duty in the world. Monks and citizens were to do exactly the same things. (See Chapter IV) Serving is seen to be a worldly thing which derives its self-validation from its very success judged in terms of a humanly defined project. Even though it was faith that "saved" us, still it made the whole world field of our action. A kind of spiritual calculus of humanly alleviating things became the sign of holiness. Did we boycott the right grape growers? Did we march in the right protest organization? Were we against the right weapon or right war? This was doing God's work. Purely religious or contemplative vocation is challenged even by many current schools of theology because it does not "criticize" or "protest" against things presumably wrong in this world, which of course does in fact have many things wrong with it as befits the environment of the truly free being. Nothing spiritual is allowed to escape the absolutizing presence of worldly success.

The healing function of religion, then, comes to be seen in humanistic terms which posit no intrinsic value beyond this life except on the condition that the purpose of life, even its God-given purpose, is to alleviate and remove all its on-going evils. Religion becomes what Wilton Wynn once aptly called a kind of "fussy benevolence." No authentic vocation pierces the clouds, none transcends any and every temporal order no matter what its human condition. Since nothing flashes beyond the worldly tasks, "eschatological" theology is transformed to make the ultimate City of God depend upon success in re-fashioning the world. Success is attributed to willed human efforts and plans. General Sherman's famous aphorism is quite literally turned around. Now hell is war, a worldly phenomenon.

Religion, then, is re-cast in terms of war and peace. Sin is bad social conditions attributed to groups not individuals. Paradise is stretching out scarce resources to as many future generations as possible. Apocalypse is a nuclear bomb or a consumption of oil.[8] Paradoxically, this subtle influx of this worldly perfectionism is undoubtedly the major reason why many religious men and women often feel they can participate whole-heartedly in these ideological movements claiming to improve man's lot. A Maritain or a John XXIII tried to distinguish within such movements what can and what cannot be accepted.[9] The belief that men can apply themselves and their minds to achieve better health or society cannot be identified with the meaning of reality itself.

Since we practically identify, often, the ways of God and our finite success in establishing 'a kingdom of health and justice' in this world, we should also expect to find less and less possibility of conflict between law and morality. Morality will be what the law says. This will seem ironic, at first sight. But if we refuse to admit the reality of suffering and death, particularly in their traditional religious meanings, if we insist on the worldly possibility of absolute justice, if we repropose evil as a project to be removed by political means, if we are taught first to seek "the political kingdom," as a famous African politician (K. Nkrumah) once advised us, then we have to begin to identify the health we have or can achieve with our present technology with life itself.

We will likewise have to identify the justice we legislate with justice itself. We will find that our existing state will necessarily come to be considered the ideal state. Anyone who then disagrees with its concrete values and practices will be considered to be advocating "injustice" and will be forced to conform to the political practice or leave the community should that still be allowed. The present philosophical attention to immigration, its right, its world-wide lack of opportunity, arises at this very point. The refusal to accept anything the people by democratic process decide as just or unjust will be tantamount to rejecting the only norm on which it is legitimate to decide any question once a transcendent criterion is identified with a worldly politics. Will there be any longer a place we are permitted to go to? Needless to say, this overturns the very fundamental cleavage Christianity initially introduced into the political world, that is, the possibility of knowing and therefore judging the things that are Caesar's by the things that are God's, as from a valid, independent source. This is the point where Christian and medieval traditions become again central to our thinking about the public order and its theoretical limits.

Thus, when we give up this latter criterion of the things that are God's, for whatever reason -- and the most subtle and dangerous way today is to identify Christianity with a worldly movement in the name of justice itself -- we must come back to equating the existing order with what is possible to man. This possibility will be seen as an expression of a realized political order based on "justice" according to some humanist "right" or inspiration. We legislate

135

and administer political formulae for amelioration. We carry them into being by political, court, or revolutionary action. But once we arrive at this point, we must reject further criteria, because we have excluded the sources of criticism itself by identifying our ideology or religion with the on-going movement to establish health, abundance, peace, or justice. The revolutionary "cleric" unable to distinguish tyranny from justice will be more and more a common figure in our time. We should not be overly surprised by his sudden appearance.

And if we do not so identify ourselves with the worldly movements to establish ideological justice, the failure to improve the world will be directly attributed to our religious concern for something beyond politics.[10] The ancient charge against Christians that their worship made them ignore the worldly order, that charge that incited St. Augustine in the first place, is constantly being reformulated. But since this is the charge that is now denied, we must end up identifying our movement with our ideal. When this point is reached, control of media, religion, education, economy, and parties becomes necessary to prevent any suspicion that men's problems are not being met by the existing order so earnestly established according to the highest ideals.

This latter tendency is obscured from our sight, it seems, because we still deal, at least in much of the West, with an existing society that has not been afraid to admit its defects and limitations. This society did not pretend even in theory, largely because of its Christian origins, that perfect justice or health could be achieved by political, legal, or medical means. Therefore, problems of death and personal destiny were not just matters of housekeeping within a system that itself defined the major problems of man. What we have not yet fully grasped, hidden in these newer enthusiasms for medicine and law, is a broader social attitude transferred into a political project designed to make the ideal system actually "work."

Again and again, we are told of our impatience with the "results" of two thousand years of Christianity or four hundred years of Europe or two hundred years of America, as if the main criterion of spiritual movements were to produce an approved worldly system. The "possible" no longer limits what is feasible politically. The strange and curious

136

human condition no longer acts as a check or restraint on efforts to make a perfect life on earth. And failure to produce such a system comes to be assignable to definite groups and persons living in the world and said to be the "cause" of this failure. Their political punishment is the modern equivalent to the last judgment; their reward is the modern hell. The unborn are perhaps the first victims of this mentality.

The sobering problem of original sin, once so dominant in our historical religious reflections, comes to be socialized into a project to remove its worldly signs, signs whose very definition goes back to Christian and medieval theological and political reflections. Thus, the human condition is rejected as an outworn thing standing in the way of realizing this newer, projected world. The slowly accumulated wisdom of man is dispensed with as unscientific. Freedom is gradually separated from experience. For the first time in history, it becomes possible, even necessary, to think of man in terms of process. A definite set of realities that ought to be completely removed from his personal being and corporate life can now be targeted.

Indeed, we think of the whole human race as the proper object of this total reformation. We think we must include everyone for the project to be a success, so that our control norms are subject to no criterion other than those set forth by men. Man thus comes to consider himself great because he _makes_ himself great, not because he _is_ already created great. Therefore, anything believed to be constitutive of human worth discovered in revelation or even in nature is to be rejected as "alienating." Alienation takes on anti-theist overtones. All of this is, consequently, Pelagian in the sense that men must accomplish their essential task by their own efforts. It is also Gnostic in that the content of the human must be defined by the sole use of human reason and insight, a reason and insight that reject the historical and creative formation of man as a being subject to a God whose ways are not our ways.

What is most striking recently is exactly this sudden reappearance of "morality" as a judge of law. Perhaps the most obvious sign of this is the high level of political anger manifested in a society in which value-free social thought has been the common academic norm. Public anger, however, indicates that

137

a contradiction is believed to exist between what men "do" and what they "ought" to do, a project that reverses the influence of Machiavelli at the origin of modern political theory. He held that what is done should determine what ought to be done. There is, however, a rediscovery of the ought coming from the radical attempt to overturn existing society.

We are again hearing that law ought to be also moral, not merely technically correct. This has been one of the ominous results of the '60's, '70's, and '80's throughout the world. There has been a sudden and determined influx of revolutionary ethics into every Western political order, usually from a radical point of view, itself strictly Western in origin. Recently, too, there has been an ethical impact from the ecological approach which seeks to make the criterion of the ethical broader than the human.[11] These two approaches in practical politics and in theoretical origins are usually at diametrically opposed poles in analyzing what is wrong with man. The conservationist tends to see people as the problem. This position generally, in the name of man or perfect man, pits men one against another for presumably scarce resources. Thus, a kind of advanced Hobbesian thought is reintroduced as the basic relation among those who do and do not participate in the "remaining" resources. The social revolutionary school of thought tends, on the other hand, to see institutions and their reorganization as the way to a temporal salvation.

This clash of theory about what is to be expected of man, earth, and human institutions is the context of the great intellectual struggle of our time. Much modern thought is a search for the perfect social order. This theoretical controversy lines up the Third and Marxist worlds directly against the so-called developed world. Within this latter, there is still room for a more conservative-scientific view that finds its origin in an older view of man and his limited progress on earth, the one most likely to make at least some improvement. But both the conservationist and socialist theories are, in some basic sense, "heretical" in the way they look at man and his prospects in the world, heretical because of their utopian elements. In both cases, morality comes to be seen primarily in terms of the corporate group. Private, individual or personal morality is, in a way, dead in such views. It is considered theoretically unimportant.

138

We are left, then, with various corporate moralities which judge the individual in terms not of his freedom or contemplative wisdom or nature but in terms of his relation to a "cause" or a corporate possibility based on unlimited expectations of what man ought to do for himself in this world. (See Chapter XI) This, of course, is logical and consistent, once we grant that individuals belong to no transcendent drama independent or separate from secular history, something never granted in scriptural and medieval traditions.

The result of this is that political mobilization becomes our effort to confine man to his worldly expectations, to convince him thereby that the satisfaction of these are all the human enterprise consists in. The essential concern of morality in this context, therefore, is not a rediscovery of some higher principle but an attempt to identify morality with the effectuation of this-worldly ideologies considered to be salvation-bearing in the sense that they conceive themselves to be carriers of all the truth which is available to man.

In this context, consequently, and with this background, it is useful to look at the Prologue and first questions of the Prima Secundae of Aquinas' Summa Theologica, which deal with man as free and master of his own actions. The whole burden of the Second Question is to exclude any finite or earthly definition or goal as that which can make men happy. Classical Christianity consistently excluded any hope of human happiness that did not consist of the vision of God. As a direct result of this, considerations of the locus of beatitude, of hell, evil, and human nature in grace rejoin political theory proper, in the consideration of what in principle men can expect of the political order, if they cannot expect ultimate happiness from its structure and proceedings.

The basic definition of law in Aristotle was simply "reason without passion."(1287a32) This disarmingly concise formulation was written with full realization that Plato wrote The Republic without incorporating the need of law, because law could not provide for the particular cases of justice with which all our individual actions deal. Plato expected the ordinary man to be deflected by his own passions from seeing and doing what is right. Justice, in The Republic, was for each man fully to exercise his

139

talent in contributing his share to the variegated whole.

The philosopher-king, in this context, was a living substitute for law, designed to make up for a glaring deficiency in the very structure of the law itself, namely, its generality. Law could never avoid leaving the ultimate decision to the individual doer, except when the individual conformed directly and probably determinately to the good. Law was not providence. But this jeopardized the individual's own act either on the grounds of alien intelligence or ignorance of the real good. Further, there was always a disruptive element in the heart of each man in all existing states because man could be expected to choose mainly for his own self-interest.

Plato saw that the ordinary human community could not be expected to be ruled by the philosopher-king, even though Plato persisted in believing that man could only be truly just if so ruled. No existing state, therefore, could avoid injustices in this life while the operation of pride and envy could always be anticipated. In The Laws, Plato suggested that law might substitute for the philosopher-king in the second-best state, a theme to be taken up more fully in the following chapter. Law at least could limit passion and regulate its effects. The change in society that Plato found so dangerous could be mitigated by conformity to the laws. The major task of society is thus to restrict the excesses of greed, pride, coveteousness, and envy.

Classical political thought, consequently, always held man's own internal control over his nature was the first norm and requirement of order. Law was the instrument by which this was accomplished insofar as the individual's actions were public and affected others. Law freed man from the tyranny of his own passions and protected him from those of others. Reason without passion constituted law. But law as such was second-best; that is, it did not put man directly in contact with the good.

The greatest of the law-giving peoples of the ancient world were the Romans. For them, law was both administrative and customary. The eventual codification of the Roman Law sought to rationalize a long series of practices and principles by which judges decided what was fair and equitable among differing, often conflicting legal and national

140

practices. Thus, each and every type of case at controversy had some norm or precedent rooted in experience by which justice was set in practice.

Further, the various types of authority, or ways authority projected from one basic "imperium" or sovereignty gave a hierarchy to legislation and defined its validity. A universal political system imposed on all people demanded a common law so that all came to live according to the same procedures and criteria. An abuse could be appealed to the law-giver or to tradition. Such civil procedure protected the subjects of law. A Paul of Tarsus could thus appeal his case to the Emperor.(Acts, 25:1-12) The philosophic doctrine that all men lived according to the same law of reason found, apparently, a civil counterpart which endeavored to identify this natural law with the Roman justice system.

It was no accident that Cicero's second-best state came to be equated with the existing Roman Republic, while later Roman Law came to be coterminus with the Empire. Thus, law met in part the lack of a philosopher-king whose real existence would have meant ex hypothesi no injustice in the world. The absence of the philosopher-king meant the approximate justice of law. And Roman law came to be identified with the best law possible because it was the most universal and the most detailed, the one that decided controversies most adequately.

However, law was never theoretically designed to solve man's deepest problems with justice. Plato recognized this impossibility when he proposed the immortality of the soul in the last book of The Republic as the answer to the political dilemma of how injustice is finally punished and how justice rewarded in the universe when it often is not in this world. This is why political reflection, from its very beginning, never has escaped from the religious problem of the nature of the ultimate good in its efforts to establish a perfect and just state.

The question thus remains: how and where is this curious, often disruptive longing for complete happiness, the question that also began Aristotle's reflections in both The Politics and The Ethics, to be achieved? We are ever tempted to believe that this is something for us to achieve by ourselves. One of the main reasons the ancient world was spared the destructive implications of this tendency was

Aristotle's ability to distinguish metaphysics and politics, each with a proper kind of good and happiness to which men were called, the same men in different ways. But Aristotle clearly insisted that political happiness, the kind we mortals could achieve in this life, was not ultimately the same as the contemplative happiness which placed man before the First Mover and the order of the cosmos. The two were related as means to end. The state at its best made it possible for men at leisure to transcend this political world.

Christianity, as we saw in our considerations of the death of Christ, has political significance in its relation to the Platonic question: namely, is ultimate happiness to be achieved in this life by human means? (Chapter II) The Christian God was a gift not "due" to anything in nature or the cosmos. In the Christian version, the "guardians," furthermore, also gave up family and property in their own way to devote themselves to the revealed good. (Chapter IV) This fulfilled their corporate purpose of mediating salvation to those to whom it was given so that monasticism became a kind of higher level guardianship.

Christianity, of ourse, was imbued with Genesis, Amos, James, the Beatitudes, and the Good Samaritan. It insisted that men could improve their lives and societies. But it has even more firmly insisted that man's destiny is not the product of political action nor is man's happiness in this life exhausted by even the best states. Human personhood is essentially and mysteriously a relation to its creator. Political messianism, however currently popular, is seen as a goal degrading what the Christ came to preach and promise. Politics received no divine mission in scripture, even though it was honored.

Emperors, then, were to be obeyed, taxes paid, even law courts had their place. The two greatest men in the ancient world died unjustly at the hands of the state. Socrates did not want to live elsewhere than in the greatest city in Greece, so he condemned its injustice by observing its law to the letter. Christ told Pilate that his Roman authority was from God. He died asking forgiveness for his judges, saying they did not know what they did. The death of Socrates forced Plato to inquire whether the good man could ever live in any existing state. Christ died because a chosen people somehow rejected Him. The testimony of the ancient world is that the tragedies of politics confronted by truth and really good men cannot be reconciled by politics itself. Christianity's frank recognition of this freed men from the overwhelming burden of ever thinking that their salvation will ultimately come from the political order.

St. Augustine bluntly told the Romans, who believed their Empire so good, that justice even by their own standards could not be found within its confines. St. Augustine was so adamant on this point that he felt it necessary to exclude justice from the very definition of the state. (Chapter III) Men would be deluded were they told that true justice could be found in the civil state. So St. Augustine forcefully and dogmatically separated out the city of man from the City of God. Neither the Church nor the state were to be simply identified with these destinies.

The state, for St. Augustine, then, was conceived at its best as a remedy for the excess of pride and greed. The Fall tainted all men and all human institutions. Man could not, then, recoup the losses sustained by the Fall through any merely institutional or moral reform, let alone by a technological or political one. These losses were defined as death, coercive government, and private property. Only by unmerited grace could most earthly improvement be had. The state, to be sure, could and ought to be used to limit the extremes of man's vices. But it was not and could not be a salvation-producing instrument.

The City of God embodied the primary drama of creation. It consisted of all those ever to enjoy the vision of God, the only true happiness and justice for which man was made. History was the record of the City of God and the city of man in reaching their respective goals. Secular history, the rise and fall of nations, had no intrinsic meaning except insofar as it touched some divine purpose -- as the Roman Empire did indirectly because of the incarnation.(Luke, 2:1-7) St. Augustine would never allow the belief that politics or economics could gradually or abruptly solve man's deepest problems.

Furthermore, St. Augustine would never allow a lesser goal than the City of God to be defined as the destiny that would satisfy men. The only kind of order or peace available to man was a tenuous one, one that did not contain true justice in its construction. In a sense, the intellectual history of mankind since St. Augustine has been a desperate attempt to deny the force and logic of his argumentation. "All the grand sources, in short, of human suffering are in a great degree, many of them almost entirely, conquerable by human care and effort," John Stuart Mill wrote in his Utilitarianism. (Chapter II) St. Augustine would have considered anyone who could write such a thing to be singularly unobservant of human nature, even slightly mad.

When we examine Aquinas' theory of law, it also becomes obvious that what he called human positive law, the law men make for their own society, is an imperfect enterprise. Aquinas was more willing than St. Augustine to grant some positive function to the political state, provided it did not overreach its limits, limits rooted in natural law and eternal law, law not made by men. Aquinas posited the necessity of divine positive law (revelation) largely for the reasons Plato posited a philosopher-king and immortality. That is, law touches only the generality, only the external act, while man is also ordained to a goal beyond the state.[12] Aquinas held that human law was made for the communality of men, that it ought not to legislate all virtue but only that minimum to which most men could be expected to attain. This was how Christian political philosophy was able to come to terms with the positions it took on evil, hell, happiness, and grace.

The higher reaches of ethics and holiness were beyond the competence of politics and law to deal with.[13] Therefore, considerable leeway was left between the perfect and the ordinary. Indeed, the perfect were not, properly speaking, subject to civil law at all. All human law, furthermore, was itself subject to natural law such that there was a norm to judge civil law itself which transcended any human political project no matter what the form of political rule. The purpose of this was to keep man to be man since his creation as man was the norm of his being and not the political order itself.

Political and legal theory after Aquinas came to be dominated by positive or historical concepts of law which were similar in that they sought to eliminate any source of legal justification outside an earthly source of law whereby the law itself might be judged. Throughout the modern period, something of the older tradition remained, but it has only been in recent years that the question of morality has again arisen as a criterion to judge existing law. This is why the source of the authority of this newer morality is crucial.

Usually in the modern era, normally defined as the period after Machiavelli and Austin, any challenge to law from the angle of a broader morality was considered unacceptable, basically because there was believed to be no religious or philosophic source beyond law and politics capable of grounding a critique of legal practice. The Nuremburg Trials after World War II, to be sure, gave some attention to the problem of the need effectively to judge every civil legal structure. But these trials came to be viewed as conservative, even reactionary attempts to judge the validity of all states, especially when the question of judging other states than Nazi Germany arose. The treatment of South Africa currently presents the same kind of issue, as does that of the Russian dissidents, abortion, or America's human rights policies.[14]

Helmut Schlesky has reminded us that in Germany today radical legal movements often overtly attempt to destroy law and take over the state by simply insisting on law's absolute and perfect fulfillment in every technicality.[15] Law thus becomes a destructive affair when every case, every controversy within a society is fought out exhaustively through the entire legal system. When the whole society and all relationships within it become adversary relations of presumed justice, all relationships are subsumed into law. The legal process becomes paralyzed in the very mass of decisions that need to be made to assure "justice." The law becomes so complicated in its enforcement that the whole mechanism becomes suspect. Few in the society believe that law is achieving its purposes.

Thus, the current trend of many students to study law can be rather ominous from this point of view. Law becomes potentially destructive because its practitioners seek to straighten out all conceivable injustices by its processes. There is a curious missionary zeal in many of these new legal recruits which seems oblivious to the dangers implicit in turning everything into justice, in insisting that all justice problems have a good lawyer to confront them. When everything is legalized, when men think of little else but their particular or social rights -- to which they may be entitled, to be sure -- when the principal function of society is to guarantee "rights" irregardless of the limits of what is feasible in law and justice, then, the capacity of the legal system to do what can legitimately be expected of it is jeopardized.[16]

Justice, we should recognize, is the harshest and most ruthless of the virtues. It is no accident that Christianity never considered justice to be the basic virtue. Indeed, Christianity has always been at pains to distinguish its concept of God from an image of earthly justice. The instant God is conceived primarily as a justice-giving Being conceived in political and economic terms, the whole of human life is torn apart.(I-II, 65; See Chapter XII) God's ways are not our ways -- this is the reassuring theme of scripture. The Imitation of Christ, that classic of medieval piety, has a famous chapter called "The Royal Road of the Holy Cross," whose very title reminds men of spiritual primacy.[17] Christ's life did not primarily teach of the adequacy or even the significance of justice, but of something quite beyond it. God is a God of mercy, not justice. (See Chapter XII) "See how they love one another" does not even begin to translate as "See how just they are to their fellows." Thus it says in Luke's Gospel:

> Give to everyone who asks you, and do not ask for your property back from the man who robs you. Treat others as you like them to treat you. If you love those who love you, what thanks can you expect? Even sinners love those who love them. And if you do good to those who do good to you, what thanks can you expect? For even sinners do that much ... Instead, love your enemies and do good, and lend without any hope of return. (Luke, 6:31-35)

Clearly, something more than justice is going on here.

This means at least that the drama in which men are involved in their earthly, often tragic lives transcends the accomplishment of worldly justice, however valuable it might be. This must ever be so if we have any empirical sensitivity to the kind of lives most men live. If we insist that justice is all there is or pretend that our religious relation to others is to bring them "justice", we will inevitably and tragically delude them. We are not to deal in abstractions. No human on earth has, strictly speaking, ever lived in a completely just and human society. St. Augustine was quite right. Unless we think to make the purpose of our generation or era sacrificial to some other generation long down the paths of history which will somehow eventually be "just," then we must recognize that the justification for the life of men on earth, the reason we need not despair and defy, cannot be conceived in terms primarily of justice. If in fact our real enterprise on earth is about establishing complete justice among men, then we ought to despair, for that is our only realistic alternative.

We are beginning to see recently a large scale questioning of modern civilization itself.[18] The history of modern Catholic social thought in particular has long held, on its conservative side, that "modern civilization" contained something basically ruinous to the human spirit in its ethos. Because this social thought persisted in believing this, it was looked upon as reactionary and backward. The last two centuries have been so enamored with ideas of progress, science, evolution, and secularism that due attention was never adequately given to this critical aspect of social reflection. Currently, the themes of the revolutionary socialists and the conservationist schools from different angles have taken up the attack on modern civilization itself. Both agree that the kind of civilization produced by science, technology, and capitalism is exploitive and destructive. Both propose a complete revamping of productive and distributive mechanisms, though each takes a rather opposite view of the causes of the situation.

What these criticisms have in common is a view of man which subordinates his activities, well-being, and meaning to the functioning of a system. Morality becomes identified with the laws of the system designed to reach the goal of an ideology. Morality is conformity to the values judged necessary for the success of the system. There is granted little room for classical Christian thought, which insisted that there is a standard outside the system itself according to which human worth in its essentials whould be evaluated because each person had a destiny beyond any worldly accomplishment, however noble. Thus, throwing a beer can in a forest or stealing a tool from a state factory becomes a political crime,

147

not a personal fault. Christians are constantly being confronted with laws and attitudes with which they are quickly realizing they cannot fully accept because laws and attitudes are presented as rigid, logical conclusions within the structure of a social system that demands conformity, even spiritual conformity, and assent because the good it hopes to achieve is considered the good for which men ought or have to strive.

In one sense, the secularizing tendency to eliminate religion and ethics from formal, normative consideration in education and law has left us intellectually helpless before any moral ideology claiming any sort of value. The history of behaviorism in the light of the radical value systems that followed it reveals this clearly enough.[19] We are stripped of any intellectual discipline recognizing that critical judgments of values are the essence of all morality, this in the light of a goal or destiny. The elimination of value and religion from the academic sphere, a project made possible and aided by our legal system, has merely resulted in exposing student and professor alike to every variety of moral enthusiasm from witchcraft to ecology to Maoism. Classical religion and ethics are forbidden entry on the odd grounds of separation of church and state.

But the newer ideologies are frankly moral, brutally objective about the weakness of a society that has little intellectual and public place for religion and values. The newer ideologies identify morality and legal forms such that man is forced to equate value with the observance of a new set of laws designed to effect the new goals. At first sight, this is well and good. Law should aid morality and achieve a public good. Yet "law" and morality are not coterminous except, as Aristotle said, when the good man is in the good state.

Even here, however, man's life is broader than his legal rights, so that morality may have to go against the law to achieve its purpose. Political regimes are not wrong in seeing in religion especially a disruptive force against any existing status quo. But the contemporary issue, for which Christians have been unprepared, is rather that religious people are caught in having to defend the state at a moment when many of the laws of the state are inspired by values that are contrary to human worth and value as such.

No particular insight is needed to see that the major area in which this dilemma will appear is in that of the right to life and the conditions of death.

Christian leadership has been oddly slow to grasp the significance of this problem. With little adequate thought of how public policy works through existing political structures, with little understanding of the limits of law, Christians find themselves forced to acknowledge law according to the systems that inspire its newer formulation on the books. When law becomes the expression of ideology, the kind of obedience it demands is problematic, even though the kind of coercion to be used to force its exactitude increases. Many development theories today, as well as most environmental theories, embrace a form of authoritarian coercion. Without agreement on the kind of being man is, law comes to represent an attempt to redefine man in terms of the ideology.

Law has been held to have an implicit and far-reaching educative function. Morality was broader than law but for this very reason, what the law did command and enforce was considered minimally necessary for common life. This is why laws that violate human values are so dangerous. This too is why the efforts of someone like Alexander Solzhenitsyn to insist that good or noble laws written in state constitutions be observed by the authorities in them are valuable and crucial efforts. Men naturally assume the law is wiser than they as individuals, more apt to be right than individual judgments.

Law, too, is to express collective wisdom and agreed upon goals which inform most men what they can achieve. This is why the control of the law-making process is so important. Not merely does law becomes identified with correct process, but also observance comes to be equated with justice and goodness. If there is felt to be no question of morality over against and beyond the law, then, whatever is not contained in the law becomes a matter of ethical indifference. And since law can really take cognizance of only basic requirements of the public order, the area of ethical indifference broadens to include anything man chooses to do, while real "morality" is restricted to those things commanded and enforced by the state according to its ideology.

At first glance, this would seem to be a process for weakening the state. Indeed, it does weaken the

non-ideological state. But, as Irving Kristol has
pointed out, lack of independent morality and
self-discipline leads in the long run to ideology and
authoritarianism because individuals who do what they
please have lost the very facility of ethical
discrimination.[20] When morality is current law,
there is no reason why the state cannot expand its
sphere to include those actions necessary to achieve
ideological goals, ever presented as noble and even
spiritual. Everywhere, we are seeing covert revivals
of authoritarian theories in the face of modernization
problems and resource issues since there is no longer
any way to gain and secure a private sphere that does
not belong to the state because, supposedly, of the
overriding goals its ideology drives it to achieve.
We are left only with our public interests and these
are politicized in some kind of effort to achieve a
complete and total human happiness. Private actions
become either frivolous or futile.

We are angry, Bruno Bettelheim remarked, because
we see men violate our value-free laws. This glaring
contradiction speaks with its own eloquence.
Fundamentally, it means that we are no longer
value-free in our basic feelings. Our question then
is: what kind of values do we want? What kind are
being offered? In a sense, a value-free society may
be a safer one than a society shot through with wild
and dangerous values. The American tradition at its
best recognized this and made a consistent case for
it, though, as we shall consider in the following
Chapter, a better theoretical basis can be found from
classical and Christian philosophy. But it remains
that the crucial issue ever comes back to the one that
knows and preserves the limits of law and politics.
And the most fundamental thing we can know about law
and politics is that they do not satisfy man's
ultimate desires and destinies, even though the very
existence and power of ideology today is unquestioned
testimony to the drive in men to find some ultimate.

Thus, we should realize that the feeling that law
and politics can achieve our ultimate desires in
whatever form they take is the most subtle and
difficult temptation man has to deal with. That God
be conceived in political terms, that holiness be
presented as successful worldly accomplishment for the
ultimate cause of the ideology, usually of
development, or of peace, or of earth, none of these
is unintelligible. But it is a narrowing of the
vision Christianity gives to man. If religion itself

150

yields to this temptation in practice, we can begin to expect the rise of a newer and deeper frustration among us, the frustration that comes when we enter into the Cathedral only to find nothing there but poor boxes and aid-giving agencies of various sorts.

"My purpose was to put you on your guard against the serious," E. M. Cioran wrote in the context of the decline of Christianity, "against that sin which nothing redeems. In exchange, I wanted to offer you ... futility."[21] What we must recognize currently is that religion is in serious danger of becoming "futile" to the degree that it identifies its role with projects of law and politics that do not preserve the difference between man's personal destiny and what imperfect things he can accomplish in the world. There is, indeed, a kind of futility in all our earthly projects which religion should call to our attention and keep before our eyes. There is a worth in the world which should be valued and which flows from the Old and New Testament appreciations of worldly things. But the world is not that for which we were made.

In his memorable essay, "De Futilitate," C. S. Lewis wrote:

> If there is anyone present whose fear of futility is based solely on such local and temporary facts as the war (World War II) or the almost equally frightening prospect of the next peace, I must ask him to bear with me while I suggest that we have to face the possibility of a much deeper and more radical futility....

> ... Everything suggests that organic life is going to be a very short and unimportant episode in the history of the universe. We have often heard individuals console themselves for their individual troubles by saying: "It will all be the same 100 years hence." But you can do the like about our troubles as a species. Whatever we do it is all going to be the same in a few hundred million years hence. Organic life is only a lightning flash in cosmic history. In the long run, nothing will come of it.[22]

And this is the problem that law, medicine, and the

enthusiasm for them bring up -- does it all end in futility? When this perfect city we legislate passes away, what then?

When Aquinas noted that the observance of any law, even human law, is necessarily also a participation in the natural and eternal law of God, he was suggesting that our worldly institutions do link us with the divine, that our accomplishments for the common order are worthwhile. But this was only because we knew where our public efforts belonged, what we could accomplish in them. Of themselves, they were futile if we wanted to identify them with those desires and hopes for which we were created. Behind much of the political, legal, and medical concern of our time lies a confusion that bears upon religion, its historical and intellectual roots, on its public task. This is the effort to overturn the limits placed upon the worldly order by removing from it the impossibility of making man fully happy. By promising in our projects for justice and earth and health a hope that man will finally be able to be at peace is to introduce a sense of futility in the hearts of man more profound than anything hitherto known.

Mankind as a whole has often known the despair of failure, poverty and suffering. The promise of this age is the promise of success, not just individual but political, ideological success. It is this futility that looms on the horizon, that is connected with the fundamental issues of the history of political theory. The crisis of the Christian religion in particular today, in the light of its own ancient and medieval history, can be simply put: Will this religion come to be justified essentially in terms of its contribution to the worldly projects of our time? In other words, will the worship and praise of God remain the first task of the faith?

We cannot properly worship God, when we see our brother hungry, as the Apostle James wrote in his Epistle, something that is at the roots of Christian and Western tradition.(James, 2:1-9) Nevertheless, we are told also in the New Testament that there are two commandments, the love of God and the love of neighbor. And we are told that if we love our neighbor, we have fulfilled the law. Current ideologies are spiritual because they all tell us in one way or another that there is only one commandment, only one law. This, surely, from the standpoint of Christian thought, is the best definition of futility

152

in modern times. The limits of the Second Commandment
are the First. This is the mystery of   our   existence
which we must all   confront   in   the   privacy   of   our
hearts,   our restless hearts, as St. Augustine   called
them.

Footnotes:

1. See Burton Y. Pines, Four Hard Truths for Higher Education, Washington, Heritage (#20), 1983; John Naisbitt, Megatrends, New York, Warner, 1982; Alan Bloom, "Our Listless Universities," National Review, December 10, 1982.

2. See James V. Schall, "Possibilities and Madness: A Note on the Scope of Political Theory," The Review of Politics, April, 1975, pp. 161-74.

3. See Jacques Maritain, Man and the State, Chicago, University of Chicago Press, 1951, Chapters I and II.

4. See James V. Schall, "Intellectual Origins of the 'Peace' Movement," in Justice and War in the Nuclear Age, Washington, University Press of America, 1983.

5. See James V. Schall, Human Dignity and Human Numbers, Staten Island, Alba House, 1971; Christianity and Life, San Francisco, Ignatius Press, 1981.

6. See James V. Schall, "The Abiding Significance of Gnosticism," The American Ecclesiastical Review, September, 1962; See E. Voegelin, The New Science of Politics, University of Chicago Press, 1952; "Liberalism and History," Review of Politics, October, 1974, pp. 504-20.

7. See Max Weber, The Protestant Ethic and the Spirit of Capitalism, New York, Scribner's, 1956. See also, James V. Schall, "Luther and Political Philosophy," Faith and Reason, Suer, 1982, pp. 7-31.

8. See James V. Schall, "Apocalypse as a Secular Enterprise," The Scottish Journal of Theology, #4, 1976, pp. 357-73; Michael Novak, "Moral Clarity in the Nuclear Age," Catholicism-in-Crisis, March, 1983, pp. 3-23; "The Challenge of Peace," the Pastoral Letter on War and Peace, Origins, May 19, 1983, pp. 1-32. The English Editions of the French and German Bishops' Statements on War, along with Basil Cardinal Hume's Letter, are published in a single volume by Ignatius Press in San Francisco, 1984.

9. See Maritain, Men and the State, ibid., Chapter on Democratic Charter; John XXIII, Pacem in Terris: 1963; John Paul II, Redemptor Hominis: 1979.

10. See W. Gurian, Bolshevism, Notre Dame, University of Notre Dame Press, 1952.

11. See James V. Schall, "On the Christian Love of Animals," Vital Speeches, November 15, 1976, pp. 81-86.

12. See James V. Schall, "The Totality of Society: From Justice to Friendship," The Thomist, January, 1957; also last Chapter of Redeeming the Time, New York, Sheed and Ward, 1968.

13. See James V. Schall, "Interior and Exterior Spirituality," The American Ecclesiastical Review, September, 1975, pp. 490-503.

14. See James V. Schall, "Culture and Human Rights," America, January 7, 1978, pp. 14-17.

15. Helmut Schelsky, "The New Strategy of Revolution," Modern Age, Fall, 1974, pp. 345-55.

16. See James V. Schall, "Second Thoughts on Natural Rights," Faith and Reason, Winter, 1975-76, pp. 44-59.

17. See James V. Schall, "On the Love of Enemies,"; "The Experience of Hatred," in The Distinctiveness of Christianity, San Francisco, Ignatius Press, 1983; see also "On Remaking Man and the World," Christianity and Politics, ibid., Chapter XI, pp. 295-314.

18. See for example, Robert Heilbroner, The Human Prospect, New York, Norton, 1974; Alasdair MacIntyre, After Virtue, Notre Dame, University of Notre Dame Press, 1981; Russell Kirk, Reclaiming a Patrimony, Washington, Heritage, 1982; Paul Johnson, Modern Times, New York, 1983.

19. See C. A. McCoy and J. Playford, Apolitical Politics, A Critique of Behaviorism, New York, Cowell, 1967; G. Graham and G. Carey, The Post-Behavioral Era, Perspectives on Political Science, New York, McKay, 1972.

20. See Irving Kristol, "Some Thoughts on Education, Garbage, and Moral Authority," The San Francisco Chronicle, November 24, 1974.

21. E. M. Cioran, <u>The Temptation to Exist</u>, New York, Quadrangle, 1968, p. 82.

22. C. S. Lewis, "De Futilitate," <u>Christian Reflections</u>, Grand Rapids, Eerdmans, 1967, pp. 57-58.

CHAPTER VIII

THE BEST FORM OF GOVERNMENT

No man has a right to any good without
partaking of the evil by which that good is
necessarily produced; no man has a right to
security by another's danger, nor to plenty
by another's labour, but as he gives
something of his own which he who meets the
danger or undergoes the labour considers as
equivalent; no man has a right to the
security of government without bearing his
share of inconveniences.

Those who increase the expenses of the
public ought to supply their proportion of
the expenses increased ... If by forsaking
our native country, we could carry away all
its happiness and leave its evils behind,
what human being would not wish for exile?
--[Samuel Johnson, "Lecture on the
Government of Ireland and the American
Provinces," in Samuel Johnson, by John Wain.
New York, Viking, 1974, p. 272.]

I. THE POLITICAL FORM OF NEW STATES.

From the Old and New Testament sources, from St.
Augustine, from the reflections on hell and evil, from
the locus of beatitude and the resultant place of
human law in Christian philosophy, it is possible
within this tradition to reconsider, restate the
classical problem of the best form of government. But
this will be accomplished in a way that is impossible
to comprehend in an Enlightenment or perfectionist
position.

Certain apparently philosophical and theological
issues, moreover, have to be presented and argued
because without them, "the political" will not be
clear and in its proper place. One of the essential
faults of much modern theory is very often its claim
to intellectual independence, not in the classical
sense wherein political theory found place within an
overall intellectual or theological order, but in a

157

more absolute sense of full autonomy. Nonetheless, the problem of the best form of regime is a basic one in political theory, the one that began political thought in the first place with Plato.

During the past half-century or so, the world has seen the formation of some one hundred new nation-states, while many of the other fifty odd political entities have radically altered their previous form of constitution by force, revolution, conquest, election, or change of political philosophy. This has given renewed life to the classical issue about what is the best form of rule under which man ought to live.[1] Political modernization has become a crucial aspect of political science. The external "form" of almost all these new nation-states, to be sure, even of the most absolute, has almost invariably been some legal variety of "constitutional democracy," the wording commonly given in modern times to the structure of the "best" state.[2]

In practice, however, this has not been an altogether happy result. For it has meant that one of the major tasks of political "theory" as an intellectual discipline, one devoted to truth and not merely to appearance, as Socrates taught it from the beginning, has consisted in distinguishing between proclaimed "form" of rule and actual conduct as compared to some normative standard. The United Nations itself, wherein these nation-states gain some form of public recognition, moreover, in spite of the lofty principles and norms of its Charter, has managed to exclude practically no nation from its ranks, except those which have some racial overtones, and these only if the "racism" is white against black.[3] In this context, then, Daniel Moynihan argued that there are probably not more than a couple of dozen true "democracies" existing in the world at the present time.[4] And in the perspective of nineteenth and early twentieth century political theory, beginning with de Tocqueville in the 1830's, this is doubly ironic since "democracy" was long considered to be the "ideal" form of modern government resulting from the advent of science and technology.[5]

The Marxist governments, which presently include over a third of mankind, moreover, proclaim themselves to be at another "stage" of development, advancing rapidly toward a "classless society." This is conceived to be the ideal form of government, even

158

though logically Marxism proposes eventually to eliminate the very need for government at all. All the Marxist governments in their own way, curiously showing in this manner their dependence on classical political thought, also stick to the external form of democratic structures with elections, courts, legislatures, executives, bureaucracies, parties, and well-composed, written constitutions. They invariably insist that they are "peoples' democracies." This has meant in practice that the best literature on Marxism in modern political science has been forced to deal principally with the degree to which the actual practice conforms to proclaimed ideals of society and to standards of rule from outside the narrowly arrived at Marxist system.

In effect, then, we have very little criteria for distinguishing good government from bad, even though we are in a period that insists upon high standards of public morality.[6] Further, we rarely ask ourselves any more about the best form of government, even though there is some diplomatic pressure for not dealing with so-called "fascist" rulers or regimes, or even tyrannies of a certain hue.[7] The efforts of the United Nations to exclude Israel on the grounds that it alone was "racist" revealed how much public political performance and valid political theory must be kept clearly distinguished if the intellectual integrity of the discipline is to be retained.

In a sense, we have a political ideology which, in terms of its own presuppositions, tries to gain control of political institutions to exclude the "worst" forms of government. And this very process reveals the methodological theory of the best form of rule, since the "democratic" forms are now the ones coming to be stigmatized as "exploiting," corrupt tyrannies. This too, it seems, suggests the wisdom of the classical political theorists who included a discussion of the "corrupt" forms of rule as a necessary part of a complete political science.

II. ANTI-POLITICAL NEUTRALITY.

In 1961, Professor P. H. Partridge wrote that the political thought of that era, in its attempt to imitate the other sciences, tended to accept the model of Western, particularly Anglo-Saxon democracy, as the norm of the best state. This, he felt, was a narrowing of political philosophy to manageable terms which neglected the broader moral deficiencies in the democratic states.[8] But political thought in the ensuing years became controversial because of the doubtful validity of the "scientific" democratic model since it neglected, especially in its behavioral form, the broader ethical questions.

Christian Bay, further, developed this argument by pointing out that behavioral political science did not recognize its implicit value presuppositions. "My argument will be that much of the current work on political behavior generally fails to articulate its very real biases, and that the political impact of this supposedly neutral literature is generally conservative and in a special sense anti-political."[9] And this "anti-political" element meant that choices of preference and value were hidden. Some of the New Left in the 1960's and 70's were so enterprising even to suggest to the behavioral school that, since it was ex professo value-free, it should have no objection supporting various activist programs, whatever their values.

Professor Bay, for his part, went on to advocate a normative approach which was itself much in the tradition of Saint-Simon's value of the elimination of poverty.[10]

> I propose as a normative basis the proposition that politics exists for the purpose of progressively removing the most stultifying obstacles to a free human development, with priority for the worst obstacles, whether they hit the many or the few -- in other words, with priority for those who are most severely oppressed.[11]

This orientation of politics to the least advantaged can be also itself an anti-political position in the sense that this function was never conceived in classical political theory, such as in the first book of Aristotle's Politics, to be properly a "political" one, but rather one proper to the household or economics.

The focus of attention on the poor and the oppressed, the dominant theme of politics during the late sixties and seventies, is now, however, being challenged by a renewed attention to quality and to the best. Some universities are even moving from remedial and quota systems to high quality, even classical education. This newer concentration can, indeed, be dangerous when it uses the criterion of quality against life itself. Nevertheless, the question of the best is justifiably the central issue for men, one that cannot be avoided for long in any valid political thought. "'What's new?' is an interesting and broadening eternal question", Robert Persig stated in his Zen and the Art of Motorcycle Maintenance,

> but one which, if pursued exclusively, results only in an endless parade of trivia and fashion, the silt of tomorrow. I would like instead, to be concerned with the question, What's best?, a question which cuts deeply rather than broadly....[12]

And this question, "What's best?", in political theory, is not only an ancient one, but one that presupposes the validity of the human being as such for its answer. Politics does not make man to be man, but taking him as already man makes him to be good man -- such is the Aristotelian tradition which has warned us about changing or re-creating "man" for ends of our politics rather than limiting our ends by what man already is.

III. JUDGING REGIMES.

At first sight, in the light of the history of political theory, this lack of attention to the theoretical importance of the best form of government seems strange since this very question was considered by classical thought as almost the most crucial philosophical issue arising within the political realm.[13] The Republic, from which all subsequent political theory derives, was little less than a direct confrontation with this question. To be sure, adequate and complete political theory always recognized that bad or corrupt forms of government needed to be included as an essential element in political theory. Socrates left us in something of an enigma in Book VIII of The Republic when he suggested that the reason why a less good state could ever arise from the one ruled by a philosopher-king was because "everything which has a beginning has also an end."(#546a)

But Socrates was quite sure that states were not made of "oak and rock." Rather, they were composed of "the human natures that are within them."(#544d) The question of the best, then, was related to the worst.

161

Indeed, tyranny, the worst, was the political possibility that made the discussion of the best form of government necessary, for in absolute tyranny, as Aristotle suggested, even the minimum of civic friendship and speech would be destroyed. Men would be reduced to sheer silence.[14]

The lack of general concern for the best form of government reveals something basic about the contemporary status of political theory itself, with its relationship to its own classical and medieval past. This is especially pertinent since the result of two World Wars was a concerted endeavor to establish the good, even the best form of rule as a response to the erroneous political practice which, supposedly, resulted in these very wars. And the Second World War especially was pictured as a struggle against the worst form of rule ever known among men.

Thus, self-determination, making the world safe for democracy, and the four freedoms were slogans not unrelated to the idea that we know what forms were "good" because we fought to reject what was "bad." And even the much-abused notion of "colonialism," a totally pejorative word today, in its Greek, Roman, medieval, and even League of Nations' forms, had intrinsic to it the belief that a people can be educated and trained to live under the best form of rule or at least not coerced to live under the worst.

The contemporary paradox of all of this is that we now live under quite intricate and minutely detailed "forms" of rule which do not in fact correspond to political "reality." We require philosophical and religious insight into good and evil themselves, as well as high moral integrity, to escape the rigid control of the self-professedly good "forms" of government now actually in power. This has caused us, to some extent, to look again at the tradition of St. Augustine in political thought.

This tradition, to recall, denied the very possibility of the "best" form of political rule in this world, because all existing governments act selfishly and contrary to justice. (See Chapter III) The best thing that could be expected was a kind of broken peace imposed upon our unruly desires and greeds. Thus, the maddening, even destructive pursuit of justice in this world, pure politics, must be put aside for a higher and more realistic view of the possible. Love, not justice, becomes the norm of even the world.

In this context, too, one of the principal reasons why Alexander Solzhenitsyn causes so much controversy in current political culture is because he insists upon using philosophical and theological criteria to judge states that profess themselves to be good. For Solzhenitsyn, those who live in the worst state are deprived of everything. The only thing they can have left to them is a form of moral will not to co-operate with the lie, with evil, itself something of a classic problem, as we have seen. Indeed, the Russian even arrives at the paradox that those who live in the worst of states can, through their suffering, become the best of men.[15]

Thus, Solzhenitsyn has persisted in seeing Marxism in moral terms and chastizing the free powers for going along with it to keep men slaves.

> (Communism) has infected the whole world with the belief in the relativity of good and evil. Many people besides the communists are carried away by this idea today. Among enlightened people, it is considered rather awkward to use seriously such words as "good" and "evil." Communism has managed to instill in all of us that these concepts are old-fashioned and laughable. But if we are to be deprived of the concept of good and evil, what will be left? Nothing but the manipulation of one another.[16]

And Solzhenitsyn's address on the BBC was perhaps one of the most morally shattering accusations ever made against a free people because they refused to see their responsibility to others suffering under tyranny.[17]

What is of interest in this matter, however, is the kind of response often made to Solzhenitsyn, a response that has to negate his implicit argument that the division of good and evil is an essential element in politics. An Editorial in The Washington Post (July 4, 1975) attempted to do this by identifying Solzhenitsyn as a Russian moralist who seeks to impose his "moral crusade" on all people. He thus became a "fundamentalist," often today the reductio ad absurdam of all classical liberal argument. "Human dignity ... is a high moral value. But so is the avoidance of

163

nuclear war -- this is the overarching goal of detente."

Solzhenitsyn had an opportunity to respond to this line of criticism which sought to separate moral value from political reality. He pointed out that he wanted no crusade, just a decision to cease helping the Russian government to enslave its own people. Further, he felt nuclear war would never happen because of this same lack of moral will in the free world. Indeed, he maintained that World War III has already been fought and lost by the West on these very moral grounds.[18] He argued, in other words, that placing politics higher than morality would inevitably lead all the world into the slavery of his own nation, which ironically claims to be the embodiment of the good state, while it is in fact the worst state.

IV. A HUMAN POLITICS.

The question of the good form of regime, consequently, the one in which man can best achieve his highest ends embodied in actual political practice, cannot be avoided in contemporary politics and thought. And to understand further the intellectual import of this issue, we must see the evolution of the discussion in the light of the history of political thought and the relation of classical and medieval theory to American theory which has, in fact, been grounded in the search for the "best" form of government.[19] The dilemma encountered by this question throughout intellectual history has been that of either minimizing politics or transforming it into a religion or metaphysics. How to keep politics to be politics and yet the "human", the practical science, has proved to be the most difficult of the speculative problems arising out of man's actual social nature.[20]

In the second book of the Peloponnesian War, Thucydides recounted the Funeral Oration of Pericles, his classic, unforgettable statement of the best form of government:

> Our constitution is called a democracy because power is in the hands not of a minority but of the whole people. When it is a question of settling private disputes, everyone is equal before the law; when it is a question of putting one person before another in position of public

responsibility, what counts is not
membership of a particular class, but the
actual ability which the man possesses. No
one, so long as he has it within him to be
of service to the state, is kept in
political obscurity because of poverty ...
We are free and tolerant in our private
lives; but in public service we keep the
law. (Bk. 2, Ch. 4)

Already here, there is a trace of Aristotle's acute
sense of a justice that must account both for equality
of condition and diversity of talent and
contribution. And when, some twenty-three centuries
later, Abraham Lincoln delivered a "Funeral Oration"
at Gettysburg that rang true to the spirit and even
the words of Pericles, when he affirmed that "a
government of the people, for the people, and by the
people shall not perish from this earth," he
reaffirmed the abiding concern we have for the best
form of government as intrinsic to our very political
condition.[21]

Yet, when the plague devastated Athens, the ideal
city, revealing yet again the constant inclination of
human nature, when Pericles is himself finally struck
down so that he could not carry out his professed
policy to the end, Thucydides could only reflect with
nostalgia, as we reflect on the murder of Lincoln in
the Reconstruction, that Athenian democracy could only
exist because the best man held the people "in
check." "So in what was nominally a democracy, power
was really in the hands of the first citizen."(Bk. 2,
Ch. 6) The best actual state failed because its
citizens could not keep the admonitions of its best
citizen during the rest of the war. Cleon and
Alcibiades, indeed, became the incarnation of the
vices opposed to Pericles' virtues. And they were men
of the highest talent, which again proved that
knowledge was not virtue. Meanwhile, Syracuse, the
city most like Athens, is the one to defeat her.

Classical Greek political theory was haunted by
the notion of the best form of regime for men. Each
of its monumental efforts to determine the rule under
which men ought to live ended in an intellectual
impasse, out of which succeeding theory has never
quite managed to escape. When Pericles spoke of not
being kept in "political obscurity," he touched upon
the crux of the problem presented by the best form of
government, a form that would somehow enable everyone

to escape from this obscurity in which he dwells under any less perfect form. Moreover, Thucydides' observation that Pericles was needed to keep the Athenians "in check" for their own good hinted at the structural problem that arises among citizens who are not in fact perfect, that is, among governments that include actual men. It will be about how this "checking" is to be accomplished that later American political thought will most directly address itself.

V. BEST AND SECOND-BEST STATES.

After Thucydides, Greek theory immediately confronted the figure of Socrates, confronted him in the agonizing, unending question of Plato we have often recalled: How was it the best state killed the best man? And to resolve this enigma, political theory ever since has been, at bottom, a search for a form of rule in which both the virtuous _and_ the normal could live. Greek political thought in Aristotle immediately recognized that a complete political theory needed, to repeat, to account for the corrupt forms of rule, while each of the good, constitutional forms which ruled according to law for the good of all lacked some basic factor, some essential perfection.

Monarchy did not allow the participation of everyone; aristocracy lacked unity of action, while polity lacked both unity of action and higher virtue, though it did enable the many to participate in ruling. In this dilemma, both Plato and Aristotle proposed a theory of the "second best" state. This was the burden of The Laws and of the "middle class" state. (1295b35-1297a12) They were proposed as the best "practical" as opposed to the best theoretical state, since there seemed to be something amiss with actual human nature that did not bear the best. The second best state was the one that was of "law" also, but it acknowledged the impossibility or improbability of the best.

Indeed, from the very end of The Republic, political philosophy has realized that there is something paradoxical about mankind's enterprise, his search for happiness. Socrates ended in doubt about all existing states. He believed that somehow the best ordering of society transcended any actual political arrangement. This meant, as Glaucon had suggested earlier, that any perfect man would probably be executed in any real state of men.(#361c; #592a) Yet, Socrates insisted on believing that the pursuing

166

of justice and wisdom was the primary endeavor which established men in their value. Without it, no one could know his place in the societal order.

Aristotle recognized immediately that there were two kinds of "happiness" in question: that which referred to the "practical" life, the life of politics, and that which belonged to the contemplative life, the metaphysical order. In Book Six of The Ethics, Aristotle wrote:

> Speculative thought has nothing to do with action of production, and it performs its functions well or ill according as it succeeds in reaching a true or false conclusion. To be sure, ascertaining the truth is the function of any part of the intellect. But what the practical intellect does is to reach that kind of truth which answers to right desire.(1139a26-31)

Aristotle insisted in keeping "wisdom" distinct from political science. His reason for maintaining this is seldom understood in its ultimate sense. "I find it strange," he remarked in a rare personal note, "that anyone should regard political science or practical wisdom as the noblest of studies, for that is to assume that man is what is best in the world."(1141a20-21) And because Aristotle did not assume that man was the best in the world, he was able to prevent politics from becoming a metaphysics, that is, a science of all being whose reality is defined and formed by man. "It is all very well to say that man is the noblest of the animals. There are creatures far more divine than man...."(1141b1-2)

For Aristotle, there were two "ends," one of politics, another of metaphysics, but they were related to one another. The best form of political life will end in leisure, as he suggested in the last book of The Politics, in questions and realities that transcend the best political order.

> But as our object is to find the best constitution, and that means the one whereby a city will be best ordered, we can call that city best ordered in which the possibilities of happiness are greatest ... We defined this (happiness) in our Ethics ... Happiness is activity and the complete utilization of our own powers, our goodness,

167

not conditionally but absolutely.(1332a4-10)

When Aristotle further referred to the two aspects of reason upon which he grounded a transcendent end and a worldly or political one, he concluded, "(The statesman) must regard men's lives and their choices of what they shall do. For one must be able to work and to fight, but even more to be at peace and lead a life of cultivated leisure, to do the necessary and useful things but still more those of intrinsic worth."(1333a39-b4)

Aristotle constantly recognized the difference between the absolutely best state and the "second best" state. He trenchantly remarked, in his comments on The Laws, "It is quite possible to live a virtuous life and yet be miserable."(1265a32) Further, Aristotle was conscious of the limits of the ordinary man. He therefore posed yet another form of the "best" state:

> What is the best constitution and what is the best life for the majority of states and the majority of men? We have in mind men whose standard of virtue does not rise above that of ordinary people, who do not look for an education that demands either great natural ability or a large private fortune, who seek not an ideally perfect constitution, but first, a way of living in which as many as possible can join and, second, a constitution within the compass of the greatest number of cities.(1295a25-31)

There is, furthermore, a more complicated, subtle point. No best political state answers man's highest good and happiness. This is why, in Book 10 of The Ethics, Aristotle restricted politics to the life of mortal men qua mortal, while leisure in a sense transcends this proper life of man. "The business of the politician also makes leisure impossible. Besides the activity itself, politics aims at securing positions of power and honor or the happiness of the politician himself or his fellow citizens -- a happiness obviously distinct from that which we are seeking."(1177b13-16) Aristotle, then, does not exclude or ignore either the best practical or the best theoretical state. He does not, however, hold that politics is the highest life for man.

Indeed, Aristotle maintained that if politics

168

were made to be the absolutely best life for man, it would end up by destroying politics itself.

Yes, but such a life (contemplative) will be too high for human attainment. It will not be lived by us in our merely human capacity but in virtue of something divine within us, and so far as this divine particle is superior to man's composite nature, to that extent will its activity be superior to that of the other forms of excellence. If intellect is divine compared with man, the life of intellect must be divine compared with the life of a human creature. And ought we not to listen to those who counsel us, "O man, think as man should" and "O mortal, remember your mortality?" Rather ought we, so far as in us lies, to put on immortality and to leave nothing unattempted in the effort to live in conformity with the highest thing within us.(1177b25-29)

This means that politics has a special dignity but not the highest. That is the theoretical foundation for any notion of limited political constitution. It is also the proper context for any notion of the best theoretical state.

VI. CHRISTIAN REFLECTIONS.

Post-Aristotelian thought -- the Stoics, the Epicureans, the Cynics -- was noteworthy because it no longer held that man was a social animal.[22] Rather, his perfection was not to transcend the state but to withdraw from it. The individual could only find deadly confusion and moral decadence in the post-Alexandrine political world. Yet, within this world there was a notable attempt in Polybius and Cicero to reinstitute the theory of the best state within the Stoic system. Aristotle's notion of mixed constitution was elevated into the central position of being the answer to the classical problem of the deficiencies of all pure forms.

The difficulty with this was not, however, in its structural arrangements and analyses, which were to have a long subsequent history, but in the Roman elevation, as Charles N. R. McCoy has well argued, of the practical virtues to that of the highest human virtue.[23] This had the effect of eliminating

169

Aristotle's carefully calibrated limits on the
political order. The best form of rule was
theoretically confused with the highest human good and
thus subjected man's highest faculties to politics.

The arrival of the Christian religion takes its
theoretical significance from the impasse of ancient
thought which, in despair, had ended in a kind of
escapism in the post-Aristotelian theories. Men were
perfect only if they withdrew from the state, the very
opposite of Aristotle's notion that man is by nature a
social animal. At first, Christianity found itself
quite congenial both to Stoicism and to Plato.
Stoicism had a certain sense of universal law and
brotherhood which corresponded, apparently, with
certain New Testament themes, even though, as Ernest
Cassirer suggested, on the very issue of the
self-sufficiency of the individual, the two radically
parted company.[24] The spirituality of Plato, too,
seemed designed to open a way to the Christian concept
of God. The good came to be identified with the
Trinitarian Deity.

But Christianity did not place man's purpose and
happiness in any political order, as the death of
Christ clearly showed. Christianity, at the
beginning, had a certain diffidence about politics
which made it almost an a-political faith. St. Paul
and St. Peter advised Christians to obey the
Emperor.(Romans, 13:1-7; 1 Peter, 2:1377) On the other
hand, this seemed to correspond with certain truths
already discovered in classical thought about the best
and second best states. Christianity appeared to have
relativized the gods of the ancient city.[25] The
Romans were not wholly wrong in feeling this religion
undermined the all-encompassing scope of the
Empire.(See Chapter III) Furthermore, St. Augustine
quite clearly sensed, to recall our earlier
discussions of him, that the City of God must not be
identified with the Church nor the city of man with
the Empire.[26]

From its Jewish origins in the Old Testament, the
Christians had felt that the state was not all that
necessary. God ruled Israel and men were a fallen
lot. In St. Peter and St. Paul, authority came from
God but the state was to remedy our sins and faults in
order to keep some kind of "peace," as St. Augustine
would call it.[27] Thus, when St. Augustine formulated
his concept of the state, he deliberately removed
justice from Cicero's classical definition, since St.

170

Augustine believed, as Plato did, that no existing state, certainly not republican Rome, Cicero's best, ever was or could be just. Some states were better than others, to be sure, but men tended to evil so that the principal function of the state was to prevent the worst. St. Augustine was the classical realist from whom all subsequent political pragmatism derived. Yet, St. Augustine did not despair of man's ultimate city. He was quite prepared to admit the reality of the good from Plato and of happiness from Aristotle. He merely was quite careful about just where to locate it, certainly not in this world.

VII. THE LIMITED LEGITIMACY OF POLITICS.

The medievals, heeding St. Augustine's various warnings no more carefully than the Athenians listened to those of Pericles, were tempted to confuse the City of God with Christendom. It seemed quite illogical to many of them that the effect of the faith should not be to establish a better earthly city. Yet, feudal political practice was based upon the limitation of all power. The Church visibly stood for the truth that no state was absolute. Everything was defined and confirmed by law and custom, by charters and promises. The king and the pauper were equal before God. Each had his station in life, as he did in The Republic, each had his own destiny which did not prejudice one in favor of another except on the ground of holiness.

Something of the flavor of this spirit, with its sense of virtue and vice in all men, can be found with pleasing bluntness in Piers the Ploughman:

> Besides all this, a hundred men in silk gowns stood swaying from side to side and making speeches. These were the lawyers who served at the bar, pleading their cases for as much money as they could get. Never once did they open their mouths out of love for our Lord; indeed you could sooner measure the mist on the Malvern Hills, than get a sound out of them without first producing some cash!....

> For though you speak the truth and are honest in your dealings, and as chaste as an innocent child that weeps at its baptism, unless you love men truly, and give to the poor, generously sharing the goods God has

given you, you shall have no more merit from
your Masses and Hours than old Molly from
her maidenhead, that no man wants....

Love is the physician of life, the
power nearest to our Lord himself, and the
direct way to Heaven. Therefore, I repeat
from these texts, that when all treasures
are tested, Truth is the best. Now I have
told you what Truth is, and shown you that
no treasure is better....[29]

The medievals had this realistic sense of the
difference between holiness and status or rank. They
manifested also in most of their theory a vivid
awareness that ultimate perfection was a gift of God
and not, as it seemed in The Ethics, something which
evidently resulted from practical reasoning.

Yet it was into this medieval world that
Aristotle re-entered, as it were, with Aquinas. Here
the problem of the best form of regime came to be
reformulated. Neither classical nor Christian
solutions had seemed wholly adequate. Even though the
"mixed" state appeared to be a good and practical
arrangement, the question remained whether the best
state could exist. From the time of Joachim of Flora
on,(A. D. 1135-1202) Christendom would be haunted
with the notion that perfect happiness could be
achieved as a result of some human or divine
historical process -- an idea which will, in its
secularized form, have enormous significance in modern
political theory.

Furthermore, the Platonic-Old Testament notions
of the Fall and ability of men to rearrange the social
order -- the guardians had no wives nor property to
themselves; before the Fall, nature provided for man
-- seemed to fit in with the belief that government
was eventually to be eliminated. Man was not
naturally "political" in terms of his best state. The
so-called "effects" of original sin -- labor, birth in
pain, coercive government -- could perhaps be removed
after all to return man to his original perfect state
or better, even move him forward to a better one, one
totally man-made. This seemed to imply that politics
could portend religious and metaphysical solutions
which had been denied to it in both Augustinian and
Aristotelian political theory. The best form of
regime was, perhaps, a worldly project after all.

172

Aquinas, however, had been too perceptive -- we shall see in the following Chapter just how perceptive he was -- ever to allow politics to become the "highest" science. He had read his Aristotle well. He knew man was not the highest being so that politics could not be the highest science even for man. Moreover, the Christian notion of the gratuity of grace -- and thus of ultimate happiness -- seemed to evaporate the world and hence politics of any intrinsic meaning and worth. The main objection to religion from the angle of political theory was that it removed the essence of human action from the worldly enterprises over which politics had the highest competence. Political theory will have its deadly revenge on such a view later, beginning with Marsilius of Padua, who simply took Aristotle to mean that politics covered only what was tangible in the world. Marsilius completely despiritualized politics and thereby eliminated the transcendent from any place in the world of men, a position quite the opposite of both Aristotle and Aquinas.[30]

Aquinas, however, had posed the issue quite differently. Nature and grace were both necessary. The very incompetence of human law, a theme familiar to political theory from Plato on, became in a famous question in the Summa Theologica the very reason why revelation was, if not "necessary," at least plausible and reasonable.(I-II, 91, 4) Aquinas succeeded in restoring nature to revelation and therefore politics again became the natural end of man qua mortal, but not qua graced. This re-vested politics with a kind of ethical dimension and seriousness that it largely had lost in St. Augustine. This meant also that the re-posing of the question of the best form of government could also be placed in an atmosphere in which it had never before found itself. That is, the problem of the ultimate destiny of man, his personal happiness, related to his individual life no matter what its context, could be considered a different question from that of the life of the polis.

Yet, Aquinas held, rather unlike Plato or Aristotle, that the divine ultimate destiny offered to human persons was a life that in fact made living in this world different and better such that the classic weaknesses of human law were changed by grace's non-political influences.(I-II, 92, 1; 94, 3; 96, 4) It is, of course, such a conclusion that even the most classically oriented of contemporary political philosophers like Leo Strauss and Eric Voegelin strive

173

to avoid. They prefer a theory that is complete without the issues caused by the factual presence of grace and its consequences as elaborated by Aquinas, without denying the possibility or fact of revelation.

Thus, since grace built upon nature and is in part corrective of it, politics and salvation were related but they were not the same.[31] Politics, which had begun to attain a certain religious autonomy with the Christian notion that there were properly things "of Caesar," such that religion could not claim all, now could also be considered man's highest life not insofar as he is contemplative but as that proper to him during his stay on earth as such. But this did not foreclose his higher "immortal" destiny -- something Christians applied to the fragile individual not to the polis or the species, as Hannah Arendt has pointed out in The Human Condition. Politics, thus, was limited and checked by what was not political. With their contemplative religious orders, their distinction between regnum and sacerdotium, the medievals were capable of recognizing these classical theoretical issues much more clearly than previous or subsequent political thought. (See Chapter IV)

For Aquinas, in a commentary on the Old and New law, the best form of regime could be seen as the one that was composed of men subject to law beyond politics and therefore men who could act as full citizens in a way in which their inclinations to evil -- inclinations documented minutely since Thucydides among the Greeks and St. Augustine among the Christians -- were minimized and accounted for.(I-II, 105; 106; 108) The best form of human government did not bear that strong hint of divine destiny that it did with the Platonic tradition. "By the dog of Egypt, he (the philosopher-king) will! (accept rule)," Socrates said sadly at the end of Book IX of The Republic.

In the city of his own he certainly will, though in the land of his birth perhaps not, unless he have a divine call.

I understand; you mean that he will be a ruler in the city of which we are the founders, and which exists in idea only; for I do not believe there is such a one anywhere on Earth?

174

In heaven, I replied, there is laid up
the pattern of it, methinks, which he who
desires may behold, and beholding, may set
his own house in order. But whether such a
one exists, or ever will exist in fact, is
no matter; for he will live life after the
manner of that city, having nothing to do
with any other. (592a-b)

Christianity had accepted that a divine call was
necessary to establish the City of God, and this City
was not a political one in this world. Yet, Aquinas
also managed to suggest that the transcendent aspects
of Aristotle's leisure did have an effect on the
subject of politics in Christianity so that something
more than a second best state was possible, yet it was
only a state, not a salvation.[32](I-II, 108, 3)

The best form of government could contain all
three of the pure forms and this not as a second best,
nor as elevating political experience to the highest
reality, as Cicero was tempted to do. Politics was
not man's ultimate end but was what was most proper to
him as man. There was no longer any need to confuse
destinies and institutions devoted to one end or
another. The "best" form of government need not be
confounded with the City of God nor with Joachim's
"Third Age". It would quite properly refer to the
highest life of mortal man insofar as he was mortal,
while he lived out his years. His ultimate destiny
did not deny that his worldly life was significant,
even ultimately so since salvation dealt with the real
person who did or did not give a cup of water on
earth. But politics was not salvation.

The tension between metaphysics and politics, as
Aristotle already sensed, goes very deep. What is
termed specifically "modern" political thought began
with Marsilius of Padua and Machiavelli, with the
theoretical separation of ethics and politics, with
the Reformation and absolutism. Here the political
state, in its modern form of nation-state, gained
practical and theoretical ascendency over religion and
metaphysics, that is, over what had previously limited
it. The question of the best form of rule, of course,
did not disappear. Indeed, the modern political
enterprise, in a basic sense, has been the search for
the best form of rule after the scientific,
technological, and industrial revolutions. Even a
Hobbes, who must still be considered the most radical
of all absolutists, sought to base his theory on

175

liberal, scientific principles which produced the best state men could expect. In retrospect, in the tradition of classical and Christian political thought, it is not without its irony that Leviathan would come to be considered as the best form of rule. (See Chapter IX)

VIII. RESTRUCTURING MAN THROUGH POLITICS.

Modern political philosophy, then, has valiantly sought to make politics a "science" on the modern model. Yet in doing this, the older tradition of man's special status in nature, his own individual and species uniqueness, continued to be presupposed as "self-evident" in some sense. Aristotle had placed man's perfection qua mortal man in freedom, virtue, and intelligence. The modern mind, as a result of certain of its own presuppositions, has more and more begun to wonder if absolute perfection could not be achieved by refashioning man himself by means other than choice, virtue, and grace. This has come to mean that men might restore to themselves by their own means all things "alienated," supposedly, by the traditional view of the human condition and its improvement by moral means. All through the modern era, this "revolutionary" project became more central, became, as we shall see in the next two Chapters, almost a secular continuation of certain problems classical Thomism discussed in speculation about the ultimate status of the human person.

This project as "revolutionary" began, consequently, with schemes to restructure man by reshaping property and society, specifically in those areas that were thought to have been caused by original sin. More recent theory has begun to speculate on improving man by "genetics" rather than politics, such that the classical norm of politics, the good man, is projected into biological, not political, theory.[33] And in the ecological movements, there is a definite shift of emphasis from man the individual to man the species, only with a pessimistic rather than an optimistic notion of the progress of mankind.[34] Yet, these revolutionary projects of the modern world were considered to be necessary alterations of man's freedom, his earth, or even his genetic form if the inherited and volitional imperfections keeping him from his best future were to be removed.

Previously, in this context, Aquinas had held
176

that politics or law ought not to try to prohibit all vices nor should it command all virtues, that politics was for imperfect man, the vast majority of whom would not be able to adhere to the highest standards conceivable among men.(I-II, 92, 1; 96, 3) Therefore, the political order ought to limit itself to what could be expected of the plurality of normal men who were not in fact saints.(I-II, 96, 5; 97, 2) This meant that the laws and institutions of government could and must deal with those imperfect forms of action that men in reality did do to one another.(I-II, 95, 1 and 2) This seemed to reformulate the project of Plato in The Laws and Aristotle's second best state.

But there was a clear recognition that ultimate happiness was not a political project so that the mixed form of rule was in fact the best theoretical form of government for the humans who do actually exist. And it was this actual existence of finite persons who bore a unique sacredness in themselves beyond all politics that came to bear the true meaning of the central notion of a "common good," a good that reached each person in his actual particularity. (See Chapters VII, XI)

IX. AMERICAN POLITICAL THEORY.

The question, then, has come to be re-posed in recent times by Hannah Arendt in her On Revolution and, in another sense, by Ben Wattenberg in his The Real America.[35] Hannah Arendt argued to the best theoretical form of government, while Wattenberg stands within the middle-class theory of Aristotle, that is, the second best state. The focus of the two is sufficiently different to clarify the distinction of the two questions, yet close enough to recognize the nearness and continuation of classical and Christian political theory within the more modern context. Wattenberg is most sensitive to the difference between desire and performance. Indeed, he has held that the expectation of absolute improvement of perceived status is, in fact, the major cause of political unrest. Therefore, there is a moral basis to the social turmoil of recent years.

Wattenberg's major thesis, however, was simply that the physical conditions of well-being were now reached, or soon will be, such that the problem of the proper life of man can now be discussed in terms other than those of mere physical well-being. And this is the significance of the United States within the history of political thought.

> After examining the data, the conclusion here is that the human condition in America -- as measured by the data -- has in fact improved rapidly in recent years. Indeed, it may well be that conditions improved more rapidly than at any time in recent American history, in fact, improving to such a degree as to create a new human situation, a society whose massive majority is "middle class." The emergence of this Massive Majority Middle Class, it is suggested here, is a benchmark of major historical importance, and its ramifications are enormous.[36]

The significance of this claim in the history of political theory should not be lost. It is a revival in a way of de Tocqueville, but more especially of Aristotle's second best practical state. This is the state, it is to be recalled, that does not itself achieve virtue but only "imitates" it by assuaging the vices and desires that cause society's ruin, those especially recounted in Book V of The Politics of Aristotle, Books VIII and IX of The Republic.

Hannah Arendt's On Revolution, did attempt to address itself to the crucial question of the best theoretical state within the context of ancient, medieval, and modern theory. Hers was a remarkable and largely successful attempt to clarify the troubling intellectual curiosity of why the American Revolution was politically successful, while the French was not, and yet why the French was followed even though the American Revolution was the more profound one. Hannah Arendt distinguished carefully between the "social" revolution which attempted to eliminate poverty and necessity -- the burden of Book I of The Politics -- and the political revolution that sought to establish freedom in the public order.[37]

Modern revolutionary thought, unfortunately, has consistently confused these issues such that political freedom is now seen to be the utopian vision at the end of the long historical process in which poverty is eliminated. This was a theme familiar to Saint-Simon's "New Christianity" and, as such, a non-political, though moral, purpose. Also, it lies within the tradition of Joachim of Flora in which the

Parousia is seen as a worldly process. The Hegelian system is the major mode in which this thought has been filtered into modern thought.[38]

Thus, the Kingdom of God, in this sense, is more and more seen as an earthly, political project, however it be called, yet something it never could have been in orthodox religious thought. But its secularized forms keep bringing it back because the imperfect human condition that real politics deals with cannot, evidently, be accepted by men for long in lieu of some transcendental immortality theory.[39] Furthermore, the French revolutionary tradition bequeathed a necessitarian outlook and model to subsequent reform theory such that no one has believed that a revolution actually took place unless the political process imitated the historical progress of the French Revolution from the Bastille to the Terror.[40]

X. POLITICAL AND NON-POLITICAL.

One of the central intellectual problems in Western political theory is whether American political theory is logically and essentially a part of classical Western theory. Daniel Boorstin, in a famous thesis, argued that it was not, that its "genius" was so particularized, so pragmatic, accidental, that it was to be imitated elsewhere only in the vague sense that each people is to find its own peculiar way.[41] Much of modern thought accepted this view at face value even though the influence of de Tocqueville's prediction that America was to be the wave of the democratic, egalitarian future was widely accepted at the time.

Yet, as Hannah Arendt argued, the American founding fathers were first-rate philosophers, in spite of European intellectual reluctance to admit it. They knew their classical and Christian traditions. They did not accept Rousseau's notion that man was good by nature, while his institutions made him evil. Rather, they followed classical and Christian political theory in recognizing that men did have a tendency to evil. This led them to follow Montesquieu's (and hence Polybius') separation of powers and Madison's federal theory as the most important elements in their political experiment. And this "experiment" was the proper political question of the best form of government in which imperfect men are to rule and be ruled.

179

Political freedom implied something very
different from the elimination of poverty, which the
French revolutionary tradition came to accept as the
primary human task. As a result of its confusion
between politics and poverty, the revolutionary
tradition was never able to stop violence. The
American tradition, however, recognized that a
revolution had to stop, had to build a space for
public freedom which controlled man's vices. The
worst of these vices needed to be recognized as such,
as Aquinas insisted government must do. Yet
government needed to allow men also to participate
actually in ruling and being ruled.

This meant a multiplication of local units of
government within a larger public order which had real
authority over its members. Madison's Number Ten of
The Federalist was, surely, cynical of the potentials
in man, very much as Thucydides, Plato, Aristotle, St.
Paul, and St. Augustine were. Madison felt, however,
that men's vices could be recognized to be vices --
and therefore not denied or ignored -- and still be
counterbalanced by political institutions such as
federalism and the separation of powers, two houses of
legislature, checks and balances. In this context, it
is interesting to note of late a return to more
medieval and local concepts as the solution of even
the world's poverty questions.[42]

This same trend exists also within the liberal
wings of the Marxist tradition which have valiantly
tried to maintain Marxism and locality. However,
Solzhenitsyn powerfully has reminded the West of
Hannah Arendt's main point that the elimination of
poverty does not mean political freedom. And this
latter is ultimately the more important human
question, even though both Aristotle and Aquinas
realized that a sufficiency of goods was helpful, even
necessary to virtue for most men. But this did not
deny the classic tradition that even the most humble
may at times be required in the face of evil to
practice heroic virtue, the great tradition of
Christian martyrdom.

Hannah Arendt was right to suggest that there are
two separate but related traditions. When men in
building the political forms of the Third World
largely choose the model of the French Revolution
calling it "democratic" rather than that of the
American Revolution, they force themselves inevitably

to reproduce the steps of the French Revolution which lead them to a new tyranny, to Aristotle's worst form of rule.[43] This is why Daniel Moynihan's remark that democracy -- the supposed future of the 20th Century, its best form of rule -- has fallen into ill-repute all over the world takes on significance. The difference between public freedom and abundance has not been understood.

Indeed, it is still arguable that democracy cannot exist outside that Western political theory which brought it forth. Modern revolutionary thought has missed the import of the Christian notion of poverty as found in the Epistle of James as well as the notion that Caesar really does have things that belong to him. Public freedom is its own reality to be constructed by the "political and social animal." Furthermore, men will not even eliminate poverty adequately if they insist on quasi-totalitarian models for development, an insistence and justification that have come more and more to be found in modernization theories.[44]

XI. LIVING WELL AS MEN.

The crisis of contemporary political theory is, then. "What is the best form of government?" The abundant middle-class state is now open to all men. But, to recall Professor Minogue's comment on Professor Galbraith, the reason it may not now be achieved is still a question of issues about the nature of man, of those issues in classical and Christian political thought.[45] Many have argued that American loss of confidence in itself, its misconception of its own potential, will have catastrophic effects on the rest of men. Noblesse oblige is still a real principle in political theory. It means, essentially, not the reduction of the best to the mean and the mean to the worst on some theory of absolute equality, but the retention of the best in the confrontation with the normal and the worst. In a sense, then, Americans have been largely talked out of their own political theory because they have not understood its broader import in the evolution of modern man.

Nevertheless, this improvement that is indeed possible to men is a fallible process involving men's control of their greed and envy rather than statistical poverty. Furthermore, the end of the process of poverty elimination and the establishing of

181

public freedom is the state of leisure, Aristotle's highest life for man qua man, the area in which the active fuses with the contemplative life to put both in their place. And the leisure of our future involves more than this very extraordinary planet in which the race of men find themselves already formed as men, as Aristotle said. The vision of the human race is undoubtedly inclusive of more than the human space of our planet, something that seems already contained in a way in Genesis.[46] Yet, as Hannah Arendt had argued in The Human Condition, it is our condition as men here on this earth that determines the quality of our politics.

The political choices about the best form of regime necessarily involve the retention of man in an environment of full abundance, in true public freedom. Indeed, it is necessary to suggest that the problem of the best and the second best state for a creature that transcends politics in a sense can be found in the same actual state. This is probably the ultimate theoretical significance of American theory at its best. That all men remain sinful and finite in themselves is the fact, even the value that we must begin with. It is not the project of politics to create another creature, but to enable men to live well as men. The undoubted locus of totalitarian thought -- that is, of the worst form of rule -- during the next century will lie in the attempt to "restructure" man himself, to remove his sinfulness and his finiteness by biological, psychological, and social means as if this will somehow produce the "good man," that man who has stood at the center of classical theory from the beginning.

But, man, good and sinful, has a project, a freedom within his mortality. He must rediscover the legitimacy and nature of the main question of political theory -- that of the best form of rule. It is this question, as Hannah Arendt noted, to which American political theory at its best addressed itself. This is the central question ignored by modern revolutionary traditions which have taken a secularized messianism as their ultimate goal rather than public freedom for finite, sinful men who do know the choice and meaning of evil. But American theory also includes the second best form of rule, the middle-class state, for those who do not know virtue directly but who can lead a better life if their poverty is eliminated and their passions counteracted.

XII. FOUNDING A CONSTITUTION.

The past decades have seen a precipitous change
in Western political theory. They have seen a decline
of ideology and behavioral thought to be replaced by
the newer ideologies of the late '60's, '70's, and
'80's, which sought, so they claimed, to re-establish
a moral politics.[47] And yet, as this newer
.enthusiasm has exhausted itself in the classical
confusion of ends and means, this world and the next,
poverty and revolution, we arrive back at the crucial
issue of the best form of government. In 1960,
Professor John Plamenetz wrote: "Even in Oxford, which
perhaps more than any other place in the English
speaking world is the home of political theory or
philosophy, it is often said that the subject is dead
or sadly diminished in importance."[48] He went on to
suggest that the purpose of political theory is "not
to tell us how things happen in the world, inside our
minds or outside them; its purpose is to help us to
decide what to do and how to go about doing it."

Nonetheless, the question is "Doing what?" This
is the need to manifest the existence of each human
being before the world in a public order in which he
is free from the necessities of life and at liberty to
discover and create what is new according to his
limited, human, often sinful life. This makes the
best political rule a legitimate and abiding issue in
political theory. "Classical political philosophy is
guided by the question of the best regime," Leo
Strauss wrote in a famous essay.[49] And it is to this
question, in all its forms, that American political
thought directs itself, as Arendt and Wattenberg in
their own ways suggested.

At the end of what is still the most gripping
book in political theory, Socrates has finally
succeeded in praising justice for its own sake and not
for any reward or pain it might bring.(The Republic,
#613a) Glaucon had earlier remarked, as we saw, that
the just man in any existing state would be wracked
and punished.(#361e-62a) Returning to this theme,
Socrates insisted that the just man even in all these
dire circumstances must see how things work to the
good.(#613a) The gods do care for those who desire to
be like gods. Thus, after all, the good are rewarded
and the evil punished. The final myth, however,
carries us back through necessity to freedom. "Your
genius will not be allotted to you but you will choose

your genius ... Virtue is free, and as a man knows or
discovers her he will have more or less of her; the
responsibility is with the chooser -- God is
justified."(#617d-e) So men should seek to find and
follow the one thing necessary, to be able "to learn
and discern between good and evil, and so to choose
always and everywhere the better life as he has
opportunity."(#621c)

So in the history of political theory, the
"deciding what to do" is also the more profound
enterprise, that of distinguishing good and evil in
politics. The political order, as Aquinas and the
Americans perceived, must account for this
difference. But it must also recognize that this
difference, in its very establishment, lies beyond
politics itself, though politics and law can, as
Aquinas argued, determine truly this difference within
the reality of the human itself.(I-II, 95, 1; 96, 4)
There is, further, a difference between a sufficiency
or even an abundance of goods and the good life, as
Aristotle already pointed out. And within the kinds
of polity men can form, some are based on norms quite
contrary to the human good. And because this is so,
we are free to contest these latter. That tyranny,
the worst form, should become the prevalent form of
rule in the 20th Century, that it can lead to a
Hobbesian view of the state as a rule needed to bring
men peace and abundance for their own good -- such is
the intellectual disorder of our political thought.

Thus, the decision men actually must face is that
of the political form which can account for their
evils, while not proposing to remove them totally by
political, genetic, or sociological means such that
man's very being is altered or threatened. The proper
political task is the form of regime in which fallible
men can rule and be ruled in order to place before
themselves the freedom and leisure in which newness
and uniqueness are brought forth from obscurity while
checking their bad choices and desires institutionally
and legally. That the American tradition has known
how to "found a constitution," to use Hannah Arendt's
phrase, witnesses to its direct relationship to
classical and Christian theory as well as to its
unique place in the contemporary political context
which is so much concerned with new regimes, with
their proper ordering.

The American political experience and thought,
then, have taken up in a new way the question of the

middle-class state, the second-best state of the classical theory, and of the best form of government, while recognizing the limits of politics itself. That American thought has not been understood by Americans themselves, let alone European, Third World, and revolutionary theory, is itself in the central line of political theory, in its dependence on both choice and intelligence for its own order, continuity, and integrity.

Footnotes:

1. See Lucian Pye, <u>Aspects of Political Development</u>, Boston, Little, Brown, 1966, Chapter I.

2. "Democracy is probably the greatest political symbol of the modern age," Francis Graham Wilson wrote in 1936. <u>The Elements of Modern Politics</u>, New York, McGraw-Hill, p. 187.

"The dominant political idea in the modern world is democracy. Most of the contradictions of contemporary politics find their place under the democratic umbrella ... And where are the political theorists of democracy today? ... Liberal democratic principles ceased to evolve in the nineteenth century ... but the world did not stop at that point, and it has become a very different place since. Meanwhile, democracy, for lack of thought, has ceased to be a living political idea." Alfred Cobban, "Ethics and the Decline of Political Theory," <u>Contemporary Political Thought</u>, New York, Holt, 1969, p. 293. See Jeane Kirkpatrick, <u>Dictatorships and Double Standards: Rationalism and Reason in Politics</u>, New York, Simon and Schuster, 1982.

3. See Michael Novak and Richard Schifter, <u>Rethinking Human Rights</u>, Washington, Foundations for Democratic Education, 1982. Vols. I and II.

4. See D. Moynihan, "The Caged Revolution," <u>Harper's</u>, January, 1975; "Is Democracy Dying? Verdict of 8 Leading World Scholars," <u>US News</u>, March 8, 1976, pp. 50-67.

5. "I confess that in America I saw more than America; I sought there the image of democracy itself, with its inclinations, its character, its prejudices, and its passions in order to learn what we have to fear or to hope for from its progress." Alexis de Tocqueville, <u>Democracy in America</u>, New York, Knopf, 1956, Vol. I, p. 15.

"At the beginning of the twentieth century no political idea seemed more solidly entrenched than that of democracy. Among most bourgeois liberals, intellectuals, and socialists it was esteemed as gospel. Only a few die-hard conservatives, disgruntled cynics, and hard-bitten defenders of direct action appeared to hold out against it. From the great revolutions of the seventeenth and eighteenth centuries it had been handed down as a shibboleth to nearly all who were dissatisfied with the relics of despotism and feudalism that still remained as encumbrances to progress in many countries. So strong was the faith in democracy that it made some headway even in such backward nations as Spain, Russia, and Turkey." Edward McNall Burns, Ideas in Conflict, New York, Norton, 1960, p. 3. See also James V. Schall, "America and Recent Catholic Social Theory," in Christianity and Politics, Boston, St. Paul Editions, 1981, Chapter X, pp. 267-94.

6. See James V. Schall, "On the Teaching of Ancient and Medieval Political Theory," in Christianity and Politics, ibid., Chapter II, pp. 42-64.

7. See Anthony James Joes, "The Fascist Century," Worldview, May, 1978, pp. 19-23.

8. See P. H. Partridge, "Politics, Philosophy, Ideology," Political Philosophy, A. Quinton, Editor, Oxford University Press, 1967, pp. 32-52.

9. Christian Bay, "A Critical Evaluation of Behavioral Literature," Contemporary Political Thought, ibid., p. 139.

10. See Henri de Saint-Simon, "New Christianity," Social Organization, the Science of Man, and Other Writings, F. Markham, Editor, New York, Harper, 1952, pp. 81-116.

11. Bay, ibid., p. 158.

12. R. Persig, Zen and the Art of Motorcycle Maintenance, New York, Bantam, p. 8.

13. See Charles N. R. McCoy, The Structure of Political Thought, New York, McGraw-Hill, 1963, pp. 138-50; Leo Strauss, City and Man, Chicago, University of Chicago Press, 1964.

14. Politics, Book 3, Chapter 14; Book 4, Chapter 10; Book 5, Chapters 10, 11, 12.

15. See Solzhenitsyn's Harvard Address, "A World Split Apart," The National Review, July 7, 1978, pp. 836-41; also in Solzhenitsyn at Harvard, Washington, Ethics and Public Policy Center, 1980.

16. See Solzhenitsyn's Speech of July 9, 1975, Washington, AFL-CIO, 1975, p. 30; See also Solzhenitsyn's "Men Have Forgotten God," The National Review, July 22, 1983, pp. 872-76.

17. Address on BBC in The Times, London, April 2, 1976.

18. Speech of June 30, 1975. See also Interview, Le Monde, May 30, 1975.

19. See James V. Schall, "Theory in American Politics," The Modern Age, Spring, 1960; see also Irving Kristol, "The American Revolution as a Successful Revolution," America's Continuing Revolution, Doubleday Anchor, 1976, p. 1-21; Joseph Cropsey, "The United States As a Regime," Political Philosophy and the Issues of Politics, Chicago, University of Chicago Press, 1977.

20. This is, of course, the burden of much of the work of Eric Voegelin. See especially his The New Science of Politics, Chicago, University of Chicago Press, 1952, Chapters 4 and 6.

21. See Harry Jaffa, The Conditions of Freedom, Baltimore, Johns Hopkins University Press, 1975.

22. See McCoy, Chapter III; see also James V. Schall, "The Significance of Post-Aristotelian Thought in Political Theory," Cithara, November, 1963, pp. 56-79; Mulford Q. Sibley, Political Ideas and Ideologies, New York, Harper and Row, 1970, Chapters 6 and 7.

23. See McCoy, ibid., pp. 82-87.

24. See E. Cassirer, Essay on Man, New Haven, Yale, 1944, Chapter I.

25. See F. de Coulanges, The Ancient City, Doubleday Anchor.

26. See especially Christopher Dawson's two remarkable essays on St. Augustine in St. Augustine, New York, Meridian, 1957; see above, Chapter III.

27. "Let every person be subject to the governing authorities. For there is no authority except from God, and those that exist have been instituted by God. Therefore, he who resists the authorities resists what

God has appointed, and those who resist will incur judgment. For rulers are not a terror to good conduct, but to bad.... " <u>Romans</u>, 13:1-3; see also <u>John</u>, Chapters 18 and 19.

28. See H. Rommen, "The Genealogy of Natural Rights," <u>Thought</u>, Autumn, 1954, pp. 403-25; J. Morrall, <u>Political Thought in Medieval Times</u>, New York, Harper, 1962.

29. William Langland, <u>Piers the Plowman</u>, J. Goodridge, trans., Penguin, 1959, pp. 69, 75.

30. See Leo Strauss, "Marsilius of Padua," <u>History of Political Philosophy</u>, Strauss and Cropsey, Editors, New York, Rand McNally, 1963, pp. 227-46.

31. See below, Chapter XIII.

32. See James V. Schall, <u>Far Too Easily Pleased: A Theology of Play, Contemplation, and Leisure</u>, Los Angeles, Benziger-Macmillan, 1976.

33. See J. Lederberg, "Experimental Genetics and Human Evolution," <u>The Bulletin of the Atomic Scientists</u>, October, 1966; see also James V. Schall, "On the Non-Existence of Christian Political Philosophy," <u>Christianity and Politics</u>, ibid., Chapter I, pp. 16-41; <u>Christianity and Life</u>, San Francisco, Ignatius Press, 1981.

34. See James V. Schall, "Revolution and Conservation in the Christian Social Perspective," <u>Studies</u>, Dublin, Summer, 1974, pp. 153-66; "Apocalypse as a Secular Enterprise," <u>The Scottish Journal of Theology</u>, #4, 1976, pp. 357-73.

35. Ben Wattenberg, <u>The Real America</u>, New York, Capricorn, 1976; Hannah Arendt, <u>On Revolution</u>, New York, Viking, 1965.

36. Wattenberg, p. 5. See also in this context, Herman Kahn, <u>The Next 200 Years</u>, New York, Morrow, 1976, and Norman Macrae, "America's Third Century," <u>The Economist</u>, London, Survey, October 25, 1975; Julian Simon, <u>The Ultimate Resource</u>, Princeton, Princeton University Press, 1981; George Will, <u>Statecraft As Soulcraft</u>, New York, Simon and Schuster, 1983.

37. See also Jacques Ellul, <u>The Betrayal of the</u>

West, New York, Seabury, 1978, Chapters I and II.

38. "... Political philosophy can coincide with the philosophy of history because the final state replaces the best regime." Allan Bloom, "Georg W. F. Hegel." History of Political Philosophy, ibid., p. 651.

39. See Carl Becker, The Heavenly City of the Eighteenth Century Philosophers, New Haven, Yale, 1932; Robert Nisbet, History of the Idea of Progress, New York, Basic, 1980; see also James V. Schall, "Reason, Revelation, and Politics: Catholic Reflections on Strauss," Gregorianum, #2 and 3, 1981.

40. Arendt, ibid., Chapter I.

41. D. Boorstin, The Genius of American Politics, Chicago, University of Chicago Press, 1953.

42. E. F. Schumacher, Small Is Beautiful, New York, 1973; see also Roger Heckel, Self-Reliance, Vatican City, Justice and Peace Commission, 1978; and James V. Schall, "Christianity and the 'Cures' of Poverty," in Christianity and Politics, Boston, St. Paul Editions, 1981, Chapter VIII, pp. 178-212; John Naisbitt, Megatrends, New York, Warner, 1982.

43. Daniel Moynihan has argued that the Third World leaders followed most often the theories of the Fabian Socialists; see his "The United States in Opposition," Commentary, March, 1975, pp. 31-44; see also Moynihan's "The American Experience," The Public Interest, Fall, 1975.

44. See James V. Schall, "Conservatism and Development," Cultures et Developpement, Louvain, #2, 1977, pp. 315-34; see also P. T. Bauer, Equality, Development, and Third World Delusion, Cambridge, Harvard University Press, 1981.

45. See Chapter VI, Footnote 1.

46. See Robert Jastrow, "Have Astronomers Found God?" The New York Times Magazine, June 25, 1978, pp. 18 ff.

47. See Max Mark, Modern Ideologies, New York, St. Martin's, 1973; see also James V. Schall, "Impossible Politics -- Review of Henry S. Kariel: Beyond Liberalism: Where Relations Grow," Review of

Politics, 1977, pp. 423-26.

48. John Plamenatz, "The Use of Political Theory," _Political Philosophy_, _ibid_., p. 29.

49. Leo Strauss, "What Is Political Philosophy?" _Contemporary Political Thought_, _ibid_., p. 64.

CHAPTER IX

ON WAR AND THE WORST REGIME IN POLITICAL THEORY

It is difficult to see how Gandhi's
methods could be applied in a country where
opponents to the regime disappear in the
middle of the night and are never heard of
again. -- [George Orwell, Collected Essays,
V. 4, p.469.]

The same kind of defect, the flaw of a
consciousness lacking all divine dimension,
was manifested after World War II when the
West yielded to the satanic temptation of
the nuclear umbrella. It was equivalent to
saying: Let's cast off our worries, let's
free the younger generation from its duties
and obligations, let's make no effort to
defend ourselves, to say nothing of
defending others -- let's stop our ears to
the groans emanating from the East, and let
us live instead in the pursuit of
happiness. If danger should threaten us, we
shall be protected by the nuclear bomb; if
not, then let the world be burned in Hell
for all we care. The pitifully helpless
state to which the contemporary West has
sunk is in large measure due to this fatal
error: the belief that the defense of peace
depends not on stout hearts and steadfast
men, but solely on the nuclear bomb. --
[Alexander Solzhenitsyn, "Men Have Forgotten
God," The Templeton Prize Address, National
Review, July 22, 1983, p. 873.]

In classical and medieval political theory, the
best form of rule conceptually involved knowing about
the worst forms under which mankind could live. St.
Thomas' Treatise on the Governance of Rulers devoted a
considerable space to the question of tyranny, the
classical word given to the worst regime.[1] For both
Plato and Aristotle, as well as for the medievals, the
worst regime was in some sense "possible," even though
it was not conceptually to be confused with the
theological notion of hell. (See Chapter V) A

tyranny, to be sure, would be rather unstable, since its definition was the rule of the one worst man for the good of this one worst man. Such a regime has no extension beyond the self-definition of the tyrant himself with his ability to control the populace over which he had absolute control. The classical tyrant exercised his control, as Aristotle understood (1295a-25; 1313a34-b33), by preventing any kind of friendship or communication to arise within his regime. All things had to be public. At every point, tyranny was the opposite of the human good.

The Book of Revelation in the New Testament (Chapter XIII) at least raised, in the context of political theory, the further idea that a civil order could itself be erected against the divine order.[2] This possibility was not intended to deny either the power of God or the freedom of man, but rather to bear out the full meaning of each for a being whose nature is political. The polis seemed to be the most likely arena in which the worst defiance of God's order could take place for a free, finite being. This possibility could even be extended to include the whole "City of Man" arrayed against the divine order as known to the human intellect. In this sense, it was possible to conceive mankind, in its political institutions, structured on the basis of norms and laws of good and evil erected not from reason or revelation, but from man's own self-definition of what he chooses to call good, presupposed to nothing but human will itself with the intelligence to carry it out. (See Chapter II)

If we consider this line of analysis very carefully, it will be clear that the ideas of heaven and hell are actually necessary religious and philosophical postulates. They reflect metaphysical realities, once we grant the limits of any actual political order. The realization that, in the end, the polis will never reward all good actually occurring in it, nor will it punish all the evils, leads naturally to the idea that this complete reward or punishment is not the purpose of real states in this world. But this does not suggest that the range of evil in actual states cannot be very extensive. It is. When Socrates did not choose banishment to Thebes in The Apology rather than death by Athenian law, he tacitly acknowledged that there is a large array of disorder to be reckoned with among states, even though all were at least capable of executing their philosophers. Christian tradition has likewise held

194

that all states are capable of killing the Man-God within them. The resolution of such disorder is not finally or exclusively political.

But do states "need" to become the worst? In The Republic, the military guardians appeared in the process of expanding greed and the consequent need to protect one's polis from the similar greed of neighbors.(373a-74d) War, in other words, arose in political theory first as an aspect of the question about the stability of regimes, the worst and the best. Diversity of virtue, which was at the root of the diversity of actual regimes, implied that there were many different kinds of political forms, classified generally as monarchy, aristocracy, polity, democracy, oligarchy, and tyranny, or mixtures of some or all. The nature of certain vices, moreover, particularly greed and envy, made it necessary to guard one's own regime, if it did not choose to become like its enemy.

The multitude of virtues and vices, furthermore, made the existence of a wide diversity of actual regimes, if not ideal, at least better than a world-wide tyranny, a fear that arose especially with critics of Alexander of Macedon and Rome. And yet, in all this, as Plato saw in Books I and II of The Republic, there was an argument to be made, one very difficult to refute actually, that the worst regime in theory was really the best regime, because there were no philosophical standards other than the will of the tyrant, however conceived. That is, no natural standards of justice or order existed in the cosmos. The logical conclusion was that tyranny was the best regime. Thus, men should accept this consequence voluntarily.

Behind the discussion of war in Western political theory was the question of regimes and their diversity. This latter distinction between regimes was philosophic in definition and prudential in recognition. A polity that did not allow philosophy because it was itself a dangerous or threatening thing to its civil order necessarily ended up with a form of civil religion or philosophy. In this latter sort of regime, any philosophic questioning of the regime's explanation of itself would undermine that regime's order. War, in this sense, was a consequence of the difference between chosen goods or evils in differing political orders. Differing goods often came into conflict. War itself was thus not looked upon as the

195

worst of evils.

Indeed, the centrality of the virtue of courage in classical political thought, of the knight in medieval life, meant that things worse than fighting or death were quite possible, things worth preventing even by war. Soldiering was a noble profession in any regime that did in fact have something worthy of defence, the definition of which was itself a question of political philosophy. To have nothing worth defending was merely another way to deny any ethical standards whatsoever. Death in war was far better than cowardice, which meant continuation of life at the expense of value, at the expense of others.

The notion of just war from Cicero to St. Augustine to St. Thomas and the later scholastics was not merely a sort of grudging admission that the best state or Christian charity was not wholly possible or practical in this world. Rather just war theory was the means by which moral and political philosophy carried on the discussion about the tremendous ethical import of the diversity of regimes actually existing among men.[3] The Thomistic discussion of law had already argued that not all men were saints or virtuous so that a certain amount of evil is to be tolerated, expected, and accounted for in all existing polities. (See Chapter VII) Not to realize this is not to inaugurate the best regime, but to corrupt political life further.

On the other hand, if it be possible to speak of a "just war" and its conditions, this meant that men could prudentially apply their reason and strength in the public order to remove some obvious evils, known to be such by philosophy or religion, and to limit others.[4] Capitulation before known tyrannical rule was not itself seen to be virtuous, even on a theory of non-violence. For Christianity particularly, this was not meant to deny that other means might also exist and be effective in a way beyond reason, provided this did not fail to acknowledge the problem of coping with evils that did exist.

The classical and medieval problematic of the worst regime and the just war theory seemed, therefore, to enable regimes to protect themselves without necessarily becoming themselves like the distorted regimes against which they fought. They could prevent tyrannical rule from being imposed on them. This, of course, necessitated including within

196

war theory a discussion about the right to go to war or to defend one's society (jus ad bellum) as well as a discussion about what means could be employed in warfare and how these means related to enemy soldiers and the members of society who were not soldiers (jus in bello).

The history of this question is, no doubt, well enough known.[5] Yet, it seems that certain branches of contemporary thinking on war have argued that this just war theory must be rejected, on its own grounds, because its classical formulation cannot be adapted to current issues, particularly those relating to the nature of the Soviet state and nuclear weapons. This is but an aspect, of course, of the broader questions relating to classical and modern theory, particularly the idea that modern science and democratic relativism can supply whatever sort of life men choose for themselves. Political ethics remains, on this hypothesis, indifferent to human ends and therefore to a distinction of values. The ends of public and private action are said to be in theory unknowable, so that the "modern" political regime must be built on this theoretic premise.[6]

As this intellectual discussion has worked itself out in modern thought, the question of the philosophical nature of the worst regime, now seen in the context of 20th Century totalitarian societies as a highly nuanced sophistication of this sort of worst regime, again becomes proposed as an issue of political philosophy. Briefly, the question is posed such that nuclear weapons, in their possible destruction of the human race on this planet, require, as a matter of virtue, surrender of all regimes to the worst regime that possesses such weapons, on the grounds that nothing is worse than the death of the race.

Clearly, neither classical nor Christian theory taught that death, even the physical death of the whole human race, was the worst evil, but yielding to evil to save one's life was. The question arises, then, is it really true that the philosophical arguments about war coming from classical and medieval theory are rendered obsolete by modern scientific and military conditions seen as instruments of modern political philosophy? Or rather, is the real question, posed by nuclear weapons and the Marxist state, the modern context of the argument begun in The Republic about whether the worst regime, with its

197

philosophical premises and physical power, must be considered, morally, the best after all?

Since the terms of war and regime are part of our intellectual inheritance, it seems valuable here to reconsider them as abiding aspects of medieval theory, which acknowledged that not all wars were just and tried to define why. Likewise, this same theory recognized that not all surrenders were just or moral, again with an effort to indicate why. From the context of previous discussions about the locus of ultimate evil and beatitude, it seems clear that the obliteration of the human race by war or natural disaster cannot be considered to be the final evil for a race which dies daily. The City of God remains the central question when all humans have disappeared from this planet, as they must eventually. The final evil must be in the order of freedom and intelligence, not mere physical destruction. This final evil ought to correspond to the highest faculties and powers which are discovered to be given in human kind.

The tradition has, interestingly enough, often thought of this evil in political terms, as a <u>city</u>, in which men would deliberately embrace, as the only good, whatever the human will, as a public choice, would so define, regardless of any natural or revelational norms. If the political project in history is posed so that the removing, even by violence, from mankind such natural and revelational norms as the sign of human dignity itself, then mankind's voluntary embracing of purely man-made rules would be considered by classical and medieval theory alike as not the "highest good" but the "highest evil" open to man as a free creature. The issue of political theory proposed here is whether the voluntary embracing of the worst regime by free rational beings as the "best" choice, as the "moral" choice, is not, in terms of the tradition, the overturning of the whole heritage of the West about the meaning of human life and the higher good.

Against this classical and medieval background of worst regimes and just wars, where does the modern "ethics of virtuous surrender" to a worst regime take us in terms of classical and medieval political philosophy? That is, has the nuclear war issue "proved" the inadequacy of the tradition, or has it rather merely carried the so-called "modern project" (Leo Strauss' phrase) to its ultimate conclusion, which would correspond to the classical discussion of

198

the moral rightness of tyranny as the "best" regime?[7]

What is further at issue here is the abidingness of human political discourse, the question of whether human philosophical questions are, in fact, persistent, so that an adequate understanding of one's present involves entering into arguments and norms discovered and passed on in active intellectual history. This will suggest that what is really dangerous to mankind is not so much "war" as "thought" about war. Is it moral, in other words, to avoid war of whatever kind by embracing the worst regime? And if this is done, is the result virtue or the voluntary abdication of all moral principle before a system that presents violent physical death as the worst of evils, the principle of modern political thought from Hobbes?

A cartoon showed two generals walking out of a building looking suspiciously like the Pentagon, both carrying bulging briefcases. The first general mumbled to the second, "There is talk in some quarters that the pen is mightier than the sword."[8] This is, of course, an old saying with the new twist. What is pertinent and even comical about it is that we find it used not by the clergy or the journalist or the academic, but by the soldier himself, who seems to be unsettlingly aware today that the craft of arms may well be rendered obsolete by the art of words or argument, by what Aristotle knew as rhetoric. That words should replace weapons, ploughshares replace swords, constitutions replace feuds, no doubt, has been considered to be itself a sign of moral progress and has a long history.

However, something more ominous seems to surround this discussion today, for the craft of words, including the "word of God," appears to accept as "necessary" the very consequences which the craft of arms was designed to prevent. The very possibility of there being an order of speech to replace the order of coercion, so that speech and prayer could proceed in liberty to accomplish their purposes, this was the "good" the craft of arms was to make minimally possible when threatened by a system which did not allow them. Arms in classical and medieval thought were not ends in themselves, but rather instruments sometimes needed when enemies of speech, prayer, and pen did appear. These enemies could be recognized by both soldier and politician because of terms provided by political philosophy.

199

Throughout the contemporary discussions of nuclear war, there has been, for many, a remarkable lack of attention to political theory and the reality of politics. Indeed, the current debate arose first not in politics but in religion, with religion's conception of itself.[9] What political means and political understanding might mean almost seemed not to have entered the discussion, even though particularly Catholic thought traditionally left a wide and esteemed place for both political experience and political philosophy.

Politics is, after all, that side of the human endeavor which is responsible directly for war prevention. Scripture itself leaves little doubt that this is one of Caesar's responsibilities. Part of human dignity consists in mankind itself discovering what politics does and can do.[10] Nowhere was it suggested in the tradition that a replacement of politics by religion would either itself prevent war or render war less burdensome. Not a few, in fact, have held that the intrusion of religion into politics has made wars worse, not better, a proposition that is no doubt true in some, though not all, cases. Politics has its own laws and rules which must be discovered and employed if men are to achieve those ends of life which politics naturally serves. The political theory of Aquinas especially stands for these principles.

The classic issue, then, in the light of the recent discussions, must be constantly reposed, namely, why was not the worst regime, the interest of the stronger defining its own ends, itself the best regime, which men should embrace as a result of moral argument? Why was not the subversion of all morals the only feasible or "right" choice open to mankind? And this was all to be presented not in the context of being "tricked" into embracing the worst form of rule, but in concluding to it as a clear result of moral discrimination. The advocate "knew" what life in the worst regime was like while he was recommending it as a necessary moral conclusion.

The case for living under the worst regime, to be sure, has often been made from passages in Plato, to Machiavelli and Hobbes, wherein Christian morals were, most often, seen as obstacles to the successful functioning of the worst state. Only by changing this religion, it was thought, did the worst state have a chance of succeeding. What is thus new in this current consideration is a sudden change in the relationship of the worst regime and Christianity. To put it graphically, it now appears to many that to establish the worst regime in fact, the Christian religion need not be changed, as Machiavelli might have urged it to "lower its standards," but rather it should only follow loyally its highest preachings and norms.

Thus, not merely on philosophic but also on religious grounds the argument is made that we must, as a matter of ethical principle, embrace the worst regime, if this latter, by a process of political understanding and persuasion, can employ the religious-ethical principles for its own ends, but addressed to a religious people. Free men "ought" then to open themselves to the worst regime, without any necessity of being defeated in war, as the "virtuous" thing to do, since it is, presumably, "immoral" to prevent this result by the only workable means.

The only workable or reasonable means, of course, is effective nuclear deterrence.[11] Using this deterrence or even "intending" to use it, in this view, makes the society employing it to be itself the "worst regime." The conclusion, then, is that free societies "should" live under the actual worst regime, because the world is so structured that, evidently, they can do nothing else. This is true even if life under the worst regime, by everyone's admission, corrupts every value civilization and religion have claimed they stood for.

In effect, this means that the real "war" is currently being fought in the mind, with the pen, as it were, as anyone with the slightest insight into the way Soviet leaders, to their credit, eagerly follow the religious arguments about the morality of war in the West recognized.[12] Soviet strategists clearly understand that if the West, by its own ethical and religious testimony, must live under their regime to consider itself "moral," then those sectors and segments of the free world, who have accepted the terms and logic of the argument, for whatever reasons, even religious ones, are to be encouraged, supported, and relied upon. Even a minimum sensibility to self-interest would acknowledge this.

Likewise, since this "ethics of surrender" to the

worst regime, as it shall be called here, the notion
that moral argument dictates not defending oneself,
implies that morality demands living under the most
powerful Marxist system in its present manifestation,
some, at least, begin to grant that such a life might
not be so bad after all. However, in spite of
testimony from Solzhenitsyn, Shafarevich, Bukovsky,
Sakharov, and many others about what in fact happens
in such a regime, we do find not a few in the
churches, universities, and the press arguing that the
"worst" regime is the solution to the Western ills.
While in practice, the advocates of "an ethics of
surrender" usually have a very benign view -- and to
that extent violate their obligation to fact -- of
life in the worst state in its full consequences, here
the argument is with the group which admits the worst
consequences imaginable, yet which still insists that
we ought to live under such a regime because we can do
nothing else on moral grounds.

The current debate is almost wholly premised on
"might be's" or worst scenario cases. The nuclear war
is considered not as a question of politics to
prevent, but of imagination to scare. There seems
almost a dogmatic refusal to face the probability of
limited nuclear war which could well be far less
destructive than future conventional wars or even
World War II, which in some sense must be considered a
just war. But the real issue has to do with minds and
wills. The free nations are free enough to protect
within themselves those who, on what they consider
"ethical" or "religious" grounds, refuse to protect
their own freedom, which the worst regime certainly
would not allow. As C. S. Lewis once wrote in this
regard, so long as the pacifist position does not gain
political control in a free society, so that it
continues to defend itself, pacifist argument remains
possible. Once it does gain political power, it must
in turn be submerged by regimes which do not permit
it, so that it disappears.[13] Pacifism and the
"ethics of surrender" depend, ultimately, on their not
being true.

The last thing the Soviet regime on its own
principles wants is a nuclear war or any war that
would jeopardize its own rule. Clearly, the Soviet
regime understands deterrence, which is why, as
Margaret Thatcher has remarked, it works.[14]
Unfortunately, however, even if the West decided to
grant the premise of the "ethics of surrender", it
would not certainly follow that nuclear weapons would

202

not be used, say against China. From the position of the worst state, the "surrender" of the West on "moral" grounds would appear also hypocritical or doubtful, so that it would be at least "rational" both for control purposes and security purposes to launch a few weapons in the process of taking over after the surrender was announced.

The Soviets and any else, then, are deterred by the present system and know it, so long as it remains in being and so long as they continue in their absolutist system and the rationale that justifies it in their own eyes. The Soviets have, furthermore, recognized that their long-term strategic military plan of imposing, preferably voluntarily, their system on the rest of mankind will not succeed as long as effective restraints continue in being, backed by a political will that allows no alternative.

The real guarantee that no war, nuclear or conventional, will happen, which ought to be our moral goal, however, is deterrence, given the present Soviet system taken in its complete being, which includes its philosophic description of itself, the ultimate cause of the problem. Professor Alois Mertes, Minister of State in the German Foreign Office, put this well:

> The West will never use weapons first, be it conventional, nuclear or other weapons. There is only one exception: the right of individual and collective self-defence enshrined in the Charter of the United Nations. The strategy of flexible response in case of attack from outside has so far proved to be a reliable basis for securing peace and freedom in Europe. The intended effect of deterrence has obviously made an impression on responsible leaders of the Soviet Union ... It is the opinion of the Federal Government that all efforts deserve support which make certain by a combination of deterrence and arms control that there will be no use of weapons whatsoever in Europe. Such a policy corresponds to the ethical command of maintaining peace.[15]

What best prudentially guarantees no use of weapons, nuclear or conventional, while at the same time preventing the worst regime to be imposed on more peoples, ought, it seems, to be seen as the most moral

203

position.

The Soviets, however, are not unjustified in seeking an intellectual road around this de facto deterrent barrier. Understanding clearly the place of will in political action, they can legitimately wonder if it might just be possible to gain their long-term objectives, or at least some short-term ones, not by superiority in or use of weapons, a path the Soviets will continue to follow, as Solzhenitsyn said when he first came to the United States, but by argument, by the pen, against a culture that has lost much of its intellectual way and no longer understands its priorities or, indeed, its own philosophic history.[16]

This latter argument, of course, need not be identifiably orchestrated by Soviet "dupes" in academic or religious garb to be effective. Rather, it could be something independent of such sponsorship, but its results would reach by its own logic the conclusions the Soviets would most desire. This would be the official Western ethical announcement that nuclear deterrence will be unilaterally renounced and no military power will be further employed because it is, specifically, "immoral" to threaten or use such force.

Here, in this argument, the questions asked by Edward Luttwak and Andrei Sakharov about whether any renouncement of nuclear weapons would in fact not demand massive reliance on improved conventional weapons which might well have as much destructive force as nuclear weapons will be set aside.[17] For the sake of analysis, it is clear that a Western announcement on political-ethical grounds, from its political authorities, accepting the "ethics of surrender," which would leave the present Soviet system intact with its present weapons and ideology, will render any other defence impossible.

Such a decision, however virtuous it presumably is, needs to be considered in itself. To state the issue in another fashion, when the virtuous, good ethical choice results, on the basis of its own act, in the establishment of the worst regime, must that choice be considered as moral? Or does it merely render the whole enterprise of ethics and religion ridiculous? Does it reveal a serious misunderstanding on the part of its proponents about what politics is about, how political morality must be based on

204

political persuasions which cannot be so easily reduced to single acts taken in isolation from overall political and ideological considerations?

Not a few leaders, religious and otherwise, have proclaimed that surrender to the Soviets is to be preferred to fighting them with the threat or use of nuclear weapons. A 1983 Calendar promoting the Nuclear Freeze reads: "The taproot of violence in our society today is our intent to use nuclear weapons. Once we have agreed to that, all other evil is minor in comparison." In this, there is a lapse into pure intentionality. The bomb is no longer the direct problem, but the "intention" to use it.

Thus, evidently, even if the nuclear weapons are never used because of deterrence which involves this intent, the society remains equally evil. Since the Soviet system also has this "intent" presumably, though it is not chastized since it is implicitly conceded to be a corrupt regime, it follows that mankind as a whole is evil in intent by virtue of its efforts to remain free to think of the difference between good and evil. Consequently, if the intention to "use" nuclear weapons is likewise the central guarantee for the fact that they will not be used -- the efforts of politics -- then the giving up this "intention" leads to the known evils of the worst regime which follow directly from the renouncing of this intention. "Morality" begets "immorality", as the cynic always suspected.

The reason offered for this sort of thinking is that "evil" acts cannot be used for a "good" cause. This implies that the use or intent to use nuclear weapons is itself necessarily an "evil" act. (Usually, this proposition needs to be qualified by saying "use on innocent people", since a nuclear weapon might be used on an isolated military target. To avoid even this latter, some hold a sort of determinism which argues that the first use of nuclear weapons must lead to the use of all of them.) Grimly or gleefully following the logic of these premises, the obvious conclusion follows that surrender is to be preferred to war.

Indeed, surrender is the only moral alternative, so that the society that does not surrender lives, as we saw above, in intentional immorality, which, of course, "makes all other evil minor in comparison." This argument is then taken one step farther, just to close off explicitly any avenue of moral escape, to hold that even the possession, intent or not, of nuclear weapons is also immoral. This leads some even to suggest that military service or working in defence plants, or holding stock in them, is immoral.

Though it is not often presented in its most graphic form, namely what life in a Gulag might be like, the consequences of surrender are to be accepted in the spirit of high virtue, in itself demanded by ethics and religion, which claims competency in this area. This suffering becomes the "cross" we must bear. Thus, we have religious people, themselves often not elected to be responsible for political power over peace and war or the consequences of their own admonitions, willing to recommend surrender to the worst state as a conclusion, inevitable as it turns out, required to retain "intentional" morality.

What is to be remarked here also is that in none of this is the bomb ever actually used. The citizens of free societies are to surrender to the worst regime and accept its consequences because it is "immoral" to do the only thing (politics) that will effectively prevent it, granting the enemy's political philosophy. In other words, this philosophy operative within the worst state, defining its form, determines the form of surrender for free societies, because it is admitted implicitly that the worst regime will not change its goal or methods. The argument for living in the worst state, then, is to be accepted as normative for those living in states far less than the worst.

At the heart of this issue, as Richard Neuhaus well phrased it, is the question of "whether we are responsible before God for the possible consequences of the positions we take, or whether we are simply to say No to war and Yes to peace, and leave whatever may be the policy implications and their consequences up to God."[18] Was it "immoral" then to stop a Hitler? If they had a nuclear weapon two years earlier, should Roosevelt and Churchill have told Hitler to stop killing Poles and Jews or they will remove, say, Berlin? And if FDR and Churchill did not use such a bomb, restrained for the above outlined ethical reasons, would they also have been war criminals for not stopping what they could have stopped? What, in other words, is the logic which would, in the name of ethics and religion, seek to persuade us that surrender is the only moral choice when an enemy seeks to place us in such a moral position?[19]

Thus far, few religious or ethical leaders have embraced the surrender view in its pure form, however great the temptation to do so may be for many. Enough loopholes have been left for an effective deterrence system to continue, or at least enough obscurity so that not even the Soviets will be able to figure out what exactly is meant. Deterrence in practice remains in place, even assuming the politicians were to accept literally everything religious or ethical leaders might come up with. The rhetoric of it all, to be sure, will probably continue to give aid and comfort to the Soviet "peace" ambitions, which see religious peace initiatives as a possible bloodless way to achieve classic Soviet ambitions, or on a less exalted scale, to keep American missiles out of Europe so the Europeans begin to doubt the American ability or intention to protect them.

On the other hand, the surrender position, whose morality is under consideration here, has a sufficient number of religious and other advocates to warrant attention to the values and consequences it must embrace to justify itself. Ex fructibus eorum, cognoscetis eos. By their fruits, you shall know them. We know bad trees from bad fruit. The worst "fruit" of politics is the worst state. Something seems radically wrong with the political tree that bears it. This is what the Western political and religious tradition requires us to consider.

Starting out with the premise, valid in itself, that it is never permitted to do evil to achieve good -- God may bring forth good in His own way from evil, which is not saying He intends evil or encourages it -- evil is defined either as the weapons themselves, a sort of Manichean position which locates evil in material things, or, as we have seen, as the "intent" to use them. The reason for this prohibition depends, naturally, upon what sort of a thing is said to be evil. In this argument, following the tradition, it is that innocent people cannot be directly attacked as a means to deter their leaders from pursuing their policy, even if it be the policy of the worst state and will only result in bringing all people into the worst state.

Soldiers, of course, usually are said to be direct objects of attack, unless the use of nuclear weapons on them in any form would "necessarily" result

207

in their use in <u>all</u> forms, again a sort of determinist
position. Somewhat dogmatically, moreover, the power
of the worst regime to force admittedly innocent
people to co-operate in evil enterprises is radically
downplayed. Thus, if, as some hold, it is "immoral"
to work in American defence plants, it must likewise
be "immoral" to work in Soviet defence plants. Why?
Following the surrender argument, it is because the
weapons themselves or the intent to use them, which
the Soviets have never denied they had, is immoral.
Logically, this should lead to the conclusion that
workers in Soviet defence plants are not "innocent."

In any case, let us further suppppose, as the U.S.
Secretary of the Navy, Mr. John Lehman has pointed
out, that Western rulers do accept the ethical
principle as it is explained in the surrender
argument, namely, that no "innocent" person may be
directly attacked. On reading Western religious and
ethical literature on this topic, the Soviets discover
that farmers, defence workers, children, women, the
aged, practically the whole population of the Soviet
system, however little they may have done to change
it, are technically "innocent."[20] Responding to the
moral sensitivity of Western political leaders, who
may not yet have renounced all defence posture, except
where "innocents" are involved, according to the
argument, what should Soviet leaders do?

First, they should seek to find out how many
"innocent" are required to make a military target
"morally" off limits. They could discover this in the
moral literature of the West and reconfirm that
Western political leaders will follow, no excuses,
what the religious and ethical authorities urging
surrender recommend. Soviet leaders would, secondly,
immediately move significant numbers of "innocent"
civilians out to where the weapons are in place
already or, alternatively, move the weapons to the
cities. Since in the ethics of surrender argument,
there is an unwillingness to question whether such
people remain "innocent" in the strategic sense, but
become rather instruments of power and coercion as
much as the soldier, the only alternative remains
surrender. Again, this surrender results not from
defeat in <u>actual</u> war but from defeat in political and
ethical <u>argument</u>, itself developed historically by
Western religion or ethics.

Since surrender in this context would come from
religious and ethical argument, then the consequent

religious and ethical "mission" necessarily would have to face the results of what it has wrought. People would have to be prepared spiritually for life under the absolute state which must be accepted because it is immoral not to do so. Churches, schools, pulpits, and universities, instead of nuclear freeze debates, would begin to sponsor "surrender seminars," to explain how life under the worst regime works. The people would be asked to see this as willed by God, because no effective deterrent can be intended or used, a deterrent which in practice even the worst regime acknowledges to work, to prevent the further spread of the worst regime. The reason deterrence "works," apparently, is that, unlike Western ethics and religion, which presumably held for some purpose in this life beyond politics and beyond this life, the Marxist system maintains that this life is all there is. Thus, even on its own terms, there is something rather unattractive about getting wiped out, since, again, life is all there is.

The real question, therefore, lies elsewhere. The "ethical surrender to the worst regime" argument, taken in its most likely form, does two things. First, it deliberately bypasses politics as it is usually understood, that is, a real concern for the safety of a people or civilization, the means to protect its way of life as a good. This involves knowing how to prevent and, if needs be, ethically fight a war, as well as knowing what would happen when a worst regime is allowed to take over.

Contrary to what might be thought, Western society already has had within it advocates of surrender who, on an earlier occasion, did not realize what their ideas would lead to. The Oxford Union debated this question in the light of the contributions of pacifism in the 1930's toward World War II and Hitler's successes. Professor John Gray reported Lord Max Beloff's moving address:

> (Beloff) described his speech as an "act of atonement" for his having voted for the pacifist motion 50 years ago (in a similar Oxford Union Debate) and as a tribute to the memory of a friend who opposed the motion and went on to fight and die for the cause of liberty in the African desert. Lord Beloff continued by pointing out that while six million Jews had been left with no option but to practice

nonviolent resistance against the Nazis, this did not prevent them from perishing in the ensuing Holocaust. The events leading up to World War II, and the crimes that Allied victory allowed to be revealed in Nazi-occupied Europe, illustrate a depth of moral nihilism at the heart of civilized Europe against which the postures of pacifist optimism had no force. An absolute choice of nonviolence may be right for a private citizen ... but it cannot be a basis of a national policy.[21]

Secondly, the ethical surrender argument establishes, as the center of morality, the thesis that the continuation of life on earth, taken as a human collectivity, is the highest good to which all should be subordinated, no matter what the results. This argument, in the history of political theory, stems not from Christian sources but from Hobbes. What we are now, apparently, witnessing is the acceptance by many Christians of the validity of the modern philosophy of Hobbes, now as a necessary religious option.[22]

This latter principle, which would hold that the continuing life of the human species is the highest good, must be taken literally. Absolutely no value is worth upholding if it can be so presented that the only alternative involves death. To this end, of course, the Soviets, who substantially agree with these philosophic premises, have managed to structure the argument. Therefore, the human "good" in practice, by an act of virtue, must embrace the worst regime to be "moral." This is where the argument actually leads and is said by many to be a "demand" of religion and ethics. This is also a very ancient argument in political philosophy, already in The Republic in its essential outlines.

Western civilization, moreover, was built on the rejection of the proposition that the only moral choice is to accept rationally the worst regime as the good. Western religion agreed with this rejection of the worst regime and reinforced it by suggesting that the Kingdom of God was our only true home, so that those who died resisting the worst regime did not simply perish forever. The ethics of surrender to the worst regime argument, thus, represents something more fundamental in political theory than we might at first sight realize, however much it might bear the aura of

210

virtue. This argument is willing to sacrifice all value to staying alive in a system that itself subverts free, natural standards towards which the human enterprise ought to be directed in and beyond life. Further, the ethics of surrender argument permits the removal from the earth of any political system that would argue that anything more than staying alive is important. The ethics of surrender, therefore, implies the disappearance of ethics and religions themselves, this in the name of morality itself.

Michael Walzer has considered this problem from another angle. Could pacifist means be successful in the worst state to which free societies give up on allowing it to take over the whole world? Up until now, resistance within the Soviet world, as Solzhenitsyn has often remarked, has much to do with the existence of a free world to which at least some could escape and which prevented the worst excesses from happening. Suppose, however, on surrendering for morality's sake, as we have been considering it here, the churches and schools try to instruct everyone on the latest means of non-violent resistance. Would this "work" in a totalitarian state now with no external enemies? Here, be it noted, we prescind from the position that "morality" need not account for any "consequences," however dire, and from the position that God would somehow, ex aliunde, protect those who so surrender by supernatural means, the legion of angels not sent at the time of the Crucifixion of Jesus, for instance.(Matthew, 26:53)

Elaborating how pacifism might work in the worst regime, Walzer remarked that it could only work

> if the invaders are committed to the war convention -- and they won't always be committed. While nonviolence by itself replaces aggressive war with political struggle, it cannot by itself determine the means of struggle. The invading army can always adopt the common methods of domestic tyrants, which go well beyond curfews, fines, and jail sentences; and its leaders, though they are soldiers, may well be tempted to do that for the sake of a quick "victory." Tyrants will not, of course, lay siege to their own cities or bomb or bombard them ... But there are other, probably more efficient, ways of terrorizing a people

211

whose country one controls, and of breaking
their resistance....

    Nor would civilian resistance work well
against invaders, who sent out squads of
soldiers to kill civilian leaders, who
arrested and tortured suspects, established
concentration camps, and exiled large
numbers of people from areas where the
resistance was strong to distant and
desolate parts of the country. Nonviolent
defence is no defence at all against tyrants
or conquerors ready to adopt such
measures.[23]

Again, the difficulty with the ethics of surrender to
the worst regime argument is its failure to understand
the tradition of politics, to understand that
political will and political power are what prevent
wars. The surrender premise, far from preventing,
encourages the worst regime, indeed legitimizes it.
Surely, if religion presents itself in the
contemporary world as the chief instigator in the West
for living in the worst regime on a world basis, in
claiming that this is our <u>only</u> moral choice, this
wrenching of ideas and experience, this narrowing of
vision can only lead to the conclusion in argument, in
speech, that such a religion must be wrong.

    Aquinas himself had said that reason and faith do
not contradict one another. If we are told that the
worst regime, the ultimate contradiction of politics,
an area "natural" to man, as Aristotle held, is the
<u>necessary</u> conclusion of "religion," as some are
saying, increasingly many will simply conclude that
such religion is mad, even on its own grounds.
Winston Churchill wrote in <u>The Gathering Storm</u>:

    The Sermon on the Mount is the last
word in Christian ethics ... Still, it is
not on these terms that Ministers assume
their responsibilities of guiding states.
Their duty is first so to deal with other
nations as to avoid strife and war and to
eschew aggression in all its forms, whether
for nationalistic or ideological objects.
But the safety of the state, the lives and
freedom of their own fellow countrymen, to
whom they owe their position, make it right
and imperative in the last resort, or when a
final and definite conviction has been

212

reached, that the use of force should not be excluded. If the circumstances are such as to warrant it, force may be used ... These are tormenting dilemmas upon which mankind has throughout its history been so frequently impaled. Final judgment upon them can only be recorded by history in relation to the facts of the case as known to the parties at the time, and also as subsequently proved ... It is baffling to reflect that what men call honour does not always correspond to Christian ethics.[24]

What I wish to suggest, in conclusion, is rather that sometimes, particularly in the case of the worst state, Christian ethics, rightly understood, and honor do correspond. The argument for ethical surrender, even when proposed by clerics, is not Christian but Hobbesian.

Christianity, to be sure, as St. Augustine taught us, is also responsible to know how men even in the worst regimes act, to teach us that our basic transcendent hope remains even in the worst arrangement of office and rule we can imagine. To allow the worst regime to come upon us because we can think of no moral way to stop it, not only argues to a very limited political imagination, but to a very cavalier concept of Christian ethics that would presume to embrace as "necessary" everything traditional religion and philosophy had held to be wrong. St. Augustine put it well:

What is the charge brought against war? Is it that some men, who will in any case die sooner or later, are killed so as to establish order for people who will live in peace? To make such charge is the part not of religious minds, but of timorous minds. The real evils in war are the love of violence, revengeful cruelty, fierce and implacable enmity, wild resistance, and the lust of power, and such like; and it is generally to punish these things, when force is required to inflict the punishment, that, in obedience to God or some lawful authority, good men undertake wars, when they find themselves in such a position as regards the conduct of human affairs, that right conduct requires them to act, or to make others act in this way.[25]

Mankind seems more and more to be confronted by "timorous minds," who would allow a system of violence, cruelty, enmity, willed resistance, and lust for power, to control civilization in the apparent name of classic virtue.

Right conduct then requires action to prevent such things. Today, the most crucial "right action" is not war itself, but argument, the pen, which would instruct both the worst regime and its advocates in the ethics of surrender, that accepting the worst, however noble in a grizzly sense, is not an act of virtue. Doing no evil act to promote a good end includes, in the first instance, the failure to posit an act that would prevent giving the worst regime universal dominance. That the "act" that would most effectively accomplish this prevention is an intellectual act only adds to the irony of it all. The "truth" of the ethics of surrender is the "end" of religion as a viable option for mankind, not to mention politics.

Most normal men, I think, understand this without the elaborate argumentation presented here. This is why, in the nuclear debate, religion in particular, or at least that part which accepts the ethics of surrender, is contemplating its own suicide, with a position that would undermine any credibility to religion's claim to uphold the human good. Fortunately, Western religion need not, and hopefully will not go that way. But even it has the choice, in some confused way, to allow us to be uncertain what it is about.

The pen remains mightier than the sword except when the pen has lost contact with any reason to prevent the worst regime from using this same sword. In the end, then, without political philosophy, political power conquers politics and religion bloodlessly. All values merge into their opposites. The worst regimes become the "moral" regimes. Political theory is turned upside down in the name of the pursuit of virtue. Classic and medieval theoreticians would have been astonished. This is why we must continue to study them and think within their civilizational terms when considering the second greatest problem of political philosophy, that of war and the worst regime. This is why embracing the worst regime to stay alive, to avoid war, is, at the same time, a denial of philosophy itself, a denial that

214

anything higher than staying alive at any cost can be thought.

Footnotes:

1. St. Thomas Aquinas, On Kingship, trans. by G. Phelan, Toronto, Pontifical Institute of Medieval Studies, 1949.

2. Oscar Cullmann, The State in the New Testament, New York, Scribner's, 1956. See above, Chapter II.

3. See F. Stratmann, War and Christianity Today, Westminster, Newman, 1956; Paul Ramsay, War and the Christian Conscience, Durham, Duke University Press, 1961; Herbert Deane, Political and Social Ideas of St. Augustine, New York, Columbia University Press, 1963, Chapter V.

4. St. Thomas Aquinas' discussion of war is in Summa Theologica, II-II, 40.

5. See John Ferguson, War and Peace in the World's Religions, New York, Oxford, 1978; Quincy Wright, A Study of War, Chicago, University of Chicago Press, 1965; William V. O'Brien, Just and Limited Wars, New York, Praeger, 1982; Michael Walzer, Just and Unjust Wars, New York, Harper Colophon, 1977.

6. See Leo Strauss, Natural Right and History, Chicago, University of Chicago Press, 1953.

7. The best statement of this analysis is Joseph Cropsey's "The United States as a Regime," Political Philosophy and the Issues of Politics, Chicago, University of Chicago Press, 1977. See James V. Schall, "Religion and National Security," International Security Review, Summer, 1982, pp. 135-54.

8. Washington Times, February 18, 1983.

9. See The Apocalyptic Premise, Washington, Ethics and Public Policy Center, 1982; L. Bruce van Voorst, "The Churches and Nuclear Deterrence," Foreign Affairs, Spring, 1983; Michael Novak, "Moral Clarity in the Nuclear Age," Catholicism-in-Crisis, March, 1983; U.S. Catholic Bishops, "The Challenge of Peace," Origins, May 19, 1983; States on Peace and War by the German and French Bishops, with the Letter of Basil Cardinal Hume, San Francisco, Ignatius Press, 1984; Central Committee for German Catholics, "On the Current Peace Discussions," November 17, 1981, also in

<u>Catholicism-in-Crisis</u>, May, 1983; Albert Wohlstetter, "Bishops, Statesmen, and Other Strategists on the Bombing of Innocents," <u>Commentary</u>, June, 1983; Andrei Sakharov, "The Danger of Thermonuclear War," <u>Foreign Affairs</u>, Summer, 1983; James V. Schall, "Freeze or Freedom: On the Limits of Morals and the Worth of Freedom," <u>Vital Speeches</u>, May 1, 1983; "Peace, War, Poverty," <u>The Hillsdale Review</u>, Fall, 1982, pp. 3-8.

10. See James V. Schall, <u>Christianity and Politics</u>, Boston, St. Paul Editions, 1981.

11. See James V. Schall, "War, Religion, and Political Philosophy," <u>Catholicism-in-Crisis</u>, January, 1983; "Military and Civil Responsibilities for a Just Peace," <u>Vital Speeches</u>, November 15, 1983.

12. See V. Bukovsky, "The Soviet Role in the Peace Movement," <u>Commentary</u>, May, 1982. (Also found in <u>The Apocalyptic Premise</u> in Footnote #9). Rael Jean Isaac and Eric Isaac, "The Counterfit Peacemakers," <u>American Spectator</u>, July, 1982; John Barron, "The KGB's Magical War for 'Peace'," <u>Reader's Digest</u>, October, 1982. (Barron and Bukovsky are in <u>The Apocalyptic Premise</u>, <u>ibid</u>.)

13. C. S. Lewis, "Why I Am Not a Pacifist," <u>The Weight of Glory</u>, New York, Macmillan, 1980.

14. UN Address of June 23, 1982, in <u>The Apocalyptic Premise</u>, <u>ibid</u>.

15. Bonn, German Foreign Office, February 3, 1983.

16. Alexander Solzhenitsyn, Addresses of June 30 and July 9, 1975, Washington, AFL-CIO, 1976; see David Satter, "Soviet Threat Is One of Ideas More Than Arms," <u>Wall Street Journal</u>, May 23, 1983.

17. E. Luttwak, "How to Think About Nuclear War," <u>Commentary</u>, May, 1982 (Also in <u>The Apocalyptic Premise</u>; A. Sakharov, <u>Bulletin of the Atomic Scientists</u>, November, 1982.

18. Richard Neuhaus, <u>Eternity</u>, October, 1982, p. 28.

19. John Paul II has held for a theory of the validity of deterrence in the context of agreed, verifiable arms control, see his addresses of December

13, 1981; January 1, 1982; June 11, 1982, and January 1, 1984. See in particular the Pastorals on War and Peace by the German and French Bishops, together with the Letter of Basil Cardinal Hume, published by the Ignatius Press in San Francisco, 1984.

20. Wall Street Journal, November 15, 1982.

21. John Gray, "Oxford Resolves to Fight for Queen and Country," Wall Street Journal, February 17, 1983. See also Taro Takemi, M.D., "Remembrance of the War and the Bomb," Journal of the American Medical Association, August 5, 1983, pp. 618-19.

22. See James V. Schall, "The Intellectual Origins of the 'Peace' Movement," Justice and War in the Nuclear Age, Washington, University Press of America, 1983.

23. Michael Walzer, ibid., p. 332. See also Jacques Maritain, "The Ethics of a Barbarous Society," Man and the State, Chicago, University of Chicago Press, 1951.

24. Winston Churchill, The Gathering Storm, New York, Bantam, p. 286.

25. Contra Faustum, XXII, 74.

CHAPTER X

ON THE CONDITION OF HEAVEN: A THOMISTIC REFLECTION ON POLITICS AND THE COMPLETION OF HUMAN NUMBERS

> Adam, therefore, was instituted in such perfection as was fitting to the beginner of the whole human race. And therefore, it was necessary that he generate for the multiplication of the human race, and thus that he use food. But the perfection of the risen will be a human nature totally coming on its own perfection when the number of elect is already complete. And therefore generation will have no place (in heaven), nor use of food. --[St. Thomas Aquinas, Summa Contra Gentiles, IV, 83.]

In the beginning of Chapter VIII, Samuel Johnson was cited, his very Christian remark that we should all be exiles if we could leave our native land, taking only the happinesses and leaving all the evils behind. A constant theme in Christian political thought and in Christian piety from the scriptures themselves is that we are here only pilgrims and wayfarers. (Hebrews, 11:13; 1 Peter 2:11) That there can be a proper kind of happiness in this world, that it is in the city, that some kinds of political life are better than others, these have been the various political themes in the history of thought which have been traced here.

These issues, of course, most need being put in proper political and theoretical perspective. The importance of understanding and clearly distinguishing the kinds of happiness and destinies, political, metaphysical, and theological, then, remains the fundamental one in political theory. The slightest unclarities and confusions in this sphere have the greatest of consequence in the practical order. Indeed, the modern absolute state, the most dangerous totalitarian form yet conceived by this human race, has its direct origin in the confusion of the locus and nature of human happiness. (Chapters VIII and IX)

There is a further consideration that these

reflections on themes from medieval and Christian
theory serve. They recapitulate the limits and nature
of political theory itself. This involves the
ultimate number and status of the actual individual
persons that will ever have existed on earth, those
members of the Two Cities of which St. Augustine
wrote. Thus far, we have argued that the Christian
doctrine of personal resurrection is the locus of the
human person's ultimate happiness.[1] The ultimate
hope of political theory from The Republic on, that
man has an immortal destiny, has served to free
politics to be politics and prevented it from being a
pseudo-collective or corporate happiness whose terms
are to be confined to this world in its history.

The great "atheist" project was thus to produce a
"human" and "social" world in which only the signs of
the human race were to be found.[2] The great
contribution of Christianity to political theory has
been its refusal to permit a strictly political
definition of human happiness.[3] What needs finally
to be argued here is that ideas connected with the
ultimate status of man in his final happiness in
Christianity are now returning in a rather peculiar
form as a project to be achieved by reforming man in
this world, initially by genetic technology, but
finally by complete rational planning.

Estimates about the total number of human beings
who already have lived on this planet, earth, are, of
course, highly problematic. In any case, whether or
not the number be around the eighty five to ninety
billions several responsible calculations judge, there
have been a finite number of humans during the course
of the aeons and centuries since the human race first
appeared.[4] Recent attention, furthermore, has
concentrated not so much upon the men and women who
have already lived, nor even the four to five billions
now alive, but upon the supposedly vast numbers who
will yet live -- the "futurables," the objects of
"futurology."[5]

We know now, moreover, that there is a vast
difference between the number of people potentially
capable of existing from any one human couple --
several hundreds on the part of the female should all
ova be fertilized in one lifetime, a distinct
possibility now that Louise Brown was conceived
outside the womb, perhaps billions on the part of the
male -- and the number who actually will exist. The
selection of just what few potential combinations will

be allowed, if any, to come to pass is becoming a serious social and moral question, once men recognize that the reproductive process can be controlled by will, force, politics, or science.

All of this has become a key contemporary issue because the earth is popularly believed to be reaching its so-called "finite limits" or carrying capacity.[6] Indeed, "morality," what it is to be a "good man," is currently coming to be interpreted in terms of population density such that the control of this human population becomes the _prima lex_ which, it is held, gives any certainty to the _salus_, the well-being, of a republic, or of the world. Men's primary enemies are coming to be seen as the very existence of other men against whom a kind of "incipient" warfare is to be waged. That is, many hold that we must eliminate most human conceptions or terminate them before they can break into the light of day in birth when they are assured the protection of the rights of life, liberty, and happiness, rights whose origins come classically from ancient, Christian, medieval, and certain strands of modern thought.

In this modern reflection on population, moreover -- a questionable one in many ways -- men conceive their "function," that is, the justification for the whole collectivity of men to exist at all, to be to transform the earth in such a manner that there will exist only a finite, steady number -- say three to five billions -- on earth at any given time.[7] The "purpose" of the human race on the planet -- seen in its temporal sequence -- is held to be the keeping alive and in well-being this privileged collection of humans permitted to exist at any one time for as many centuries as possible until the sun finally burns out or some other cosmic event terminates life on earth or until the race succeeds in transferring itself to another planetary system and so on until the cosmos itself ends, if indeed it does end finally.

Ultimately, humans who do not fall into this planning do not have a "right" to exist, since they threaten the collectivity that the earth, purportedly, can support. And even when the earth can no longer support _life_, as Werner von Braun remarked when men first walked on the moon, the earthly race of men itself may now be "immortal" since it has now the potential of sending its own kind to populate the myriads of planets similar to the earth, planets that evidently dot the cosmos.[8] This new ethico-political

221

goal proposed to the human race, it should be noted, does deserve more critical attention than it has been receiving, especially from Christians. They have not been quick to recognize how this thinking radically diverges from essential religious views which propose that the purpose of the cosmos is that rational persons have a period of choice in which they decide their stance for or against evil as such.

At first sight, such contemporary issues do not appear relevant to the kind of thinking Aquinas engaged in some seven centuries ago. It is still difficult for a generation unaccustomed to ideas and their connections to recognize that the intellect itself does have a "history." Philosophy cannot wholly forget what once was thought. Yet, especially in the Contra Gentiles, there are several remarkable considerations that reflect issues that have now, as we have suggested, become "secularized" or "politicized." Indeed, it might well be argued that the form in which these notions of ultimate human numbers and purposes appear today is the direct result of rejecting basic values and positions underlying the system of Aquinas.

The rise of so-called "political theology," furthermore, so strikingly absent in Aquinas, flows almost directly from de-emphasizing the human soul and the final locus of its beatitude. Aquinas never questioned that the number of human beings to be created was itself limited.(Summa Theologica, I, 23, 7) But the notion that social ethics could be reduced to a proposition of keeping alive a fixed number of men down through the ages would have seemed to be a little less than a revival of Greek biology applied to the human level wherein the immortality of the species was the purpose of generation. The individual existed for the species in this view and was not willed except in collective terms. That this can be proposed as an alternative "morality" to that envisioned by Aquinas, which was based on the free creation, election, and personal destiny of each human, is of some moment.

The Summa Contra Gentiles was written specifically for a non-Christian and non-Jewish audience so that it might appeal directly to men who only held their humanity in common.(I, 2) The structure of the Contra Gentiles is global. It seeks to establish the nature of God, man, and the universe, especially to locate and define man's ultimate happiness. This involved Aquinas in the famous

222

position that each man contained all the intellectual powers within himself for knowing, such that the destiny of man was open to God as to all knowledge.(II, 59; III, 84) The end of any intellectual creature can only be to know God, and this is the purpose for which men were created.(III, 25) In all of creation, there is a freedom since the world need not have been at all, nor was it from eternity.(III, 23, 31; I, 81)

The plan of the universe is achieved when, through Christ, men are able actually to achieve a complete life with God, body and soul.(Book IV) Undoubtedly, for modern ears at least, the most difficult part of Aquinas' approach is that each member of the human race who historically existed <u>can</u> in his very particularity achieve full beatitude. This was, as Hannah Arendt pointed out in <u>The Human Condition</u>, that which most distinguished Christianity from Greek reflection. And this is, for Christian thought, what constitutes ultimately the dignity of the person. But this accomplishment is not something that arises out of an exact performance or a merit due directly to the individual <u>or</u> the race.

It is manifest that predestination and election are not caused by any human merits not only from the fact that the grace of God which is the effect of predestination does not come from merits, but precedes all human merits, but also it can be manifest from the fact that the divine will and providence is the first cause of that which happens. Nothing however can be the cause of the divine will and providence. (III, 163)

This is not intended to deny, to be sure, that men really have something to do in the universe. Secondary causes are real causes. But it does confront directly any proposition that would locate human happiness and destiny outside of that to which it is ultimately open through God's graciousness.[9] This cautions, in other words, the definition of man in terms of his inner worldly condition and its temporal successions.

The last Chapter of the <u>Contra Gentiles</u> -- <u>De Statu Mundi post Judicium</u> (IV, 97) -- is at first sight a curious mixture of medieval astronomy and theological speculations which seeks to justify the continuance of man in the universe but without his

223

being further subject to those celestial motions that caused or influenced supposedly his begetting on earth. The import of the consideration, in other words, is how men in a resurrected state can survive when the normal conditions of the cosmos no longer apply. For Aquinas, there are indeed things made "ad perpetuitatem," made forever, though with a beginning; among these are the souls of men by which they transcend the universe itself. And in the Christian dispensation, the body shares this destiny also, even though God must supply what is lacking to it -- _Deo supplente sua virtute quod eis ex propria infirmitate deest_. This is the result, further, not of some natural "self-transcendence," but of the concrete history of salvation to which this race of men are subject.[10]

Following from this, two observations are especially relevant to the way the contemporary problem seems to be working itself out. The first is that Aquinas regarded the number of humans to be finally limited.

> The end, therefore, cannot be a multiplication of souls in infinity because infinity is contrary to the notion of an end. Nothing inconvenient, therefore, follows if, when a certain number of men is completed, we posit a cessation of the motions of the heavens. (IV, 97)

Just what should determine this completed number is, as Aquinas noted in the _Summa Theologica_ (I, 23, 7), of some dispute. God knows the number both materially and formally. That is, he knows the total number and who each one of the total is.

Physical creation is, indeed, ordained to achieve man's purposes, and more particularly, for those who in fact choose God within the confines of the drama of history. Aquinas seems to have suggested that God does not directly choose the number of damned -- who, of course, also make up part of the universe's total -- since that would imply that God chose their fallen lot directly. (See Chapter V) This would conform to the theme previously argued (Chapter VI), that the best possible universe may include choices of evil, even confirmed choices in it, since otherwise the purpose of creation in the first place would not be completely possible.

224

And what is this total number? Aquinas cited various comparative speculations -- that it is equal to the number of fallen angels, or to the number who did not fall, or to the number of angels created.(I, 23, 7) But he is skeptical of all this. "It would be better to say that the number of elect who reach supreme happiness is known to God alone." What should be emphasized in all this is that the ultimate number of humans is limited because men are in fact to reach their end, which is seen to be the personal vision of the Triune God and nothing else.[11] This relativizes any ethic which conceives man's corporate function on earth as that of preserving himself as long as possible, such that standards and values which define man's dignity and destiny become subject to this continuation or survival ethic and not to God's distinctions of good and evil in the human. For Aquinas, it is the other way around, therefore, preserving or developing the natural and Christian ethic is that according to which we should order the world.

Yet, the goal of knowing all things, earthly things, is the normal function of the human intellect in its immediate object. The ideal often proposed for earth, its preservation as a natural place of beauty and abundance -- the Garden of Eden myth modernized, so to speak -- is also present in Aquinas, but again posed as a problem for the ultimate status of physical creation.

Since then corporeal creatures are finally disposed through conformity with the status of men, the status of men will not only be freed from corruption, but also will put on glory. And it is necessary then that also corporeal creatures in their own way receive a certain glory of this clarity.

These are, in fact, the last words of the Contra Gentiles, except for the brief citations from Apocalypse XXI and Isaiah LXV about the new heavens and the new earth. What is noteworthy here is that the kind of reflection that Aquinas posited after resurrection and judgment is more and more to be found posed as a this-worldly project.

The pertinence of these approaches can be seen by recalling Aquinas' views about the existence of sex in the Parousia. This is of especial interest because recent proposals and technologies do tend either to

eliminate sex as an organism for procreation or at
least restrict reproduction severely to such an extent
that it has little to do with actual human lives.
Indeed, clonization proposals do eliminate the
connection between birth and sex altogether. So do
those notions which propose refashioning the human
corpus on the model of existing genetic structure so
that no really "new" human persons be created -- which
is the case with each new human "birth" in the present
order of reality.

Aquinas held firmly that there would be no
reproduction of new human beings after the
resurrection. His views are not dissimilar to those
contemporaries who insist that no more children ought
to be produced, granting the difference of locale and
condition.[12] But for Aquinas, the reason for no
further human birth was that all men had to receive
resurrection and Parousia at once. Any children born
after that time would be exempt from the condition of
the historical race of men -- and their finite number
-- to whom salvation was promised and achieved.(IV,
83, 88)

Sexual characteristics, moreover, were to remain
in resurrection as these are essential to the person.
Women were even to discover why they were created to
be women!

> Similarly, also neither will the
> weakness of the feminine sex be obviated by
> the perfection of the resurrection. For
> this infirmity is not from a deficiency of
> nature, but intended by nature. And this
> distinction of nature in humans will be
> shown to be a perfection of nature and
> divine wisdom disposing all in a certain
> order. (IV, 88)

Aquinas calmly rejected the notion that personal
relationship or enjoyment would be reason enough for
sexual relationships apart from reproduction after
judgment. The reason for this is, in his view, that
each person on reaching his final goal -- along with
the universe itself -- would not need to achieve a
lesser happiness, especially one without its own
natural purpose. Aquinas is very much of the opinion
that men are made for ultimate happiness and that they
do achieve it.

Aquinas also held that it was the purpose of the

226

intellect to know all things.

> Our intellect, then, is in potency to knowing all forms of things. It is reduced to act when it knows some one of them. Therefore, it will not be totally in act, nor in its last end, except when it knows all things at least the material ones. But this man cannot obtain through the speculative sciences by which we know the truth in this life. It is not, therefore, possible that the ultimate happiness of men be in this life. (III, 48)

This is a significant passage from a contemporary point of view also for another reason. The current "secular" argument for severely limiting human numbers is based largely upon statistics of "available" resources. These are believed, though not always accurately, to be in very short supply in comparison to population. Rapid population growth, it is held, will soon "exhaust" such resources so that men will reach secular apocalypse precisely by "increasing and multiplying," by fulfilling the divine command of Genesis.(1:28)

However, most of such dire predictions are themselves products of the philosophy that defines man's purpose as a "continuance of the species down through the ages." The level of scientific development upon which calculations are based, furthermore, is very narrow and does not account for the nature of human intellect as such. As more perceptive scholars are beginning to point out, there is really only one "natural" resource in the universe. This is the human brain -- something already implicit in Aquinas' definition of intellect as that faculty "open" to all being.[13]

In a very real sense, it is ultimately possible to transform anything into anything else -- except the human person -- so that resources are not "limited" in any meaningful sense compared to human population, or at least they need not be, for men can choose to refuse what they can and ought to do. This would suggest that the earth is adequate for its purpose -- which is to minister to men to achieve their trans-worldly destiny. Aquinas again placed the ultimate realization of all knowledge beyond this life, suggesting perhaps that the race of men are not in fact likely to achieve all that is possible to them

227

by themselves.

Aquinas never doubted that the number of humans to be created was itself limited. Further, the fact that he spoke of the number of "elect" suggests that this number is determined rather by the personal drama of each created person in selecting his own destiny -- and this within whatever social order or era he might find himself in. The Contra Gentiles does not deal with the destiny of nations or other collectivities. What divides men ultimately and even in this world is their personal moral and spiritual stature.

Indeed, in the one question in the Contra Gentiles that seems to bear most directly on the subject -- Quod felicitas non consistit in potentia mundana (III, 31) -- Aquinas was mainly concerned with showing the intrinsic instability of earthly power so that it cannot be that which men ultimately seek.

> If some power is the highest good, it is necessary that it be most perfect. Human power is however most imperfect, for it is rooted in the wills and opinions of men in which there is the greatest inconstancy. And when the greater power is reputed to exist, so much more it depends on many. And this pertains to its weakness since it depends on many who can destroy it in many ways. Human power then is not the highest good of men.

The import of this is that the norms of human destiny govern what man does with his temporal existence and not vice versa. It is really the rejection of the argument that man must change his morality and his life to conform to his earthly exigencies rather than trying to be the kind of man God created him to be.

Modern thought, as Karl Rahner pointed out, strives to give meaning to the earthly enterprise as such, its meaning in all time. But it consistently ignores the fate of persons, individuals, very easily subordinating them to the collectivity and its supposed higher mission.[14] Since Aquinas did not seek human meaning ultimately in some form of worldly state of human society, however defined, he could concentrate his attention upon the meaning of each person taken in his particularity as such -- "If then the body of risen man will not be of these bones and of this flesh from which it is now composed, the man who rises will not be the same in number." (IV, 84)[15]

The destiny of mankind, then, --its numbers and completion -- is seen from the viewpoint of what does happen -- men, persons, do die -- of what is permanent, of God, the soul, and through them, the body and the universe. Modern analysis resulting from theorizing about the implications of population often, paradoxically, treats positions that Aquinas saw must be handled -- the ultimate destiny of sex and reproduction, the relation of human intellect to knowing all corporeal things, the number of humans, the purpose of human creation -- in the Parousia.

In the Prologue to Scriptum Super III Sententiis, there is contained this famous passage: "For man is, as it were, the horizon and frontier of spiritual and corporeal nature, as almost the medium between both, he participates in both goods, corporeal and spiritual." This means, of course, that the authentic values and destiny of earth are, indeed, man's to accomplish. Man is the horizon and the frontier. The "completion" of human numbers is a definite project. Yet, we must recognize that men's relation to what they themselves are created to be is itself the primary determinative factor in how many there can and will be.

Furthermore, human numbers in Aquinas are never seen to be a question of numbers as such but as the "universitas" of persons who achieve the goal for which the universe was created -- that is, the free choice to respond to God's initiative and invitation to share His inner life. The "inner" meaning of the world -- the rise and fall of nations, the hominization of nature, even the peaceable kingdom -- by itself can neither aid nor hinder this more essential drama. The "horizon" of man, in all his numbers, in all his accomplishments, is always God. "For the end of the divine law is that men adhere in God ... The end of human law, however, is ordained to some worldly good."(II-II, 140, 1) Even from the best of earthly organizations we do now know whether men are really achieving the goal to which they as persons are called.

What a reflection on these elements in Aquinas provides today in the area of human numbers, the material object of all political theory, is a reminder that when questions, in their ultimate import dealing

229

with the Parousia and its condition, come to reappear
in essentially secular, political terms, it means that
mankind has lost contact for the individual person
with the radical destiny to which he is called.
Christianity's validity as a religion, as the Contra
Gentiles seems to argue even in rational terms, is its
refusal to allow men a lesser destiny that the highest
which must include the happiness of the singular,
individual person or else it is merely an abstraction
and despair. (See Chapter XI)

Contemporary speculation on human population and
sexuality, however, should not be seen for less than
what it is -- an effort to provide the answers to
ultimate questions in a this-worldly context. It is
not enough to maintain that the answer cannot be found
there, in this world no matter how long it lasts or in
what conditions. We must also recognize that the
effort itself to subsume these kinds of questions into
a manageable political, technological or ecological
prospect is resulting in a refusal to accept the kind
of men that in fact were created -- and their destiny
"post judicium." And it is this choice to accept the
human condition as such that defines this particular
human race's hope to escape nothingness -- but this
not by itself.

We live in an age, then, which seeks both to
exalt the human enterprise and fears to accept its
conditions. The new "original sin" has ironically
almost become -- what it was not for Aquinas and the
medievals -- sex and its consequences in population.
Perhaps the last words should be those of Aquinas
also: "... Humility essentially is located in the
appetite according to which it refers to the impulse
of the soul (or refrains it) lest it tend inordinately
into greater things. But it has a rule of cognition,
namely, that no one esteem himself for more than what
he is."(II-II, 161, 6)

In the end, we are told not to esteem ourselves
for more than we are, yet we are ultimately given
everything. This is the mystery that is being worked
out in the history of the world and beyond it, when
the certain number of men is completed -- certo numero
hominum completo. The proper historical intelligence
of political theory finds its limits and dignity
within such a context. Without it, political theory
becomes almost automatically a metaphysics and
religion by itself. That is, it destroys itself. The
proper function of Christian reflection in political

230

theory is precisely to prevent this.

Footnotes:

1. See James V. Schall, Redeeming the Time, New York, Sheed and Ward, 1968, pp. 227-35.

2. See James V. Schall, "Atheism and Politics," Christianity and Politics, Boston, St. Paul Editions, 1981, Chapter IV, pp. 94-117.

3. See James V. Schall, "Political Theory: The Place of Christianity," Modern Age, Winter, 1981, pp. 26-33.

4. See James V. Schall, Human Dignity and Human Numbers, Staten Island, New York, Alba House, 1971; Welcome Number 4,000,000,000, Canfield, Ohio, Alba Books, 1977; "Population: The Bomb that Will Never Go Off," Homiletic and Pastoral Review, June, 1977; Christianity and Life, San Francisco, Ignatius Press, 1981.

5. See Marcel Leroy, "Neo-Malthusianism, Foreign Aid, and International Relations," International Journal, Canada, Winter, 1975-76, pp. 26-43; John Naisbitt, Megatrends, New York, Warner, 1982.

6. See Julian Simon, The Ultimate Resource, Princeton, Princeton University Press, 1981; Herman Kahn, The Coming Boom, New York, Simon and Schuster, 1982.

7. For a more proper philosophic presentation of the meaning of this question, see Dante Germino, Political Philosophy and the Open Society, Baton Rouge, Louisiana State University Press, 1982.

8. See also John Hick, Death and Eternal Life, London, Collins, 1976.

9. See James V. Schall, "Cosmos and Christianity," in Redeeming the Time, ibid., Chapter 4; "On Taking Possession of the Whole Universe," Christianity and Politics, Boston, St. Paul Edition, 1981, Chapter V, pp. 118-48.

10. See Battista Mondin, "L'antropologia teologica di W. Pannenberg," L'Osservatore Romano, Roma, Aprile 2, 1976, p. 3.

11. See final chapter of Redeeming the Time, ibid.

12. See Igor Shafarevich, <u>The Socialist Phenomenon</u>, New York, Harper, 1980, on the question of the death-wish in modern thought.

13. This is the theme of Buckminster Fuller, W. Beckermann, P. T. Bauer, Julian Simon, and others. See Chapter III, footnote #35; Chapter VII, footnote #37.

14. "But if it is the will of modern man ... to create really new futures in creative freedom (individually and collectively in the limitations of both these dimensions), then this will mean contemporary man is ever and again rebuffed and thwarted by death, which takes on a new unique and radical quality precisely on account of its contradiction to this rather new will of man. This fatal contradiction between man's radical will to unlimited freedom and his being condemned to death, although this is suppressed in all the ideologies of our contemporary history, is obviously not reconciled for the existing individual by the fact that the succession of generations of such individuals ordained for death is thought of as going on into an indeterminate future. This fatal contradiction is not made legitimate by the fact that it is understood to be going on eternally...."

"Every man has a responsibility not only for those who follow him but also for the dead who lived before him, and not only for his own life but also for his own death. The modern mentality of an unconditional will-to-the-future, if it is not to be deceptive, must acknowledge itself to be frustrated by death." K. Rahner, "The Death of Jesus and the Closing of Revelation," <u>Theology Digest</u>, Winter, 1975, pp. 328-29.

"Adhuc. Homo naturaliter refugit mortem, et tristatur de ipsa: non solum ut nunc, cum eam sentit, eam refugiens, sed etiam cum eam recogitat. Hoc autem quod non moriatur, homo non potest assequi in hac vita. Non est igitur possibile quod homo in hac vita sit felix." <u>Contra Gentiles</u>, III, 48.

15. It is interesting that the current movements and proposals to deep freeze human bodies instead of burying them (the Christian tradition with regard to the resurrection) is based on hope of eventual resurgence and cure so that the same individual could

continue in a cycle of ages without facing death. But it is the same instinct to preserve the same individual person which Aquinas also dealt with in his belief that we will rise as the same individual. The one is based on science, the other on Christ.

It might be noted too that the interchangeability of human parts, something whose rights are now in the courts (Do I have a right to someone else's kidney?), represents the eternity of the species side of this argument. The meaning of the individual body is found in allowing other life to continue not by begetting but by giving our eyes or hearts or kidneys.

CHAPTER XI

THE REALITY OF SOCIETY ACCORDING TO ST. THOMAS

The individual man, and he alone, remains the final earthly goal of all social action, of all politics. This goal, however, can only be reached by recognizing the reality of society and its own goals. But this goal is founded in the individual welfare. The duties which we have toward society are real duties; they bind us with the same moral force as those toward individuals, for society is no fiction. Yet, it remains an instrument for the fulfillment of the individual's fate.

In my opinion, individualism is today no longer an important doctrine. The great debate behind the conflict of the parties and, unfortunately, the thunder of bombs, the essential debate concerning man's place in society is taking place between the doctrines of Aristotle and Hegel. It has seldom been so clear in history as it is today what a terrible formative and destructive force the great philosophies can be. -- [J. M. Bochenski, Philosophy: An Introduction. New York, Harper Torchbooks, 1972, p. 101.]

Throughout these analyses of political history and its perennial issues, from classical to medieval political theory, there is a fundamental issue which cannot be avoided by any political philosophy. This is the question of the reality of society. Everything turns on this ultimate issue, namely, whether the individual person is merely a "part" of a higher whole, or whether the structure of society itself is founded on the meaning and destiny of the individual person. It would be difficult to underestimate the importance of confronting this problem properly. All political philosophy depends upon the sort of answer we give to this question. Medieval political theory, particularly that of St. Thomas Aquinas, is, indeed, quite fully capable of clarifying what is at issue in this area. All other questions of human freedom and destiny depend upon the manner this issue is resolved.

In the history of political philosophy, two ideas keep recurring about the reality of civil and voluntary society. These ideas are both substantially wrong, quite dangerous, but still easily intelligible. One of the intellectual tasks of each generation of particularly Christian philosophy is to identify and isolate these ideas so that they do not undermine the possibility of faith and the truth of classical metaphysics to which they are opposed. These ideas are, first, that the state has ontological, substantial "being" transcending the individual human persons which compose it and, secondly, by contrast, that the state and other societies have no "being" at all but are merely mental fictions imposed on absolutely disparate reality by the subjective mind and will. The first is broadly Hegelian, the second nominalist and individualist.

Perhaps the name Otto Gierke more than any other in this century, with his curiously great effort to establish the ontological idea of a personality to undergird the reality of corporate law and society, comes to mind here. In retrospect, as the name Gierke also suggests, this seems to be a question somehow intimately related to medieval theory. The contemporary neglect of the force of medieval theory is understandable only within a discipline that sees the alternative between corporate entity and individualism as an exclusive one, one without further intellectual tools with which to deal with society. Gierke himself seems to have been aware that this was the case:

> As in Antiquity, so also in the Middle Ages, the idea of Organic Society failed to issue into the legal idea of Personality -- the single Personality of the group -- and yet it is only when this process has taken place that the idea which is before us becomes of service in legal science. Therefore, it is that medieval doctrine, despite all the analogies that it drew from organic life, might occasionally conceal, but not permanently hinder, the progress of a mode of thought which regards the state as a mechanism constructed of atoms. Indeed, that mode of thought lay in the womb of

medieval theory.[1]

   If we note, however, what Gierke was really
objecting to in medieval theory, we see that for him,
it failed becuase it did <u>not</u>, in spite of certain
tendencies, result in grounding the special
ontological status of the group which he felt
necessary to justify society and state. What it is
that in fact prevented medieval thought from going in
this way deserves attention in this study. Gierke, by
contrast, was looking for some justification for the
reality of the social group over against the rising
individualism of early modern political theory. He
stood in the Hegelian tradition by holding that social
well-being required the subsumption of the individual
into a proper ontological supposit beyond the
individual.[2]

   Currently, there are two types of inheritors to
this tradition over against the human person and his
ontological status. The one is socialist-Marxist, the
other ecological, both of which seek, in essence, to
discover a real social "being." Any natural law theory
based on a concept of the human person for whom
metaphysical dignity as such is not totally to be a
"part" of a whole, of some supra-personal entity,
however it be designated, is rejected.[3] The Hegelian
overtones of the socialist-Marxist tradition are
perhaps well enough known. The manner in which, in
the modern era, they have most come to the fore has to
do with the legitimacy of "sacrificing" one class or
person or nation in order that some corporate whole --
the classless society, for example -- might achieve
what is described as it "proper being" down the ages.

   In one sense, the current popularity of
"distributive" justice, perhaps best known from John
Rawls' <u>A Theory of Justice</u>, though itself rather more
Kantian, is to be located in the search for some sort
of "being" beyond the existing individuals. Rawls, in
a sense, has produced a counter-creation theory. That
is, he supposes justice to be the highest virtue --
the form -- as well as the virtue that ought to be
most operative in reality.[4] Behind this, there is a
kind of Platonism, with a form of its own being, which
bears the judging reality of justice on the rest of
reality. The socialist-Marxist tradition, however, is
usually based upon the classic tradition of the
primacy of man. That is, nature and creation are to
be judged in the light of man's being and purposes,
even if it be a collective being of some ontological

standing. This "generic" being is human and social, as Marx had already postulated in his <u>Economic and Philosophical Manuscripts of 1844</u>.

Contemporary ecology, on the other hand, insofar as it seeks a philosophical explanation for its positions, looks for an ethic or power that would harness classic individualism and socialism because ecology sees both of these generally to be products of the Aristotelian-Christian-Baconian idea of science in the service of man. There is, consequently, the need of a metaphysic that would justify the subordination of man to a non-divine reality higher than himself, to which human action, presumably, is to be directed. This reality is generally conceived to be the ongoing nature-system of the order of time which includes no hierarchy within all the grades of being. Thus it places man within a complexus which he must serve. Jonas Salk, in <u>The Survival of the Wisest</u>, sought to make mankind conform to this voluntarily, as a sign of wisdom. But the "being" of which Salk wrote so often and insistently allowed for no concept of personality that would transcend in structure or destiny the ongoing earthly-cosmic system.[5]

"Imagining that life continues in some form after death is a harmless faith", Salk wrote,

> so long as it does not promise rewards for otherwise avoidable deprivations in life on earth. Ethical or moral systems based on promises for which proof of reward cannot be established permit the exploitation of man's capacity to believe to the point where he is rendered ineffective, victimized in the development and expression of his <u>Being</u>.[6]

This is, in effect, the position of Marsilius of Padua, in the late Middle Ages, in which the reality of the spirit is reduced to a point of disappearance in the real world that, supposedly, is the exclusive field of the scientist or politician.[7] Ironically, however, the alternative to "life after death" in the classic sense, which Salk opposed, yielded in his theory to the "life after death" of the ongoing species and natural system, whose survival became the ethical norm to which man was to yield his being permanently. This ongoing system becomes in fact the only being that is real.[8]

"The order of nature ... is the best source of

social morality we can have", Professor Laszlo has
written.

> Nothing man-made can compare with it.
> The starry heavens above and the morality
> within were what amazed Kant, and we must
> establish the connection between these two.
> The starry heavens, as indeed all nature, is
> not the mechanical, soulless machine
> imagined by the Newtonian conception. The
> moral agent confronting it is not its
> spectator, passively marvelling at its
> workings. The agent here, and nature all
> around, are part of one embracing network of
> dynamic, self-regulating and self-creative
> processes....

> To be part of nature is to have a
> reason for existence. To be one of the most
> evolved systems in nature is reason enough
> for self-confidence and the wish to live and
> propagate. We are not alone; we are in
> nature....[9]

What is important in this kind of "ethic" in the
present context is the subordination of man to nature
in the hierarchy of being. The effect of this is to
allow a reversal of ethical and metaphysical priority
which grew up under the Aristotelian-Christian
tradition that decided the unique function of man. In
Salk's presentation, rather, the ongoing reality of
nature is able to determine the nature of man and, it
is not to be overlooked, to provide the same "motives"
once described by a theory of personal transcendence.
The supposit man is reduced. Man is conceived as not
surviving after death so that there is no finality to
his being except the total natural system.

The "individualist" reaction to these
collectivist tinged theories is becoming more and more
vigorous in a manner rather superior to the earlier
theories of individualism against which collectivism
grew up in the nineteenth and early twentieth
centuries. In a remarkable study, In Defence of the
Corporation, Professor Robert Hessen noted the
relation and nature of recent attacks on the
corporation to the Maitland-Gierke thesis of the state
and corporation.[10] Ralph Nader in particular, in a
well-orchestrated plan, has insisted in the name of
the public good that the modern business corporation
has no proper existence apart from the state. That

Nader should take this tack is of especial interest in the present context of the reality of society. For Nader, the corporation is a complete creature of the state, or at least the large ones are. Professor Hessen rightly suggested that individuals can create voluntary organizations whose ultimate justification and reality are independent of the state. These are organizations that arise from a proper freedom of the individuals to define and pursue goals arising out of that same freedom. Such organizations are limited and defined by their purposes. The state may have something to say, of abuses, by virtue of its own limited ends, but the essential disorder is the reduction of the vast area of freedom to state functionings.

Robert Nozick's <u>Anarchy, State, and Utopia</u> has vigorously argued a similar position against John Rawls. The alternative to some theory of collective or form-being located in nature or society is the power of the will to choose what is best for it and to associate freely with others to achieve ends which the state neither creates or justifies. Nozick is not a classic individualist in the pejorative sense. He is careful to establish the case for difference and inequality of talent and rewards in terms that do not depend on injustice. He has argued that contemporary distributionist theories in fact do become unjust by failing to understand the implications of freedom.

> The minimum state treats us as inviolate individuals, who may not be used in certain ways by others as means or tools or instruments; it treats us as persons having individual rights with the dignity this constitutes. Treating us with respect by respecting our rights, it allows us individually and with whom we choose, to choose our life and to realize our ends and our conception of ourselves, insofar as we can, aided by the voluntary cooperation of other individuals possessing the same dignity.[11]

Nozick's theory, at one level at least, seems to ignore the metaphysical basis upon which human dignity exists in the first place; this view results in a "will" able to create whatever agreed upon.

But, granting this problem, Nozick's "individualism", with its logical insistence on keeping the state in a properly defined place, is quite close to the older, and too much neglected, Catholic theory of "subsidiarity".(Quadragesimo Anno, 1931) This principle held that no authority or organization within society should be subsumed into a higher, especially state level, unless clear rational proof existed that the common good required it.[12] Nozick tried to establish a rational ground within modern philosophic tradition to prevent the theoretical subsumption of all organizations into the state's direct control in the name of justice. Finally, he argued that the basis of this limitation was freedom, whose rational effects were to produce, without injustice, a great diversity of structures, rewards, and contributions, the kind of diversity that Aristotle argued against Plato was necessary even to have a state in the first place.

Both Nozick and Hessen have rightly sensed the overtones of a "supra-being" that often envelops theories that rely on the state to subsume and justify all organisms within it. On the other hand, neither goes into the more metaphysical question of why the state or voluntary society, which depends upon and results from human nature and will, has a status which would explain why resulting orders, laws, or arrangements are not merely fictitious. The question, in other words, is what is the "reality" of society? And this is a question that was perhaps best analyzed, in medieval theory, by Aquinas himself. The neglect of medieval theory is, indeed, a theoretical choice. Its metaphysical background underscores what is wrong with both individualist and collectivist positions which subordinate man either to a supra-substantial whole, however it be described, or to man himself defined merely as will which itself has no intrinsic rule discovered or revealed to which he ought freely to conform in his activities.

To present more specifically how the Thomist tradition would approach the question of the "reality" of society, it might be best to state in rapid form the essential background positions that serve to clarify this philosophy. These are:

1. Society is not a supposit.

2. Society is real.

3. Society pertains to the actions of men, which actions have being.

241

4. Society is the order of actions, not the actions themselves.

5. The end of society is the common good.

6. The form of society is a common good.

7. The common good indicates the best order of human nature's actions.

8. Society is necessary to man that he achieve his end, the good life.

9. Actions of men in the external order receive their objective rightness from their proportion, direct or indirect, to the common good.

10. The unity of society is from the end through the form.

11. The so-called action of society does not mean that society is a supposit, because only persons are responsible for actions.

12. Society demands a multiplicity of supposits.

Such observations require one outstanding question to be answered: what is the relation between the individual and the common good? There is a great amount of controversy over this problem.[13] The difficulty, however, is not in the realm of theory as much as in the order of practical politics. The common good can never be opposed to the individual good of a person, for the one demands the other. However, what some particular government or voluntary society might claim to be de facto the common good of the group may not be the real common good, and one's obligation is always an everywhere to the real common good.

But who is to say what the real common good is? Obviously, the government, or better the people through the government. Yet, such can and do err; and when they do so, the obligation, generally speaking, is to the common good and not to the erring government or people. Since, however, man, not society or state, is the being in the substantial order, it is not correct to say that the common good is the ultimate end of men. The political common good does not satisfy all the potencies of man, nor is it the good to which men ultimately tend. It deals with moral virtues which are ordered to higher powers:

> Human happiness is not ordainable to a further end if it be the highest. However, every operation of a moral nature is ordainable to do something else. This is clear from outstanding characteristics from among the moral virtues. For the operations of bravery, which are for wartime, are ordained to victory and to peace. It would be foolish if to fight would be only for itself. Likewise, the operations of justice are ordained to keep peace among men. Through this each possesses in peace what is his. Likewise, it is clear among other virtues.(III Contra Gentiles, 35.)

How then is it that man must seek the common good if his end is a personal and apparently private good? Why not just seek that? After all, the common good of a society as such deals only with acquired virtues, not the more important infused virtues which really deal with man's ultimate end. "...The good of civil society is not the ultimate end of the infused cardinal virtues, about which we speak, but of acquired virtues...."(De Virtutibus Cardinalibus, 4, ad 3.)

The common good and a man's true personal good are not, however, contradictory but correlative. Indeed, the one requires the other. That is why St. Thomas can say simply that the common good is to be preferred to the proper good.[14] A man's personal good is only perfectly developed insofar as he deals with others. The man who neglects this truth, neglects his personhood. For from the mere fact that man is social, it follows that this perfection as a human being must be accomplished in society, that is, by seeking the common good according to which all of his actions are correctly ordered.[15] Man cannot neglect the society of others and remain human. He must consider himself as part of many multitudes, and he must remember that his perfection demands his acting with others.

> ... He who seeks the common good of the multitude seeks also as a consequence his own good, for two reasons. First indeed, because his own good is not able to be without the common good either of the family

243

or the civil society or the kingdom ...
Secondly because, since man is part of the
home or the civil society, it should be that
man would consider what is his good from
that which is prudent concerning the good of
the multitude: for the good is a disposition
of the part received in relation to the
whole.... (II-II, 47, 10, ad 2.)

Thus, it is natural to the human person to be
perfected in society so that the quality of the person
who looks to the absolute depends upon how that man
looked to society. It is true, of course, that some
can reach and in fact do reach the ultimate personal
end of man without ever seeing society, consciously at
least. But the problem here is rather one of the
ultimate perfection of man in every order. It is a
consideration of the finality of the nature as such.
Such a finality does demand society for the good of
the man himself. The real opposition between the
common good and the private one is really one of
particular circumstances.[16]

But the ontological reality of society remains to
be considered in this context. Aquinas' approach to
this question is of great interest in the context of
social theory. St. Thomas, in several places,
parenthetically remarked that society is not a
supposit or else that it has no substantial form,
which comes to the same thing. The proper category in
which to place the reality of society in the Thomist
analysis is not that of substantial being but of
relation. Aquinas did not explicitly affirm that
society is a relation, although he did call it an
order.[17] But there is little doubt that the category
of relation alone explains the various facts about
society that need to be accounted for.

A relation is real, in St. Thomas, if the
subjects, the terms, and the basis of the relation are
real. "...In things in which relations are accidents,
it follows that relation presupposes a
distinction...."(De Potentia Dei, 10, 3, ad 4.) "There
is a real relation where something really depends on
another, either simply or relatively...."(De Potentia
Dei, 7, a, ad 9. See also I, 13, 7.) Society fulfills
all these requirements. It demands many distinct
persons, and it demands them acting. Therefore, a
certain relation must of necessity exist among men.
These relations, however, are accidents in created
beings; they do not themselves constitute persons as

244

they do in God. "... Relations in human affairs do not constitute persons, since relations are accidents; person however is something subsisting in the genus of substance...."(De Potentia Dei, 10, 3. See also 8, 3, ad 7)

This ultimately, then, is why Gierke and all theories based upon some sort of superior being in nature or society are incorrect, because relations are not persons in created beings. But it also explains why the temptation to substantialize society is so alluring. For relations are persons in God.(Trinity) There is truly an accountable connection between relation and person. Thus, it is not surprising that a human mind, making only an initial error, would be strongly attracted to the position that society is a person, or that some superior being beyond it decides its true reality in this world.

Society, therefore, exists in subjects, in persons; it is not a tertium quid. It is true that in forming an idea of society, the human mind does tend to think of it as separate from the men who compose it. This tendency is further enhanced by the institutions, buildings, and other instrumentalities of existing authority. It is also enhanced by the fact that relations according to the human way of knowing must be formalized to be understood even though they themselves be not forms. Yet, the multitude does exist in the many, not outside of it. "...Just as a multitude outside the many is nothing except in reason, contrarily a multitude in many is also in the nature of things: just as also common animal is not except in reason, the nature of animal is in singular beings...."(De Potentia Dei, 3, 16, ad 16.) Relations, then, are accidents of subjects, of subsisting persons, so that society exists in the persons who compose it.

The esse or reality of a relation, however, is peculiar. Relation, "ad aliud", of itself is indifferent to existence in the sense that the relation can be in se or in alio. If the relation is in alio, as it is in the case of all relations except those of the Trinity, its esse is inesse. That is, its being is dependent on the reality of a being already subsisting together with its operation. The relation's being is not of itself ad aliud, but the being in which the relation exists is ad aliud. "... Since relation is an accident in creatures, their being is to be 'in'; hence its esse is not to be

245

related to another; but to be this way according to being <u>ad aliud</u>, is to relate itself to another."(<u>De Potentia Dei</u>, 8, 12, ad 12.) This is why society must be said to exist in persons since the relation does not have being of itself but only in a subject.

It has been held in these reflections that order is a relation or a series of relations. Society indicates this order. Thus, beings must not only be considered absolutely in themselves but in their relation to others. This implies an order in which these beings stand to one another in their actions, as the example of an army indicates whose good depends on its order. Society, then, indicates the order which exists among the active powers of men as such.

> If however relation would not be in things outside the mind, we would not be able to place a type of predicate of relation. And moreover perfection and good which are in things outside the soul, are not only attended to according to something absolute inhering in things, but also according to the order of one thing to another, just as in the order of parts of an army does its good consist ... Therefore, there ought to be in things themselves some order. This order, however, is a certain relation. Whence in things themselves, relations have some sort of being according to which one is related to another. One thing is ordered to another however according to quantity, or active virtue or passive virtue. From this it follows that only in two things can we attend to something in one, with respect to its extrinsic status. (<u>De Potentia Dei</u>, 7, 9.)

Incidently, this also explains why there can be no society among the beasts, for they do not see the end of their activity nor do they act freely. Hence, the order of their activity falls under natural providence and not society, under what St. Thomas called <u>fatum</u>.

The total reality of society comes from the fact that as a relation, it exists in a subject. Yet, this presents the problem of the continuance of society. In a sense, this latter is why ecologists can argue that the "being" that bears the individuals on in nature is the real norm. St. Thomas has said that a city was instituted to last through the succession of time. "... Neither is it ordered that it last only a certain period, but that it be preserved in all time through the succession of citizens, as Augustine said...." (I-II, 96, 1.) Why does not society change when its members change? For a relation stops when its subjects cease to be, or when the foundation of the relation ceases.[18] Obviously, every sixty or so years, societies completely change their subjects, yet it is said that the same society endures.

In one sense, of course, the order of society constantly is found to exist in different supposits, in different persons. In this sense, it is true to speak of a constantly changing society. Indeed, this fact must always be remembered if society is to avoid traditionalism and stagnancy. The change in particular individuals will demand society constantly readapt itself to this change in the new subjects of its existence. Consequently, when Aquinas said that the state lasts through the succession of time, he did not intend to imply that society is some sort of rigid form standing outside of the citizens that compose it. Rather he meant that the general type of order set up among a given group was meant to be followed by successive groups of men. But the actual order would exist in the men themselves. Society never changes all at once, but gradually, so that some die, others come to be, according to the order established for it by what Aristotle called it rule or regime.

This, then, was the position of St. Thomas on the reality of society. He always interpreted society in the light of his metaphysics and his psychology. He was not tempted to make society something substantial, something that it was not in the nature of things. The fact that society was a relation, a real one in his accepted sense, prevented him, furthermore, from making of society a mere fiction, something reducible merely to will. The true notion of society is not a mystique; it is not the Divine Idea on earth, as Hegel would have had it. It is not somehow a system beyond the persons who compose it. Indeed, the primacy of person defines its very order.

Thus, the ultimate allegiance of a sound thinker will not be to a state or to a race or to ongoing nature, but rather to a person, to a being who alone is capable of satisfying the desires and the potencies of man. And this person, this being, as Aquinas carefully pointed out in the first question of the Prima Secundae, is nothing less than God. This is why, in this context, nothing can be absolute but God and why all attempts to replace Him by nature or state end up degrading man.

Footnotes:

1. Otto Gierke, Political Theories of the Middle Ages, Cambridge, At the University Press, 1958, pp. 29-30.

2. "The Doctrine of Corporations, which was so often cited in this context, was ready to supply the idea of a Juristic Person, and a due consideration of the nature of Church and State might have induced a transmutative process which would have turned the Persona Ficta of professional jurisprudence into the concept of a really existing Group-Personality. Already the Church was conceived, and so was the State, as an organic Whole which, despite its composite character, was a single Being, and the thought might have occurred that the Personality of the Individual consists in a similar permanent Substance within an Organism. Nothing of this sort happened...." ibid., p. 68.

3. See Jacques Maritain, "Individual and Person," The Social and Political Philosophy of Jacques Maritain, London, Bles, 1956, pp. 21-27.

4. John Rawls, A Theory of Justice, Cambridge, Harvard University Press, 1971.

5. Jonas Salk, The Survival of the Wisest, New York, Harper, 1972. See Raymond Dennehy, Reason and Dignity, Washington, University Press of America, 1981.

6. Ibid., p. 85.

7. See Marsilius of Padua, Defensor Pacis, Edited by A. Gewirth, New York, Columbia University Press, 1952; Leo Strauss, "Marsilius of Padua," History of Political Philosophy, L. Strauss and J. Cropsey, Editors, 1972, pp. 251-70.

8. Salk, ibid., p. 96.

9. Ervin Laszlo, "Reverence for Natural Systems: A Social Ethic for the Age of Mankind," in Emergent Man, Edited by Stulman and Laszlo, New York, Gordon and Breach, 1973, p. 66. See also Mark Reader, "Energy and Global Ethics," The Humanist, July-August, 1979, pp. 21-23.

10. Robert Hessen, In Defence of the Corporation,

Stanford, California, Hoover Institution Press, 1979, p. 25.

11. Robert Nozick, <u>Anarchy, State, and Utopia</u>, New York, Basic, 1974, pp. 333-34.

12. See James V. Schall, "Rethinking the Nature of Government," <u>Modern Age</u>, Spring, 1979. In this connection also, it is worth citing Professor Elizabeth Anscombe: "This is one of the fundamental questions of political theory: are we to understand civil authority as arising by a transfer of rights already possessed by men without a state? Those who maintain this always assume a private right of punishment in a state of nature. We deny this and take the alternative view: civil society is the bearer of rights of coercion not possibly existent among men without government." "On the Source of Authority of the State," <u>Ratio</u>, Oxford, June, 1978, p. 19. Professor Anscombe's remark is the precise point of the weakness of the will-individualist theses insofar as they do not see the new relation arising because of the very existence of civil society. See also Johannes Messner, <u>Social Ethics: Natural Law in the Western World</u>, St. Louis, Herder, 1965; Rodger Charles, <u>The Social Teachings of Vatican II</u>, San Francisco, Ignatius Press, 1982.

13. See for example, Charles deKoninck, "In Defence of St. Thomas: A Reply to Father Eschmann's Attack on the Primacy of the Common Good," <u>Laval Théologique et Philosophique</u>, # 2, 1945, pp. 9-109.

14. "Considerandum est autem quod bonum commune secundum rectam rationem est bono proprio praeferendum: unde unaquaeque pars naturali quodam instinctu ordinatur ad bonum totius...." <u>De Perfectione Vitae Spiritualis</u>, Chapter 13 (Parma, Vol. 14, p. 87).

15. "Et quia homo secundum suam naturam est animal politicum, virtutes hujusmodi (politicae), prout in homine existunt secundum conditionem suae naturae, politicae vocantur: prout scilicet homo secundum has virtutes recte se habet in rebus humanis gerendis," I-II, 61, 5.

16. I, 76, 2; II <u>Contra Gentiles</u>, 73 and 75; <u>De Spiritualibus Creaturis</u>, q. 9; <u>Q. de Anima</u>, 3.

17. In I <u>Ethics</u>, n. 5. For a thorough and

insightful discussion on the notion of relations in St. Thomas, see Clifford G. Kossel, S. J.'s four essays in <u>Modern Schoolman</u>, January, 1946, pp. 61-81; November, 1946, pp. 19-30; January, 1947, pp. 93-107; and March, 1948, pp. 151-72. For a recent discussion of society as a relation, see the brilliant study of the Polish Thomist Mieczylaw A. Krapiec, <u>I-Man: An Outline of Philosophical Anthropology</u>, New Britain, CT., Mariel, 1983, pp. 248-52.

18. "... Relatio aliqua desinit esse dupliciter. Uno modo ex corruptione subjecti; alio modo ex subtractione causae," In IV <u>Sententiis</u>, d. 41, q. 1, art. 1, sol. 2.

CHAPTER XII

ON THE DISAPPEARANCE OF MERCY FROM POLITICAL THEORY

> (Pope) Alexander VI did nothing else
> but deceive men, he thought of nothing else,
> and found occasion for it; no man was ever
> more able to give assurances, or affirmed
> things with stronger oaths, and no man
> observed them less; however, he always
> succeeded well in his deceptions, as he well
> knew this aspect of things.
>
> It is not, therefore, necessary for a
> prince to have all the above-named
> qualities, but it is very necessary to seem
> to have them. I would even be bold to say
> that to possess them and always to observe
> them is dangerous, but to possess them is
> useful. Thus, it is well to seem merciful,
> faithful, sincere, religious, and also to be
> so; but you must have the mind so disposed
> that when it is needed to be otherwise, you
> may be able to change to the opposite
> qualities. -- [Machiavelli, The Prince,
> Chapter XVIII, 1513.]
>
> The present-day mentality ... seems
> opposed to a God of mercy, and in fact,
> tends to exclude from life and to remove
> from the human heart the very idea of
> mercy. -- [John Paul II, Dives in
> Misericordia, #2, 1980.]

The relationship of medieval to modern political
theory is an object of intellectual analysis of the
greatest moment. For an adequate understanding, this
must be seen against a background of such transcendent
questions as heaven and hell, the reason for the
limits of human law, the metaphysical grounding of the
human person and its relation to civil society. If,
moreover, faith and reason were not "contradictory"
but in fact co-existed in a common culture, whose
faith element, however obscure, was an active factor
in ongoing human affairs, then it could be suggested
that social institutions will radically change if and

when that same faith which supported them should decline and disappear.

On its theological side, Western religion has long argued not merely to the natural validity of the human reason in its own integrity, but also to its limits. This meant essentially that while the human intellect was properly "an intellect", it was not a "divine" intellect. Put differently, this meant that there were certain realities, which, while perhaps present in actual human culture, were not directly under the gaze of the unaided human intellect, even though they were not "opposed" to its basic structure and function. Essentially, the inner life of God, what this life consisted in even when revealed to human intelligence, fell under this heading.

This did not mean, to be sure, as Professor Ralph McInerny in his book on St. Thomas Aquinas pointed out, that this same revelation, as if to guarantee its own integrity to its hearers, did not contain also at least some truths that could be directly proved by reason.[1] (This was, in fact, what Thomas Aquinas did in his Summa Contra Gentiles). Nor did it mean, as Josef Pieper so cogently argued, that what was addressed to mankind from revelation did not itself, when dutifully reflected upon, cause man to think better, since the source of revelation and of intellect itself was the divine intelligence communicating to human intelligence in word and deed.[2] Whatever one might think about the truth of this revelation in retrospect, there could be no doubt about its essential outline, its form, its intelligibility, what, in the minds of the medievals themselves, was considered to be its effect in the world itself.

From the medieval view of political theory, there were present in human reality transcendent sources of intelligible order and action, personal and social, that resulted in real growth of the human good. There were new and original institutions that appeared which were not simply reducible to politics, however valid politics as such might remain. Proposals arising at the very origins of political philosophy as somehow naturally connected with a rational pursuit of "what justice is," often turned out by themselves to be somehow aberrant when carried into practice or even thought out in speculation. (See Chapter IV)

Yet, these same ideas, within a philosophical

254

reflection following on revelation, found their proper place and rational limits. The "correct" theory in a sense was derived not from "pure" theory by itself, which somehow went wrong in its own purity, but from the facts of revelation as they worked themselves out in religious and cultural life. "Christian philosophy" arose precisely in this context.[3]

The inner life of God, as can be seen in St. Augustine's _De Trinitate_ and St. Thomas' _Summa Theologica_, however, was a very delicate and profound theoretical issue even in revelation.[4] The inner life of God was not considered to be the immediate direct purpose of revelation. Rather, it was a reflection on this direct purpose which concerned men and their ultimate destiny before this inner life of God. This was the final goal of revelation.

The medieval revelational tradition itself, then, considered its most important impact upon human action, the proper area of politics, to be in the order of grace, charity, and mercy. These were looked upon as the voluntary consequences in the human creatures themselves of the communication of the inner life of God as a gift to each individual person through revelation. The purpose of this revelation, in its own terms, was the final salvation of each unique human person, not the restructuring of the political order or a guidance in scientific methodology, though these latter endeavors were not seen as necessarily opposed to the religious endeavor.

What is undoubtedly most well-known about the revelational tradition, and what is thus most directly pertinent to political theory, is its teaching about charity and mercy. These are, in effect, the same realities looked upon from different conditions in which the divine life reaches individual persons in their particularities. Charity and mercy, moreover, inhered in the human will in such a fashion that real objects of love could be recognized and acted upon, objects which would, without this something more, simply not be seen or responded to.

"Grace", therefore, meant that, since human beings were finite, intelligent creatures, their very capacity to "see" and "do" certain actions proper to the inner life of God, that is, to be charitable or merciful, required an un-merited elevation by God of the very being of man to enable humans to accomplish

255

what they would not otherwise do. To be received, grace required human freedom, but man did not "give" himself somehow elevated powers. This meant, in medieval thinking, that there were powers at work in the world which were oriented toward the ultimate and temporal good of each human person, but which were not simply the result of unaided human reasoning or power.

Both charity and mercy, then, meant literally loving oneself and one's neighbor with the kind of love (described episodically in the scriptures) proper to the internal being of God, a love which, in the life and death of Christ, showed itself to be sacrificial when it appeared visibly among men. Life was thus to be freely laid down for one's friends, even for one's enemies. This involved no necessary quid pro quo, no strict rational justice, either implied or demanded. Mercy was charity looked upon in the context of a violation of justice already having occurred as the result of actual human freedom. Mercy and sacrificial love took on definite meaning before the enormity of the free creatures' violations of the human person's existential dignity.

Part of the revelation of goodness, therefore, was a greater recognition of what violated it in its human condition. Thus, forgiveness, the power to stop vengeance from going on and on in human society, the inability of justice to be itself adequate, was the consequence of this grace, charity, and mercy. But forgiveness did not become an effort to define evil as a good. Revelation was not an exercise in overturning all standards. Rather it was a manner of responding to evil, now better understood, but responding in a manner unexpected by reason itself, thought not ultimately incomprehensible to it.[5]

The point of the discussion here is that modern political theory is unavoidably influenced by the intellectual background of the medieval enterprise, but in ways that are not, perhaps, easily ascertained without understanding what culturally existed in the medieval period. Paradoxically, and this is what will be argued here, modern political theory is not simply a reversal to classical Greek contexts, nor is it a new, "independent" theoretical discovery of the unaided human intellect. Rather it is an effort to justify goals and values originally formulated under the impetus of revelation but now recast in strictly human intellectual terms confined to political philosophy as such. By not attending to the fact that the very goals posed within modern political theory were themselves arrived at through reason and revelation, this meant that modern political theory became a kind of covert "theology" now cut off from any transcendental sources. Autonomous political theory came to claim for itself the power totally to comprehend the human.

The disappearance of the quality of mercy from modern culture, particularly from political theory is the context in which to analyze modern political theory. How is this to be understood? Why is this disappearance particularly a problem for political philosophy? Fundamentally, the reason is because the loss of mercy seen as a supernatural gift has paved the way for the rise of a secular "compassion" or "benevolence." This lies at the heart of the peculiar sort of absolute state produced by the decline of modern liberalism into an all-embracing statism or socialism, however it be defined.

The question, then, arises: how has the virtue of mercy, out of its natural context in religion, turned upon the limited natural order of politics? In becoming the objects of man's own contemplation, rather than the "higher things" of which Aristotle spoke (1072b14ff; 1141a20ff), human societies have served to politicize all areas of human life. Man no longer contemplates what is there in metaphysical being, but what he puts there by his own power.

Since initial revelation addressed itself to intellect, it was easy for men to think that some things were "natural" whereas they were not. What takes the place of mercy, however, is not "nothing" but rather, an attempt to accomplish graced and elevated ends and motives by what remains to man relying this time really on himself, on politics ultimately. This is not to confuse the "ordinary" with the "miraculous". But to the medieval mind, not only was the "ordinary" in some sense "miraculous," but something more than the ordinary was habitually in the world. This latter caused many things to come to be in the world which, within this cultural context, seemed to be "normal" or "reasonable." Mercy was one of these "normal" expectations.

In the medieval sense, then, even the ordinary is rooted in the extraordinary, or as Aquinas put it, the world was created in mercy, not justice.(I, 21, 4)

257

Thus, the abundant came before the sufficient, the giving before the taking. Yet, in its modern context, this very idea of "mercy" has come somehow to have lethal connotations, by evolving into a concept of "human rights" capable of being used to eliminate anything that could not be expected to live a normal life, anything not itself perfect. "Mercy" ironically has come to be a word commonly applied to the word "killing." "Compassion," as Joseph Sobran has pointed out, has come to be a tool whereby particularity is suppressed in the name of a group or class within the political organization responsible for "merciful" or "compassionate" activities.[6]

The so-called "modern project" was very perceptively analyzed by Professor Leo Strauss, who understood that modern political theory has in fact something to do with charity or mercy. Hannah Arendt, again, had perceived that the unique political contribution to the world by Jesus was not so much His doctrine of love, which as such was worldless, but His doctrine of forgiveness following on it. This allowed the political world to cease from the cycle of vengeance, the normal result of imperfect justice, if not of justice itself.[7] Leo Strauss put it this way:

> According to the modern project, philosophy or science was no longer to be understood as essentially contemplative and proud but as active and charitable; it was to be in the service of the relief of man's estate; it was to be cultivated for the sake of human power; it was to enable man to become the master and owner through the intellectual conquest of nature.[8]

What is to be remarked about Strauss' analysis in this context is that philosophy conceived itself to have become "charitable," a theological word. But now it is used not as a manifestation of gratitutious grace, but of mastered human power. The intellect by itself was to conquer nature. That is to say, there was nothing other than human intellect in being. This meant that the final causes were thought of as replaceable by human forms imposed on an infinitely malleable nature, including, eventually, human nature.[9]

The intellect, in the Aristotelian sense, then, was to "know" nature and to "change" it in accordance with human ends, themselves not subject to the variability of the human will. Thus, the human intellect did not create nature or substitute its own norms for the teleology discovered in nature to which the intellect was to conform if it were to know the truth. Charity and mercy, however, mean something quite different if the intellect is presupposed to no end but its own making. This is why, in the 20th Century, the most terrible crimes were often committed in the name of kindness, compassion, or mercy, because abstract perfectionism was substituted for the concrete being of individual persons in all their variety and weakness. (See Chapter XI) These latter sorts of beings were the recipients of revelation, not "perfect" human forms.

In medieval thought, what imposed limits on the human mind in all its aspects was reality itself, which was what it was and nothing else. Theories of agnosticism were seen to undermine any theories of limit, be it in politics or in science, because in them what was "known" was only what was inside the certain individual human or collective mind. There was no reality that indicated what exists to the human mind. Agnosticism thus was capable of becoming a sort of reverse omnipotence. C. S. Lewis, at the end of his remarkable book on the medieval experience, The Discarded Image, clarified the question which Professor Strauss raised about the modern project conceived in terms of a secular mercy.

"Literature exists," Lewis observed,

> to teach what is useful, to honour what deserves honour, to appreciate what is delightful. The useful, the honourable, the delightful are things superior to it: it exists for their sake; its own use, however, or delightfulness is derivative from them. In this great change, something has been won and something lost. I take it to be part and parcel of the same great process of Internalization which has turned genius from an attendant daemon into a quality of the mind. Always, century by century, item after item is transformed from the object's side of the account to the subject's. And now in some extreme forms of Behaviourism, the subject himself is discounted as merely subjective; we only think what we think. Having eaten up everthing else, he eats himself up too. And where we 'go from that'

is a dark question.[10]

The reason this "dark question" needed elaboration in the context of the intellectual importance of mercy and charity in this history of political theory was that the unique person, the basis of all medieval theory, evaporated before our very eyes in the name of political benevolence.

Doubts about the human capacity to know the whole truth about mankind, which would include the input of the revelational tradition as itself intelligible in some sense to the human intellect, however, have led to skepticism about whether the human mind can know anything at all. For if the intellect does know, certain things follow about natural limits and order. This is what is rejected in modern theory about human ends. Ironically, this methodological doubt about the human capacity to define anything human as certainly true is the basis for that monstrous aggrandizement which allows mankind to put all its moral passion into the project of creating a "truth" subject only to itself.[11]

In a passage of extraordinary insight in his famous essay, "What Is Political Philosophy?", Professor Strauss suggested why liberal moral passion, lacking an object worthy of its force, resulted in an absolutism. He indicated also why the existence of charity and mercy in the past culture has paradoxically resulted in a totalitarian justice within a secularized society, why, in other words, the whole project of political philosophy must be rethought. In criticizing terms rather reminiscent of much current religious rhetoric of "social sin" or "reformation of structures," of justice and revolutionary theology, often themselves functions of modern ideology, Strauss wrote:

> What you need is not so much formation of character and moral appeal, as the right kind of institutions, institutions with teeth in them. The shift from formation of character to trust in the institutions is the characteristic corollary of the belief in the almost infinite malleability of man.

> In Machiavelli's teaching, we have the first example of a spectacle which has renewed itself in almost every generation since. A fearless thinker seems to have

260

opened up a depth from which the classics, in their noble simplicity, recoiled. As a matter of fact, there is in the whole work of Machiavelli not a single true observation regarding the nature of man and human affairs with which the classics were not thoroughly familiar. An amazing contraction of the horizon presents itself as an amazing enlargement of the horizon. How can we account for this delusion?

By Machiavelli's time, the classical tradition had undergone profound changes. The contemplative life had found its home in the monasteries. Moral virtue had been transfigured into Christian charity. Through this, man's responsibility to his fellow man and for his fellow men, his fellow creature, had been infinitely increased. Concern for the salvation of men's immortal souls seemed to permit, nay, to require courses of action which would have appeared to the classics, and which did appear to Machiavelli, to be inhuman and cruel ... He seems to have diagnosed the great evils of religious persecution as a necessary consequence of the Christian principle, and ultimately of the Biblical principle. He tended to believe that a considerable increase in man's inhumanity was the unintended but not surprising consequence of man's aiming too high.[12]

We would be ill-advised to miss the intellectual force of these remarkable lines, what they imply in terms of political philosophy and Christian intelligence.

On the one side, from the side of the classics, what is suggested is a corruption of the public order because of mercy and charity once they are set loose in the world. This presence is said to corrupt men into striving for goals that cannot be accomplished and thus to undertake power fanatically to achieve them. On the other side, there is the warning about a civil order still retaining unattended to the heightened expectations of man's abilities and generosities which were alive within the revelational tradition. These gradually came to lack the discipline of faith, sacrifice, and sacrament, which were understood in the revelational tradition as necessary for these elevated efforts, aimed very high,

261

to come about.

Thus, having been once told that mankind could anticipate, even on earth, a life of peace and brotherhood, political philosophy was left with the ideal but not the Biblical means to achieve it. That is to say, the nation-state, the product of specifically modern theory, grew in size and ambitions when the charitable offices of the Church were secularized or abandoned by monks and nuns. The modern state assumed offices and aims which had to be fulfilled because of public expectations rooted in religion yet by those who worked to achieve them by ordinary financial or prestige motives, for aims only comprehensible in civil terms. The result has been that the absolute state, not excluding the democratic absolute state, has arisen not against the Christian vision, but precisely in its wake. The distance from the City of God to the Leviathan is not at all far once the City of God is relocated on earth.

This same thesis, perhaps, can best be seen from another related angle whereby the relationship of modern and medieval theory becomes more evident in the disappearance of mercy. This is to note that, even in religious circles, what has taken the place of mercy are "human rights," of a highly nuanced intelligibility, rights which need careful distinction from the ideas contained in medieval natural law theory. The way to alleviate the poor has come more and more to be not merely the "charitable" or "compassionate" technology of the "modern project," but the insistence on certain "rights" and "structures," usually said to be economic and social rather than civil or individual. The poor in this newer type of religious-political attitude were no longer to suffer patiently or work harder. Their self-appointed advocates rather were free to use all means to attack what was considered to be "inhuman conditions."

Religion and goodness, therefore, became an end-product, not a means with their own methods and sources. The politicization of religion itself has contributed to this notion. Indeed, what is to be suggested here, is that this very politicization of religion is leading, ironically, to an empirical rediscovery of charity, because the proposals in the modern era to replace it are not working and cannot work.[13] They are simply too expensive and dangerous if motivated by forces available to the state itself.

262

This latter discovery, interestingly, is coming from neither political theory or from theology, but from cost analysis and policy studies without a theoretical framework in which to grasp its significance.

To the medieval mind, the nearer a person or a society or a family or a friendship approached to authentic charity, to mercy and grace, the more it would distance itself from pure "justice," yet at the same time, it would make justice more real. The social action programs of the modern era, the assumptions of political theory on which they are often based, which have insisted first on justice instead of grace and faith, are exactly the opposite of the orientation of classical Christian medieval theory. No doubt, remnants of charity and even the reason flowing from it remain scattered over the political universe. To identify faith with justice, however, has resulted in eliminating both, a result that paradoxically has justified the positions of a Machiavelli or a Hobbes that calculations of power are all that remains in the public order. There has arisen recently also a sudden non-religious realization that the cost of what is lacking in modern public life is, even in empirical terms, too high.[14]

Christianity as a culture in the Middle Ages did not set itself up "against" justice, of course, however skeptical it might have been about the laws and constitutions that were called "just" in the public order to resolve human goals. Christianity believed rather that justice would exist in a society that was "more" than just, as it believed that among real friends there was more than "justice." In this context, against the background of medieval speculation about political philosophy, what has been most worrisome about the specifically religious climate of the contemporary world has been the disappearance of charity and mercy as theoretical presences to be replaced by "justice" concepts. This has been why it is not surprising to see a sense of their loss arising in those institutions that were most rooted in its origins, those relating to health, education, and general human service.

The complex relation of classical, medieval, modern, and current ideological political theory comes more clearly into focus because of the theoretical implications of the disappearance of mercy -- which is to be distinguished from ideological notions of "benevolence" or "compassion" -- in political theory.

Mercy's unattended demise is, in fact, not a reduction into nothing nor a reversal to the status quo ante. Rather, it implies the substitute erection of an elaborate political-philosophical replacement of what was effected by mercy by means that were not in any sense "graced." This is, no doubt, the force of Eric Voegelin's thesis about the "gnostic" character of specifically modern political theory, since it logically implies this project or effort as a "self-salvation" fully under the control and guidance of human intelligence.[15]

In practice, this must mean, from classical theory, that politics would substitute for mercy, yet without quite realizing what might happen. That is, following Aristotle, if man is the highest being with a theoretically autonomous intellect proposed as his humanizing mission, something Aristotle did not propose, man's highest natural activity then would be the operative solution to the question of what might replace mercy grounded in human reality but originating from sources outside it. Politics would be what must substitute for mercy. But in this context, it would be a politics wholly architectonic, but not merely in regard to the practical intellect, as Aristotle rightly held it should be.

Thus, the human intellect would now conceive itself in control of all natural ends, including those of the natural sciences, since it has no other source but itself in which to ground intelligibility. Moreover, the sciences, still considered to be in some sense "charitable" by the modern mind, will come to be used to make man as he "ought" to be, but now presupposed to no stable essence from the origins of nature. Hence, there will be no "moderation" possible for an intelligence not grounded in given, objective being.

The recent appearance of various proposals for genetic control and engineering of the human psyche and corpus, attacks on the family and property through laws and institutions which deny their classical forms, have come to exist in sophisticated projects in contemporary practice from test-tube babies to female combat soldiers, to the new global economic order.[16] Each of these proposals has an uncanny parallel to an element in The Republic. The question is, why is this so? Professor Allan Bloom had argued, brilliantly, that The Republic of Plato, the classic, elemental book in political theory itself, deliberately proposed such outlandish projects as the communality of wives, children, and property (in whatever form) in order to instil political moderation into human minds thinking on the structure of reality. The very intellectual construct, The Republic, did this by analyzing what justice-in-itself would necessarily mean.[17] The very reading of The Republic served this purpose.[18]

What seems clear, however, is that rather than rejecting this utopian direction on seeing where this intellectual process would lead, modern experience, what could almost be called "post-modern" experience since theory is put into practice, embodies that which undermines the very structure of human reality.[19] Modern practice begins to effect the extremes which Plato felt mankind would reject on their adequate comprehension.

This appearance of the extremes arrives through notions of absolute legal equality, genetic perfectionism, fetal experimentation, and the elevation of state power over all subsidiary institutions. We try to put into effect those very things Plato held would be rejected once their intelligibility was made clear in the mind by sophisticated literary argument. Since the solution of St. Augustine has also been undermined within Christianity itself in the rise of "political theology," we are left with no metaphysical or theological protection from the modern project.[20] The function of political theory is destroyed once its extremes can be put into practice without any recognition of what is beyond theory, once theory is no longer itself "moderate."

The Straussian tradition in political theory has cogently argued that the dangers implicit in the modern political theory can be corrected through a return to the Greek and Roman classics. To regain a common philosophical ground of reason prior to the revelational impact on it, it has been assumed that "practical reason," as Aristotle called it, unencumbered with revelation, would see these existential aberrations in the human good arising from contemporary science, politics, and economics.[21] This has set many an earnest scholar off to read and reread carefully the classics. What seems evident, however, is that this welcome effort, by itself, has not succeeded in averting the attack on the human good arising from a "charitable" human science in the service of a civil society presupposed to no natural ends.

At first sight, this would seem to argue for the validity of the medieval philosophical theses about these same Greek and Roman classics. The right understanding of classical theory in fact came largely not through itself but through revelation, though a revelation rooted in a common divine intellect which stood at the origin both of natural intellect and revelation itself. This was the work of Maritain, Gilson, Pegis, Mascall, Lewis, Pieper, and others who understood relatively clearly what was at issue in modern philosophy itself.

What would prevent the "democratic charity" or mercy of modern political and natural science, in alliance, from overturning the natural order of reason -- and indeed eventually the given terms of revelation itself, not opposed to reason -- would not be classical reason. Rather this would be the task of revelational philosophy, that is, reason which has likewise pondered revelation as a given. It was this latter reason that many proponents of the classical revival wanted to remove from Western intellect because it derived from "faith".[22] The intention of this endeavor, which in effect reduced the importance of medieval theory, was the erection of a common intelligence. What seems clear, however, is that this common intelligence is not fully capable of being recovered in such terms.

The endeavor to return to a revelational philosophy, however, could be considered to be more cogent if contemporary Christianity itself did not often appear to have accomodated itself to those ideologies which have come to embody the modern project in some overt or covert fashion. And there is a valid sense in which it can properly be said that orthodoxy remains the central line of Christian intelligibility about itself.[23] Nevertheless, in terms of political philosophy, the endeavor to reformulate modern culture through a return to Greek classics, however necessary at one level, seems doomed. Contemporary culture by itself appears bent upon producing existentially, in scientific and political systems, that form of "human 'being'" which was rejected by the classics in theory as "immoderate." Yet, this rejection of classic moderation is accomplished in the name of scientific and political freedom and "reason." Ultimately, this is so because mercy has disappeared from political

266

theory or, perhaps better, mercy has become
benevolence or compassion in a rational form that has
become the very motive of the modern project.[24]

In his remarkable essay, "From the Theology of
God to Theology in the Church," Hans Urs von Balthasar
noted how many ideas from the revelational tradition
remained in modern political culture to make it appear
as precisely "utopian," that is, Platonic, but not
"impossible" under the revelational impact.

> That individual and social ethics are
> only analogically one becomes even more
> obvious if we trace our steps from the
> Christian ethics, christologically grounded,
> back to its preliminary phases, namely, the
> Old Testament and non-biblical ethics.
> There is without a doubt something like a
> natural law which is congruent with human
> nature as such, both individually and
> socially considered, a law which co-achieves
> fulfilment in the biblical realm. This law
> is somehow summarized in the 'golden rule,'
> which is acknowledged by the ethics of all
> nations, and is quoted in the Sermon on the
> Mount(Matthew 7:12). But consider the
> context within which the golden rule
> occurs. In Christ, we are not dealing with
> a man-centered piece of reasoning, to wit: I
> should not do to others what I do not wish
> that others should do to me. We are dealing
> instead with the God-centered truth that the
> unselfish love which God has exhibited
> towards the good and the bad is the most
> appropriate model for man to follow in his
> individual and social conduct....[25]

This passage from a sane and leading theologian
itself is suggestive of the wide distance the
discipline of theology and the discipline of political
theory stand from each other if they do not grasp the
direction both are travelling. Maurice Cranston's
analysis of the meaning of the international documents
on human rights warns of the danger of the easy
identification of human rights and Christian
virtue.[26] Yet, von Balthasar's comments serve to
suggest that there is a revelational philosophy which
is not "utopian" but which is still not merely natural
law or rationalism. This is what Strauss himself
worried about.[27] This is the area of medieval
theory, the actuality of graced action which, as

Machiavelli saw, has been operative in Western
culture. He held this must be removed if men are not
to aim too high and thereby destroy the natural
order. The medieval tradition would argue the
opposite, that this very removal is what undermines
reason.

Both Aristotle's criticism of Plato and St.
Augustine's transformation of Plato's objectives in
the light of revelation, then, remain necessary to
protect the normal and what the normal can do when
graced, but not yet at resurrection. Joseph Sobran's
remarks are to the point in ascertaining what is the
result of the removal of both classical moderation and
Christian revelation from contemporary political
practice:

> What is strange -- at least at first
> sight -- is that this callousness about the
> unborn child should occur in a society where
> we are forever hectored to show "compassion"
> for others. Even as enlightened voices
> sternly urge us to take responsibility for
> unseen strangers, they soothingly release us
> from responsibility to our own children. If
> these two positions seem inconsistent, they
> can be politically harmonized: we can
> discharge the duties of "compassion" through
> politics, while the state relieves us of our
> nearer duties. Since this form of
> "compassion" is brokered by the
> tax-collecting and wealth-distributing
> state, the reasonable inference is that what
> we are headed for is the totally politicized
> society, in which relations among citizens
> replace relations of kinship.

> To put it simply, we are required to
> love, and provide for, our neighbor, and our
> neighbor's neighbor, and our neighbor's
> neighbor's neighbor; but not our sons and
> daughters. This has quite literally given a
> new meaning to the word "compassion," which
> now implies a strangely politicized form of
> love; a highly unnatural love, at the
> expense of more natural kinds.[28]

"Political compassion" has thus replaced theological
"mercy" or "charity" so that this same secularized
"mercy" finally ends up by turning on the very given
being of man himself.[29] Since this normal human

being in his living requires privacy, family, property, and autonomy, something the revelational tradition itself supported, the removal of these "moderate" supports leads to a this-worldly, mystical politics, a politics recalling Plato now brought to earth.

Modern political theory began with Machiavelli's "lowering of the sights" so that politics would not "expect" more than man would be able to support. The revelational tradition, of course, had, while not forgetting original sin or Thucydides, filled medieval culture with the idea that, aided by grace and following its norms, more would be given and expected of man than his "due," though not utopia. Indeed, the startling doctrine of resurrection undercut, as C. S. Lewis wrote, all political systems, however ongoing down the ages they might be, by promising beatitude to each person.[30] But as St. Augustine and St. Thomas recognized, this was not a political project of this life. These augmented expectations, with rational analogues in Plato, did, rightly considered, come from revelation. Machiavelli was quite right.

But what is at issue is whether mankind, while recognizing these elevated expectations but not their source, can let them go without reverting to something worse than "natural man."[31] This is the core of modern political theory and why the "worst state," in theory and in practice, must be considered relevant to it. (See Chapter IX) The qualitative difference between Aristotle's worst tyranny and 20th Century totalitarianism cannot be ignored, nor can the validity, again based on the classics, of the distinction between "authoritarian" and "totalitarian" rule.

In a sense, then, the "lowering of sights" has resulted not merely in the sort of politics discussed in the classics before revelation appeared, but something much worse. However nuanced, the question of "diabolism" in political theory seems to arise from contemporary political experience, as the famous anti-utopian novels from Brave New World to 1984 have intimated. Whether a Machiavelli would have been surprised by this can be questioned. What seems clear is that it results from lowering the sights in a world in which both mercy and reason were operative as normal.

The revelational tradition, however, suggested

that once it existed in human culture, any attempt to "remove" it would tend not merely to restore reason as the Greeks and Romans knew it, but result in its very perversion seen in elevating to the rank of good what reason rejected as distorted. Plato's Republic, in other words, as a necessary theoretical endeavor of the human mind to construct "what is justice" is perfectly valid and consistent as an existence in the human mind which proposes to know what is.

Consequently, the revelational tradition suggested how this Platonic reason could, even in existence, be saved, so that it would not, at the same time, destroy the natural institutions, especially the family and the polis. A proposal to return to the classics though bypassing the medieval experience should lead logically not to a revitalization of pure speculation in the mind to see where the limits of moderation lie, but to the "charity" or "compassion" of an existence now presupposed to no "moderation" whatsoever. This result, ironically, is not only capable of corrupting reason, but also revelation, when revelation itself has given up its Greek side (that is, St. Augustine and St. Thomas) in favor of a philosophy or ideology grounded in the modern project.

Mercy is, obviously, a theological concept. Essentially it implies that the consequences of violations of justice in the real order will not necessarily be requited, either in politics or in everlastingness, provided this does not imply a redefinition of evil as good. Mercy, in other words, already "corrupted" the natural political order not so much by denying its givenness in nature (Aristotle), but by deepening the seriousness of its actions and aberrations. This was seen, not by an abstract law but before the inner life of the Godhead.

Mercy and forgiveness were thus the only things that could ultimately confront the power of evil and a just response to it in the public order (Arendt). In a political culture, in this case Western culture, built upon the expectation of mercy, political theory could not come up with a moral replacement when it disappeared other than an existential endeavor to put The Republic into existence. This project was now aided by science and technology limited to no metaphysical knowledge of what man is, yet it retained the heritage of "charity" or "mercy" within itself.

"The traditional treatment of the history of philosophy and particularly of political ideas," Eric Voegelin shrewdly observed,

> recognizes antiquity and modernity, while 1,500 years of Christian thought and Christian politics are treated as a kind of hole in the evolution of mankind ... Whatever one may think of Christianity, it cannot be treated as negligible. A general history of ideas must be capable of treating the phenomenon of Christianity with no less theoretical care than that devoted to Plato or Hegel.[32]

The unity of political philosophy cannot ignore those revelational aspects of its history and intellectual character which were operative within the existing Christian culture.[33] Not to come to terms with them is to miss what is intelligible about actual political history. This does not mean political philosophy must become "theology," however much a "theology" unconnected to its roots has become itself a quasi-political ideology. Rather, it means the opposite, that both theology and political philosophy are products of human intelligence which can understand what does happen in history, but which need not "explain" what it does not yet know on the basis of an a priori theory of an absolutely all-knowing human intellect. Moderation remains.

The importance of medieval political philosophy, then, is not esoteric. It is directly relevant to costs, movements, dangers in the contemporary world which men find difficult to explain to themselves. These dangers have in fact been built into the modern social world to replace realities that arose in and through religious experience. A return to the classics of Greek and Roman political and metaphysical thought in order to avoid the problems connected with the gift structure of the Judaeo-Christian faith does not succeed in evading the aberrations of modern Gnosticism, the effort to ground human reality totally upon the knowledge rooted only in human intelligence. The "lowering of the sights," the attempt to remove the Biblical tradition, because of its supposedly corrupting influence on modern political philosophy, has its point.

Thus, Strauss was not wrong, in his general suspicions about where such ideas would lead.[34] And

271

"mercy," as a theological reality, does, as Eric Voegelin intimated, require that the Christian experience and its intellectual structures be accounted for carefully within political philosophy in order that theory might be what it is, that is, political philosophy and not ideology. In this sense, the disappearance of mercy from political theory is the key to understanding modern political theory. This, in turn, leads to an understanding of what is implied by classical and medieval theory.

<u>Footnotes</u>:

1. Ralph McInerny, <u>St. Thomas Aquinas</u>, Notre Dame, University of Notre Dame Press, 1982; see James V. Schall's review of this book "On the Recruitment of Political Philosophers," <u>Teaching Political Science</u>, Summer, 1983. For excellent texts from St. Thomas on all the topics in this area, see <u>St. Thomas Aquinas</u>, Edited by T. Gilby, Durham, N. C., Labyrinth Press, 1983, Vol. I, Philosophical Texts, Vol. II, Theological Texts.

2. Joseph Pieper, <u>The Silence of St. Thomas</u>, New York, Pantheon, 1967.

3. Etienne Gilson, "What Is Christian Philosophy?" <u>A Gilson Reader</u>, Doubleday Image, 1957, pp. 177-91; Maurice Nedoncelle, <u>Is There a Christian Philosophy?</u> New York, Hawthorne, 1960; Anton C. Pegis, <u>Christian Philosophy and Intellectual Freedom</u>, Milwaukee, Bruce, 1955.

4. St. Augustine, "De Trinitate," <u>The Basic Works of St. Augustine</u>, Edited by W. J. Oates, New York, Random House, 1948, Vol. II; St. Thomas Aquinas' main treatment of the Trinity in <u>Summa Theologica</u>, QQ. I, 27-43; see also James V. Schall, "The Trinity: God Is Not Alone," <u>Redeeming the Time</u>, New York, Sheed and Ward, 1968, Chapter III; "Trinitarian Transcendence," <u>Distinctiveness of Christianity</u>, San Francisco, Ignatius Press, 1983, Chapter VII, pp. 114-25.

5. Hannah Arendt, <u>The Human Condition</u>, Garden City, Doubleday Anchor, 1959, pp. 236-48.

6. Joseph Sobran, <u>Single Issues</u>, New York, Human Life Press, 1983.

7. Arendt, <u>ibid</u>.

8. Leo Strauss, <u>City and Man</u>, Chicago, University of Chicago Press, 1964, p. 3.

9. See Charles N. R. McCoy, <u>The Structure of Political Thought</u>, New York, McGraw-Hill, 1963; E. B. F. Midgley, "Concerning the Modern Subversion of Political Philosophy," <u>New Scholasticism</u>, Spring, 1979, pp. 168-90.

10. C. S. Lewis, <u>The Discarded Image</u>, Cambridge, Cambridge University Press, 1964, pp. 214-15.

11. See James V. Schall, "Atheism and Politics," Christianity and Politics, Boston, St. Paul Editions, 1981, Chapter IV, pp. 94-117.

12. Leo Strauss, What is Political Philosophy?, Glencoe, Free Press, 1959, pp. 43-44.

13. Irving Kristol, "Human Nature and Social Reform," Wall Street Journal, September 16, 1976; see also Sobran, ibid.; Iredell Jenkins, Social Order and the Limits of Law, Princeton, Princeton University Press, 1980; Hadley Arkes, Philosopher in the City, Princeton, Princeton University Press, 1981; Ellen Wilson, An Even Dozen, New York, Human Life Press, 1980.

14. "It is fashionable these days to view paternalism and benevolence as obscene terms. The reformers of the past are often ridiculed for failures to achieve their ends. Worse, their intentions are suggested to be motivated by unconscious self-striving ... I have little faith in the eventual success of the best intentioned of our current laborers in their efforts for equity and justice ... There will always be need for parental compassion, at the same time, there will always be the need for vigilance in recognizing the limitations of institutions of government as surrogate parents. Nevertheless, it is not paternalism that is the crime; it is what is passed off for paternalism. The language of rights, with its litigious and paranoid assumption that good can only be received from others by pursuit and protection of law, must also recognize that the good that can be received from others in that way is often quite limited ... Certain minimal rights ought to be defended even beyond the court -- in the streets, if necessary; but the solution will require that we go beyond the kind of moral behaior that can be defined in terms of plaintiff and litigant." Willard Gaylin, "In the Beginning: Helpless and Dependent," "Doing Good": The Limits of Benevolence, New York, Seabury, 1978, p. 32.

15. Eric Voegelin, New Science of Politics, Chicago, University of Chicago Press, 1952, Chapter IV.

16. See James V. Schall, Christianity and Life, San Francisco, Ignatius Press, 1981; Human Dignity and Human Numbers, Staten Island, Alba House, 1971;

Welcome Number 4,000,000,000, Canfield, Ohio, Alba Books, 1977.

17. Allan Bloom, "Interpretative Essay," The Republic, New York, Basic, 1968.

18. See James V. Schall, "Teaching the Political Philosophy of Plato," Classical Bulletin, 1982.

19. See Raymond Dennehy, Reason and Dignity, Washington, University Press of America, 1981.

20. See James V. Schall, Liberation Theology, San Francisco, Ignatius Press, 1982.

21. Strauss, City and Man, ibid., Introduction and Chapter I; see F. Wilhelmsen, Christianity and Political Philosophy, Athens, University of Georgia Press, 1978.

22. Leo Strauss, Natural Right and History. Chicago, University of Chicago Press, 1953, pp. 161-64; see the author's "Reason, Revelation, and Politics: Catholic Reflections on Strauss," Gregorianum, Rome, #2 and #3, 1981.

23. The intellectual analyses of John Paul II in this regard merit close attention. See his The Acting Person, Boston, D. Reidel, 1979; see also George H. Williams, The Mind of John Paul II, New York, Seabury, 1981; Andrew N. Woznicki, Christian Humanism: Karol Wojtyla's Existentialist Personalism, New Britain, Mariel, 1980. See especially John Paul II's address of November 17, 1981 on St. Thomas to the Angelicum College in Rome, in The Whole Truth About Man: John Paul II to University Faculties and Students, Edited by J. V. Schall, Boston, St. Paul Editions, 1981; see also James V. Schall, Church, State, and Society According to John Paul II, Chicago, Franciscan Herald Press, 1982.

24. See James V. Schall, "On the Re-Discovery of Charity," The Distinctiveness of Christianity, ibid., Chapter VIII, pp. 126-40.

25. Hans Urs von Balthasar, "From the Theology of God to Theology in the Church," The Clergy Review, London, March, 1983, pp. 93-94.

26. Maurice Cranston, What are Human Rights? New York, Taplinger, 1973; see also John Finnis, Natural

Law and Natural Right, New York, Oxford University
Press, 1980. See also James V. Schall, "Culture and
Human Rights," America, January 7, 1978; "Second
Thoughts on Natural Rights," Faith and Reason, Winter,
1975-76, pp. 44-59. See also Chapter V, Footnote #13.

27. Strauss, Natural Right and History, ibid.,
Chapter IV.

28. Sobran, ibid., p. 7. "The state was all too
willing to allocate substantial resources to the
children if they were removed from their parents. But
the state was not willing to provide equivalent
services -- probably at less cost -- directly to the
family in its own home." Ira Glasser, "Prisoners of
Benevolence," "Doing Good", ibid., p. 158. See also
George Gilder's similar point in Wealth and Poverty,
New York, Basic, 1981; see also The Wealth of
Families, Washington, American Family Institute, 1982.

29. McCoy, ibid., Chapters VII-X.

30. "He (C. S. Lewis) never supposed that
Christian doctrine included practical wisdom in any
speciality. He did think that 'nothing but the
courage and unselfishness of individuals is ever going
to make any system work properly,' but he didn't think
it was the business of the state to enforce the moral
virtues its own health depended on. In that sense,
public life was at the mercy of private life. There
was no way around it."

"And though he recognized that it was tempting to
defer ultimate questions about man and morality 'and
just carry on with those parts of morality that all
sensible people agree about,' he thought this was
impossible: for 'different beliefs about the universe
lead to different behavior.' The doctrine of the
immortality of the soul had a very practical and
urgent bearing on 'the difference between
totalitarianism and democracy. If individuals live
only seventy years, then a state, or a nation, or a
civilization, which may last for a thousand years, is
more important than the individual. But if
Christianity is true, then the individual is not only
made important but incomparably more important, for he
is everlasting and the life of a state or a
civilization, compared with his, is only a moment.'"
Sobran, ibid., p. 157. (The citations from Lewis are
from Mere Christianity.)

31. G. K. Chesterton has argued this thesis in Orthodoxy and Everlasting Man.

32. Eric Voegelin, Letter to Alfred Schutz, The Philosophy of Order: Essays on History, Consciousness, and Politics, P. Opitz and G. Sebba, Editors, Stuttgart, Klett, 1981, pp. 449-50. See Dante Germino, "Voegelin, Christianity, and Political Theory," Paper given to the American Political Science Association Convention, Chicago, September, 1983.

33. See Christopher Dawson, Religion and Culture, London, Sheed and Ward, 1948; Understanding Europe, London, Sheed and Ward, 1952; The Formation of Christendom, New York, Sheed and Ward, 1967; Religion and the Rise of Western Culture, New York, Sheed and Ward, 1950.

34. See above Footnote, #12. See James V. Schall, "From Compassion to Coercion," Vital Speeches, July 15, 1982.

CHAPTER XIII

POLITICAL THEORY AND POLITICAL THEOLOGY

> Proclaiming the Gospel -- announcing the news of creation, redemption, salvation, God's love for man, brotherly love for all, the reality and mystery of evil, the need for prayer and communion with Christ's Church -- cannot fail to transform society as it transforms men. It carries with it a multitude of implications for social and political life: the dignity of human beings, their rights, their duties. Society can be just only if people are just in their souls. Contrary to the great enterprise of modern political philosophy -- Machiavelli, Hobbes, Locke, Rousseau, Hegel, Marx -- on which modern societies have been built, justice cannot be secured by good organization, good processes, good structures.
>
> ... The critique of modern political philosophy in the light of classical political philosophy (by Leo Strauss) provides us with a starting point for analysis of the contemporary situation. Ironically, it is this non-Christian who helps make the tradition of Catholic social thought accessible to modern Catholics, who have little familiarity with it and are beset with "secularist understanding(s) of the Kingdom of God that prevail in some Catholic circles, both on the right and on the left." -- [Christopher Wolfe, "A Constructive Vision," (Review of Brian Benestad's The Pursuit of a Just Social Order) This World, Spring/Summer, 1983, p. 158.]

I. THE STATEMENT OF CLASSICAL POLITICAL THEORY.

In a well-known essay, Professor Leo Strauss

noted that the characteristic of classical political theory was that "it is free from all fanaticism because it knows that evil cannot be eradicated and therefore that one's expectations from politics must be moderate. The spirit which animates it may be described as serenity or sublime sobriety."[1] This appreciation of the abidingness of evil as a practical reality does not, however, obviate the task of political theory to inquire about the good and the kind of regimes in which it can appear in its most positive form. Moderation in expectation, then, has theoretical justifications. This is doubly so because the best possible regime of perfect order and justice runs into conflict both with the human condition and with the curiously open nature of man's speculative powers.

"The peculiar manner of being of the best regime -- namely, its lacking actuality while being superior to all actual regimes -- has its ultimate reason in the dual nature of man, in the fact that he is the in-between being existing between the life of brutes and that of the gods."[2] Built into classical political theory is a suppressed conflict, as it were, a tension between the best men can do with their public order given the presence of an inevitable degree of evil among them and the desire for an order in which these tendencies towards corruption are eliminated. For this reason too, as Eric Voegelin has remarked, the problem of the divine and the contemplative stands at the heart of political thought.[3]

With St. Augustine, St. Thomas Aquinas, likewise, held that there were two communities to which men were ordered. The human law was directed to the mortal community while the divine law fashioned men into "a certain community or republic of men under God."[4] The human law had a radically different purpose from the divine law, even though they were connected teleologically. The end of the human law is the temporal tranquillity of the city, to which goal the law achieves its purpose sufficiently by prohibiting exterior acts insofar as such acts can disturb the peaceful status of the community. (See Chapter VII) The purpose of the divine law, on the other hand, is to lead men to eternal happiness.[5] These two communities were not unrelated, of course, but they were certainly not the same thing.

For Aquinas, the duality in man was the basis for

an invitation to a community into which man could   not
properly enter of   his   own accord.(I-II, 109, 2) Thus
the   efforts   to   achieve   the   essential   effects   or
conditions of the divine   republic through the earthly
peace were   not   only   impossible   of   achievement but
blasphemous.   Politics retained its moderation for   an
even   more   profound   reason   than   man's   ontological
status   between   the   gods   and   the   beasts.   The
invitation to   man   to   share the inner life of God --
the   essence of the Christian doctrine -- transcended
any political possibility.

Can this conclusion   of   classical   and   medieval
political theory   be overcome?   That is,   are these two
"common goods"   forever   to   remain   separate   both in
theory and in practice?   The "moderation" of classical
theory   was   designed   to   prevent   man's   ultimate
metaphysical and   religious   desires   from   seeking   a
political expression.   "Hubris,"   pride, was the belief
that   the   two   endeavors   were   not   necessarily   as
separate   as   classical   and   Christian   theory   had
implied.   At least, this was   the   view   of   classical
thought itself.

The result of this is, as no   less   an   authority
than   Lemuel Gulliver had written in the   introductory
letter to his justly   famous   travels,   that we cannot
expect to remove the evils of mankind without changing
the very structure of man   himself   so that we must to
some degree live with them.

> ... Yahoo, as   I   am,   it is well-known
> through   all   Houyhunmland,   that   by   the
> Instructions   and Example of my   illustrious
> Master, I was able in   the   Compass of   two
> years (although I confess   with   the   utmost
> difficulty) to remove that infernal Habit of
> Lying,   Shuffling,   Deceiving,   and
> Equivocating, so deeply rooted in   the   soul
> of all my Species; especially the   Europeans
> ...   I   must freely confess, that   since   my
> last Return, some corruptions of   my   Yahoo
> Nature have revived in me by conversing with
> a few   of   your   Species,   and   particularly
> those of mine own   Family, by an unavoidable
> Necessity;   else   I   should   never   have
> attempted   so   absurd a Project as   that   of
> reforming the Yahoo Race   in   this   Kingdom;
> but, I   have   now   done   with   all   visionary
> Schemes forever.[6]

In other words, the scheme to change radically the nature of man is not only "visionary" but destroys the very wonder and freedom of the men who do exist -- liars, shufflers, deceivers, and equivocators that they surely are.

Any political theory, therefore, which refuses to accept this is, by definition, an anti-classical and anti-medieval theory. The theories of the good life, the best regime, and the good citizen of classical theory arose out of this context. This is why the instruments of positive improvement for classical theory were always virtue and persuasion, even though, for the same reason, the state necessarily had coercive powers. Medieval theory added to this notion of grace and supernatural virtue.

II. THE HOLY AND THE POLITICAL.

The fundamental unresolved question in the history of political thought, however, is that of the spiritual perfection of the public order in this world as such. Augustinian political thought, in one sense, deprived the political order of its aura of sanctity and goodness except insofar as it might be an instrument of providence.[7] But Augustinian theory did not for a minute forget the question of the City of God. That is, men were called to be holy and to be holy in community and in communion. St. Augustine was not loath to call that blessed life about God a "city." What he explicitly denied was that the earthly political order ever could be the proper instrument of man's ultimate destiny. In this sense, St. Augustine is a classical political thinker. (See Chapter III)

If there is one thing clear about political history, however, it is that this question of a holy public order will not disappear. Metaphysics and religion have long recognized that man's ultimate happiness is an unavoidable problem. Consequently, one of the central themes of political thought has certainly been the effort to maintain a legitimacy for the political as such in relation to philosophy and religion without, at the same time, eliminating completely a noble and ethical vision of man as a public desideratum and consideration. Even in such extremes as Hobbes, the very structure of his politics is to grant such minimal peace as the brutish and short life of man would allow. The widespread

282

appearance of "political theology" in ecclesiastical
circles recently, together with an evident and radical
dissatisfaction with the overly pragmatic and purely
descriptive or value-free standards prevalent in most
academic political theory, are signs that this problem
of the spiritual of the public order requires fresh
consideration.

We are not used to a phrase such as "a holy
politics" or "a moral polity." Indeed, for anyone at
all familiar with the evolution of political thought,
they incite rather unpleasant memories of perhaps
Byzantium or Bossuet, or even of the armies of Islam.
"To understand Byzantine history," Steven Runciman
noted,

> it is essential to remember the
> unimportance of this world to the Byzantine.
> Christianity triumphed in a disillusioned
> age because it promised a better world to
> come and provided a mystic escape from the
> world here and now. But the right eternal
> bliss, the right ecstasies, could only be
> won by treading the path of perfect
> orthodoxy.[8]

A more dynamic, worldly version of this drive has
become historically ever more to the fore.

For the early American Protestants, for example,
ecstatic bliss was not enough. "Upon that expression
in Sacred Scripture, cast the unprofitable servant
into Outer Darkness," Cotton Mather wrote in The
Magnalia Christi Americana (1703),

> it hath been imagined by some, that the
> Regiones Externae of America, are the
> Tenebrae Exteriores, which the unprofitable
> are there condemned to. No doubt, the
> authors of these Ecclesiastical Impositions
> and Severities, which drove the English
> Christians into the Dark Regions of America,
> esteemed these Christians to be a very
> unprofitable sort of creature. But behold,
> ye European Churches, there are Golden
> Candlesticks in the midst of this Outer
> Darkness; unto the upright children of
> Abraham, here hath risen Light in
> Darkness.[9]

Already, even in the religious sphere, the Dark Night

is being transformed into the Golden Candlestick. The Kingdom of God is beginning to take worldly shape.[10]

However paradoxical it may sound, during the last decades of the 20th Century, partly because of the poverty of the Third World, partly because of an inner dissatisfaction in more settled societies, there is again a widespread search for a political solution to our spiritual problems, an uneasy belief that a politics that does not also meet man's deeper aspirations must fail. Conversely, a theology which does not have tangible political effects is likewise sterile:

> The transcendence of the faith, especially if it lives under the mode of incarnation, does not only give to theology the possibility of criticizing all these things in political opinions and movements which are opposed to Truth and Charity, preventing, thereby, every absolutism; it also gives to it the possibility of finding a way to discover the line through which the concrete call of the love of the brethren passes historically. It gives it the power of advancing gradually, in fear and trembling, step by step, in assuming the risk of discernment and of corresponding engagement, which consists in placing oneself at the service of the brothers. In this manner ... will it be historical and practical. For the theos of which the logos speaks (insofar as it is theology) is the God of history, and the word (logos) which it articulates is the word of God made flesh, who gives his life to free the brothers.[11]

What the Byzantines found in mystery and the early Puritans in the Wilderness has now become the concrete political enterprise of the spiritual in this world.

The economic and cultural disorder in the world is ever more seen to be the result of theories and practices that refuse to account for man's spiritual aspirations.[12] And, it should be noted in this connection, many materialist political movements, beginning with Marxism itself, are "spiritual" in the sense that they base themselves upon a hatred of public evil with a promise to establish complete justice for man by removing all evils.[13] What is now desired and believed to be possible is a _politics_ that answers concretely man's most fundamental aspirations. Gone is the sense of moderation as well as the distinction between the two communities. We refuse to be Yahoos because we can find "the line through which the concrete call of the love of the brethren passes historically."

What is new in all of this is the transformation of politics into an aspect of eschatology.[14] The specifically "Christian" element in this approach becomes obvious because of the tradition of Caesar and God.[15] "My Kingdom is not of this world" has tended to separate the question of man's ultimate happiness from his political condition, which, to be sure, was seen also as a search for a kind of happiness.[16] Indeed, the two tendencies were seen largely to be in conflict. (See Chapter II) Yet, there has been an abiding effort to reunite these two strands into one.

"History reveals two great movements, always interlocked yet essentially independent of one another," Sir Harold Mattingly wrote,

> the movements of states and of peoples, in which the individual plays a humble and subordinate part; and the development of the individual soul, which, strong in its own freedom, need care little for political rise and fall, for _res Romanas perituraque regna_, "the might of Rome and kingdoms doomed to die." Hitherto it is in the first of these movements that the strength of paganism has been seen, the strength of Christianity in the second. Whether the quickening of Christianity is ever to work in the life of groups and societies, as it has worked in the lives of individuals, may be doubted. Perhaps it is always to be a leaven, slowly leavening the lump of societies that, collectively regarded, are still pagan. Perhaps the attempt to evangelize the state in any deep sense must fail, but one is sometimes inclined to doubt whether the attempt has ever yet seriously been made.[17]

This suspicion that the attempt has not yet been seriously made is what is becoming the driving force behind political theology. Conversely, recognition that the individual's corporate life needs moral

285

texture and spiritual depth sends all recent radical
and socialist movements in search of quasi-religious
justification.[18]

III. POLITICAL THEORY: CLASSICAL-MEDIEVAL TO MODERN.

The most famous book in all political theory
proposed that the virtue of man as man is justice.
Political thought is the search for justice. This
same book, moreover, as we saw, maintained that
justice among mortals could not be found among men and
their existing institutions. The task of politics was
to allow the good man to discover and contemplate the
good in itself. The irony of this vision, once
achieved, is that it proved to be all-absorbing,
all-consuming so that the effort to entice the good
man back into the affairs of ordering the city was no
simple one.

Nonetheless, only if this contemplating man did
return to structure the city on the model of the
transcendent good could every other man receive his
due share of happiness and justice. The weak and the
small were dependent on the perfect, while the perfect
must first discover what is beyond them. Political
philosophy began with the belief that the pursuit of
justice, the essential task of politics, required the
absolute good, which was not itself directly
political. And without justice, no state could rest.
The cycle of deterioration in Books VIII and IX of The
Republic was witness to the political turmoil caused
by the lack of the good. In other words, politics is
the reflection of contemplation. Without its
overflow, as it were, no state could save itself.

If there is anything common to the political
thought of the generations from Aristotle to the
behaviorists, it is that politics and speculative
metaphysics or religion are not the same things. The
Book of the Metaphysics was not The Book of the
Politics. A tension and a dichotomy likewise were
found between what belonged to Caesar and what
belonged to God. For the post-Aristotelian
philosophers, to be sure, individual perfection and
consolation could not be discovered in the city, as
Aristotle had held, but rather through withdrawing
from the city and politics. The locus of
self-sufficiency shifted to the individual within a
world-reason and a world-empire. Even the Stoics were

286

enamored with a politics of the vaguest and most abstract kind. Their _humanitas_, reason, and law were anti-political in this sense.[19]

St. Augustine, at the Empire's end, managed to formulate the political enterprise so that man's contemplative drives were proper to the City of God. The politics of this world were provisional, intrinsically fleeting, the coming of terms with man's darker drives and ambitions in the most expedient and workable terms. But in no case did politics define man's true home or his highest activity. Indeed, the very attempt to establish a City of God on earth was the ultimate delusion, for it offered man something infinitely less than that to which he had been called. (See Chapter III)

The freeing of politics from the immediate directive control of the contemplative or divine was, in any case, the greatest of achievements. Christianity was vital to the very structure of classical political thought because it was able to give a reason why politics, the proper science of man _as man_ in Aristotle's schema, did not have to be concerned directly with man's highest destiny or virtue.[20] Resurrection and the Kingdom of God suggested both that man's deepest personal desires would be fulfilled -- the sting of death was not absolutely defeating -- and that politics could, consequently, pursue a temporal good in a human, finite fashion.

Thus, when Aristotle said that politics was not concerned with making man to live, but _to live well_, he implied that political theory was limited by what man already was and that this "limitation" was a norm and a freedom. Otherwise, the task of politics would become directly metaphysical. That is, it would endeavor to bring forth man _qua_ man upon the assumption that no historical or reflective experience of the human could yield any criterion about man's being.

Modern political theory began with Machiavelli. The essential premise of specifically "modern" theory was the speculative indifference to political means.[21] This indicated that the theoretical check on the scope of politics -- the essentially metaphysical thesis that "the human" was already a given and thereby a limiting norm of what the state could do -- was removed.[22] Modern theory, then, was

287

a working out of the consequences of the denial of any higher judgment on politics other than politics itself.[23] The absolute states of the sixteenth and seventeenth centuries were the empirical products of this belief, while the liberal and democratic states that succeed them from the French Revolution on had the common background of a rejection of contemplative norms.

The "religious" and the "metaphysical" were thus deprived of their direct political function of providing the limits and the structures of the human conceived as something given by the order of nature and nature's God. Descartes' _Cogito_ and Grotius' dictum -- "the natural law would be the natural law even on the supposition that God did not exist" -- set up the framework of modern theory according to which politics became the architectonic science whose task was to create man as a totally independent being under whose will and choice all things exist.[24]

But while this autonomous evolution in a Hobbes, Rousseau, or Hegel was itself a kind of inverted theology which purported to explain all reality by its own independent premises -- Aristotle remarked that politics would be the highest science if man had nothing higher than himself -- still the whole effort of modern speculative political thought, be it liberalism, much of conservatism, or socialism, was to account for all reality, or at least all that mattered, without the need of God or the spiritual understood in the classical or Christian sense. Politics was its own thing. The spiritual mattered only insofar as it became some kind of worldly power demanding public attention because of its unavoidable strength. Otherwise, it was wholly private.

Consequently, the spiritual was either an aspect of the material as Marx would explain or else it belonged to a separate sphere autonomous to politics with no real influence on it. The significance of Marsilius of Padua at the origin of modern theory was undoubtedly his success in removing religion theoretically from the public order as a factor to be reckoned with. By completely depriving religion of "exterior acts" over which the public order had some control, as Aquinas had held, Marsilius removed religion from the catalogue of humanly meaningful things with some empirical effect in the world.[25]

IV. THE REAPPEARANCE OF THE HOLY IN POLITICS.

What is striking today is the reappearance in political form of the suppressed spiritual in a highly peculiar fashion, at least in regard to the history of political theory. Indeed, we are witnessing the end of "modern" political theory. We are coming to a new turning point in the history of political theory every bit a sharp as the ones inaugurated by Aristotle, the post-Aristotelians, Christianity, or Machiavelli.[26] To suggest that the essential content of this new turning point is that theology has suddenly become politics would be something of a rhetorical exaggeration if taken too literally.

The fact is, however, more and more scholars, particularly those from the Third World, many Europeans, Protestants and Catholics alike, and not excluding several notable Marxists such as Ernest Bloch and Roger Garaudy, are coming to accept the one is the other, that theology is politics and politics theology.[27] For anyone familiar with the history of Christianity or of politics, this will surely seem a most perplexing turn of events. In any case, it has spelled the doom of so-called "modern" political theory. For this reason, it is no accident that the study of ancient heresies is, in a way, the best preparation for understanding the intellectual content of the political movements of recent times.[28]

"Theology as a reflection of faith," Dorothy Solle told a famous gathering of theologians,

> has to comprehend the social situation of these who are injured and expose the social cause of their injuries. Theology has to become political theology, theology cannot afford to say out of hand to a man: "God loves you." Since every fact of reality is substantial, established by social process, such a sentence has to be actualized politically.[29]

That this also portends something of a revolution in theology goes without saying, for the medieval relation of theology to politics was always that theology was the queen of the sciences, the ultimate judge of the truly human, such that it provided a check on the aberrations of politics. Theology is now looking upon itself in a rather opposite fashion. It is a partisan advocate for political well-being. Theology tests its validity by the criterion of political performance. Even more fundamentally, at its extremes, theology is claiming to be the vision which establishes the Kingdom politically.[30]

If theology, in its own methodology, has begun to turn to politics as a matrix discipline -- for Aristotle, politics was architectonic over the practical but not over the speculative orders -- recent political thought, for its part, has reached its own impasse.[31] Revolts against academic political theories in the name of social activism and concern are symptomatic of this deeper crisis affecting all scientific disciplines.[32]

Classical liberalism, socialism, personalism, and behaviorism have all, evidently, failed in their own orders as intellectual constructs because of their human narrowness and failures to account for the spiritual hopes of man.[33] And this has not been any accidental failure but one lying at the heart of these theories. For they have all, in one way or another, failed to account for the public nature of the spiritual in the modern world.[34] What has happened, in other words, is that theology has suddenly rediscovered Plato's notion that the just man must return to the city, while political theory has been forced to recognize that it cannot escape from the good in its deepest dimensions as a criterion of its own viability.

What sparked this whole crisis both in theology and in political theory has been, it appears, the plight of the Third World together with the lot of the underprivileged in all societies along with the suppression of elementary human and civil dignities in the Marxist-socialist systems.[35] This means that the predominant political systems of the modern age have floundered by running into a radical impasse that can only be described as spiritual.[36] Even the most recent arrival on the horizon of political discussion -- the ecological-conservative thesis -- is itself suffused with a theoretical bias not only about the value and dignity of man but about any conception of the spiritual conceived in any terms but contented earthly life.[37]

Whatever be its background, however, the "revolutionary" nature of recent times is motored by the insistence that a full, "human", earthly, abundant life is both possible and available. Evil, political and moral evil, is now defined socially, not individually. That is, what prevents this full development or "liberation," as it is now more often called, from happening immediately is the true evil and proper object of political and moral hatred whether it be individually conscious or not.[38] Guilt and innocence are more and more not personal things as in classical ethics but class or functional categories which depersonalize the individual.[39]

Theology has, likewise, read, in its turn, the statistics of the worldly lot of most humans today.[40] On this basis, and even in spite of a real growth of some degree everywhere in the world, what many have decided is that theology will be judged by its results in effecting worldly progress. The very structure of the ecclesiastical is to be that of protest, of hunting down evils and bravely, as it were, yelling about them.[41]

Worldly progress or revolution is, however, dominated by hope and eschatology, by the belief that the Kingdom of God is quickly coming to all this world so that all injustices and disorders, those due to man and to nature, are overturned and revolutionized by its coming.[42] In this sense, such theology believes it can offer both a better spiritual depth and a deeper moral zeal than any of the classic ideologies. Plato had asked, "What is justice?" He found his answer in the vision of an already perfect good. Today's question is rather, "When is justice?" Any answer in terms of after life, patience, or the abidingness of political evils and imperfections -- such as both the classical and Christian traditions had assumed -- is rejected as anti-human.

In this sense, then, the significance of the current direction of practically all political theology which holds as an essential dogma that sin is social sin or, better, structural sin, becomes apparent. Original sin, indeed, is removed from its ancient context to become the complexus of worldly disorders that result in the lot of the poor -- a word which begins to take on psychological as well as economic overtones. "The poor you must not always have with you" is the new law.

Politics becomes the "salvific" instrument for removing this fundamental blight which is seen at the origin of all others. Socialism becomes a kind of

291

dogma, not necessarily because it actually relieves the poor more effectively -- it does not -- but because it proposes in the abstract a more absolute, "holy" state. The separation of economics and politics, church and state -- once considered the signs at least of political maturity -- becomes social heresy. Thus utopia, the heavenly kingdom, the classless society -- those historical substitutes for heaven where all wrongs will be righted and all desires fulfilled -- are also redemptive in this world. That is, all human and natural disorders can be removed to leave, paraphrasing Lenin's famous dictum, precisely nothing "left to be done."

V. THE STATEMENT OF POLITICAL THEOLOGY.

The objection of political theology to political theory, then, is that a completely happy state of man can be accomplished soon so that the fulfillment of legitimate human aspirations can be put off neither to the great beyond after death nor to the great withering away of the state. Political theology claims, by right, to judge the economic performance of capitalism and the civil rights performance of Marxism.[43] In short, no more generations can be sacrificed to bring about the millennium. Politics is now conceived to be the art of the impossible. This is why hope and eschatology are the form not of theology but of politics. Even the last things are subject to conquest.[44]

Everything, therefore, is being made anew. The "not yet" of scripture is accomplished when the worldly political task is completed. Political theology does not formally deny the basic Christian thesis that "the times and the moments" for the coming are in God's hands.(Acts, I:7) What it does suggest, however, is that it is scepticism to maintain that they are not being fulfilled "now" in the restructuralization of the absolutely secularized order. The "death of God" is merely the reverse side of the Kingdom of God.[45] The traditional primacy of contemplation meant that God is supreme over every now and every nation. In fact, it meant that all historical beings are equally near to God whatever their earthly lot.

St. Paul wrote to Timothy,

First of all, then, I urge that
supplications, prayers, intercessions, and
thanksgivings be made for all men, for kings
and all who are in high positions, that we
may lead a quiet and peaceable life, godly
and respectful in every way. This is good,
and it is acceptable in the sight of God our
Savior, who desires all men to be saved and
to come to a knowledge of the truth.(I
Timothy, 2:1-4)

The beggar and the tycoon, Dives and Lazarus, were,
strictly speaking, equal in their changes before the
divinity. Indeed, the beggar had somewhat the
advantage. Furthermore, while there was a "history"
of God's intervention in this world, the circumstances
of the chronological time or era of one human life did
not place it at a disadvantage over another life in
the fundamental sense of acceptability before God.
Neither the ancient Persians, the Han Chinese, the
Teutonic Knights, the Franciscan friars, the
Calvinists of Geneva, the armies of Napoleon, nor the
companions of Lenin had an "unfair" advantage over one
another.

For political theology, however, the nearness of
the eschaton is rather a function of the
accomplishment of the political task.[46] This is why
there is so little patience or willingness to accept
that the poor of the world and those subject to
injustices are near to God whatever be their lot. The
urgency for change and revolution on this score is the
result of theological analysis.[47] Politics is thus a
providence as well as a worldly enterprise.[48] Sin is
social structure, not how we are to one another no
matter what be our earthly lot.[49] Damnation is
living in unjust societies. In this view, what has
disappeared from the world is the finite, mortal,
sinful man. He is the initial being around whom
Aristotle had originally constructed a politics
separate from but dependent upon metaphysics, about
whom Christians believed was carried the substantial
burden of reality -- God loved sinners, God loved his
creation.

Political theology, it seems, has gained the
Parousia but lost the wayfarers who are expected to
inhabit it.[50] From a political point of view, the
man who is the vibrant "stuff" of politics is again
lost. This is doubly significant, for the fundamental
importance of Christianity in political theory was in

freeing politics from the necessity of fulfilling by political means man's ultimate destiny and desires.[51]

That political theology proposes to accomplish exactly this is the measure of its meaning in the history of political thought. We are at another turning point as significant as that of Machiavelli, who inaugurated "modern" political reflection by separating politics from the regulation by the speculative order of man's given being.[52] The subsequent history of modern political thought as a practical and theoretical working out of the consequences of this separation has come to the point where "the spiritual" reenters the secular as the all-consuming care of man.

As Jacques Ellul has noted,

Moreover, instead of the consoling presence -- that experience so much desired by religious people - man now experiences faith and religious conversion thanks to his participation in politics. What wa lost by the church has been found by the parties, at least those worthy of the name. Faith in attainable ends, in the improvement of the social order, in the establishment of a just and peaceful system -- by political means -- is a most profound and undoubtedly new, characteristic of our society. Among the many basic definitions of man, two are joined together at this point: _homo politicus_ is by his very nature _homo religiosus_.[53]

The sudden interest by theology in politics is, in a real sense, a belated response to an evolution that had already taken place of its own accord and by the logic of its own premises within politics. Politics, which set out to cut itself off from the spiritual in the modern world, again has become spiritual.[54]

This is why today, it seems, the religious questions are seen to be essentially practical ones and why political theory has become the locus of controversies once seen under the aspect of heresy and orthodoxy.[55] Consequently, theology recognized the need to reenter politics because it became brutally aware that the political controversies and struggles of the late twentieth century were, in truth, the

continuation and sophistication of ancient
disagreements about the nature of man and God.[56]
Political theory, meanwhile, found itself at an
impasse because the whole world was suddenly rejecting
an academic theory that limited itself purely to
material or methodological questions.

VI. THE ALTERNATIVES TO POLITICAL THEORY.

In the History of the Peloponnesian War,
Thucydides suggested that human life is inclined to
evil for the most part, that while it can also produce
many fine and noble things, its basic tendencies are
somehow against its own best interests.[57] The
revolution at Corcyra, the brutal treatment of Melos
and Mytilene, the plague at Athens were all sobering
reflections about what can be expected in man again
and again. Whether the cycle of man's tragic
inclinations can be broken in this world is, as we
have remarked, the very core of political theory.
(See Chapter VI) Certainly with the slaughters of a
Biafra, a Burundi, a Sudan, or a Bangladesh, a
Vietnam, a Cambodia, or an Indonesia, not to mention
World Wars I and II, it would be rash to conclude that
it has been so broken.[58] The theoretical discussion
over linear and cyclical history, moreover, does not
definitely mean that the "raw material" of human
nature which Thucydides described so painfully is
somehow bypassed, especially as an essential aspect of
politics which must be accounted for within theory
itself.

If this cycle cannot be definitively broken,
then, politics consists in acute analysis of human
instincts and historical trends.[59] Obviously,
Thucydides himself thought men could progress and
improve their lot even brilliantly, as Pericles'
Funeral Oration revealed. Yet, in the end, defeat was
possible, even for the best of men or the best of
cities. His judgment of Nicias comes close to being
his ultimate judgment upon what even the most noble
can expect in this life. "For these reasons, or
reasons very like them, he (Nicias) was killed, a man
who, of all the Hellenes in my time, least deserved to
come to so miserable an end, since the whole of his
life had been devoted to the study and practice of
virtue."(Bk. 7, Chapter 7, p. 486)

It is for such a reason, it seems, that Hannah

295

Arendt wisely maintained that the realm of politics is that of natality, whereas metaphysics arises at the point of death and mortality.[60] That is, politics, whatever its intrinsic glory and value, itself is subject to realities it cannot confront. This is why, then, for classical theory, politics cannot be religious or metaphysical in its very depth.

The problem of contemporary political theory, however, lies precisely in the death of Nicias. Is it possible to produce a transformation of man and his social structures such that the Nicias of today -- conceived now not as a classical politician but as the poor and the downtrodden masses -- will not be possible? The challenge of political theology to classical political theory is that an affirmative answer to this unsettling question is working itself out in hope. Revolution is bringing forth a new man freed from the bonds of the Thucydidean past.

The "new man" -- whether he be seen in the light of the eschatological hope of the Christian radicals, or of the revolutionary vision of the socialists, or the biologically good man of the genetic engineers -- defines his newness through the elimination of the dire elements of the human condition.[61] For Plato, Aristotle, and Thucydides, "revolution" was almost always and inevitably a passage from a good to a less good or evil condition. For political theology, it is coming to be considered in exactly the opposite manner, as the catharsis or trauma giving birth to a new being.[62]

Generally speaking, there are three styles of program offered to accomplish this task -- economic and political revolution, genetic engineering, and technological progress.[63] What is important to remember is that these proposals are brought forth directly to answer the classic question of the good man.[64] All recognize some radical break with the past such that historical example or tradition is, in theory, irrelevant. To put it another way, the familiar human nature to which we can still instinctively respond in Thucydides, Aristotle, Sophocles, or Tacitus is no longer a reality in this world, or at least, should not be. That is, nothing can be concluded from man's accumulated experience or philosophical reflection on it.[65] This means that the criterion of what man is or should be must find another source independent of any normative "natural" or human order.

The three dominant alternatives for this, it
would appear, are 1) theology, which claims a
non-natural source, 2) utopia, which discovers a
freedom unhindered by any past, and 3) ecology, which
makes a closed natural "ecosystem" the criterion of
"the human". That each of these proposes a
"non-political" norm in terms of classical or even
Christian political thought means that the kind of
"politics" we are experiencing in recent times is
dominated by the search for the spiritual as a
substitute for the limited kind of good life for
mortal, sinful, finite man once assumed to be the
substantial presupposition to all political thought.

VII. THE END OF IDEOLOGY.

The contemporary point of contact between the
"spiritualization" of politics and political theology
lies in the curious results of the "decline of
ideology" theory of a decade or so ago. The discovery
of the Third World as a problem of political theory
has been the instrument through which
post-Machiavellian politics has been again introduced
into the holy while the so-called "separation" of
church and state -- which Professor Sabine once oddly
held to be the main contribution of Christianity to
political theory -- comes to be gradually dropped.[66]

> The modern effort to transform the
> world chiefly or solely through politics (as
> contrasted with religious transformation of
> the self) has meant that all other
> institutional ways of mobilizing emotional
> energy would necessarily atrophy. In
> effect, sect and church become party and
> social movement....

> Whether the intellectual in the West
> can find passions outside of politics is
> moot. Unfortunately, social reform does not
> have any unifying appeal, nor does it give a
> younger generation the outlet for
> "self-expression" and "self-definition" that
> it wants. The trajectory of enthusiasm has
> turned East, where, in the new ecstasies for
> economic utopia, the "future" is all that
> counts.[67]

Thus, Daniel Bell summed up the direction of political thought in the 1960's.

Some ten years later, political thought seemed less concerned with East and West and more with North and South. The Bishops of Peru wrote, in a typical document:

> ..."Oppositions" are arising in the Christian community in favor of the oppressed; they are assuming their problems, their struggles and their aspirations. Many Christians see their commitment enlightened by a theology; which, grounded in their faith, interprets the present state of affairs as a sinful situation and a negation of God's plan. This theological vision is urging them to commit themselves to the cause of liberation, in response to the Lord who calls them up to build history.
>
> The church is thus discovering the inevitable political implications of its presence in the world; it is realizing that it cannot proclaim the gospel, in a situation of oppression, without stirring consciences by the message of Christ the Liberator. In the example of evangelical poverty, it sees the expression of the solidarity with the oppressed and the denunciation of a sin of that depressing consumer society which creates artificial needs and superfluous expenditures ... "Justice," understood as holiness, the gift of God, is the foundation of social justice; but the latter is the necessary and irreplaceable pledge of the former.[68]

The differing contexts of these two statements of Bell and the South American bishops suggest that the problem of a spiritual order which is both economically viable and morally holy is being grappled with. What is of interest is that the religious discovered its function just where the "decline of ideology" failed as a theory, namely, at the plight of the Third World.

During the 1950's, the famous debate on the decline of ideology was ignited by Professor Edward Shils speech, "The End of Ideology?", which he delivered at the Congress of Cultural Freedom in

298

Milan.[69] According to this thesis, the Western world
was experiencing a lessening of ideological divisions
between socialists and capitalists, between Marxists
and Democrats, between religion and secular humanism.
All modern social systems were discovering similar
economic and political needs, procedures, and norms.
Western democracies were, in fact, welfare states.
Communist countries were recognizing the need for a
certain amount of profit as well as for some internal
civil liberties. Christians and Marxists were
beginning to wonder what they had in common.[70]

Since this economic development evident in all
ideological systems in practice did distribute a
greater volume of wealth more evenly, the argument
ran, the result was an obvious yielding of political
and economic dogmas which only interfered with true
progress if adhered to with any absolute rigidity.
There was, therefore, considerable hope that the world
could look forward beyond the economic and political
cold war to a time of increasing amity and
prosperity. Out of this spirit was eventually to
arise economic development theories such as W. W.
Rostow's Stages of Economic Growth or J. K.
Galbraith's New Industrial State, which found all
systems tending to an empirical similarity and
structure within a logical process.

Discussing this decline of ideology theory some
five years after the Shils speech, Professor Seymour
Martin Lipset was beginning to have some trouble with
it. Is it really such a good idea that ideologies
decline? Lipset's inquiry was occasioned by his own
theory:

> A basic premise of this book is that
> democracy is not only or even primarily a
> means through which different groups can
> attain their ends or seek the good society;
> it is the good society itself in operation.
> Only a give-and-take of a free society's
> internal struggles offers some guarantee
> that the products of the society will not
> accumulate in the hands of a few power
> holders and that men may develop and bring
> up their children without fear of
> persecution. And ... democracy requires
> institutions which support conflict and
> disagreement as well as those which question
> legitimacy and consensus.[71]

For Lipset, then, democracy is itself the good society in operation which depends upon intrinsic diversity. (See Chapter VIII) Any influence which would drastically reduce the causes of change and conflict would eventually destroy the good life itself. A fresh variety of ideology seemed the best guarantee for the health of democracy even though there will inevitably be some source of disagreement in any social order.

With the decline of ideology, then, Lipset faced a problem not unlike that of Lenin when he was required to account for the failure of Marxist systems to develop according to a predicted pattern.[72]

> But I believe that there is still a real need for political analysis, ideology, and controversy within the world community, if not within the western democracies. In a larger sense, the democratic controversies within the advance democratic countries have become comparable to struggles within American party elections. Like all nomination contexts, they are fought to determine who will lead the party, in this case the democratic camp, in the larger political struggle in the world as a whole with its marginal constituencies, the underdeveloped states. The horizon of intellectual politics must turn ... to this larger context.[73]

In the Third World, there is a dire need for "intense political controversy and ideology. The problems of industrialization, of the place of religion, of the character of political institutions are still unsettled...."[74]

Left-leaning political leaders who did become empowered in the Third World, however, found that they were ever more outflanked by those more radical than themselves, while they were unexpectedly caught in the same problems of corruption, order, and efficiency that cropped up no matter what the revolutionary form of rule might have been tried. "The socialist in power in an underdeveloped country must continue, therefore, to lead a revolutionary struggle against capitalism, the western imperialists, and, increasingly, against Christianity as the dominant remaining foreign institution."[75] What this means is that ideology is ending only in the West, but it is

300

needed elsewhere to develop "free political and economic institutions in the rest of the world."[76]

VIII. RE-EMERGING VALUES IN POLITICAL CONTROVERSY.

As the 1960's rolled on their turbulent way, with their Berkeley's and Parisian May riots, it became obvious that ideology returned in an astonishing manner within the Western democracies themselves where they supposedly had declined. The discovery of the poor and the underprivileged rekindled ideological flames. Third World thinkers by the end of the decade could hardly see in any terms other than ideological ones. The very notion of scientific objectivity and discipline became suspect.

The question was suddenly asked, then, how what it possible for Western social science, of which Shils and Lipset were such articulate spokesmen, to have become so conservative in retrospect? Already there had been a considerable literature concerned with the ethically neutral strand of behaviorist political theory which had dominated especially American universities for almost two decades. The so-called "new left" politics of the late 1960's and early 1970's were, in fact, based in large part on the notion that politics should and could have an ethical context.[77] Conflict for conflict's sake, value-free investigations seemed to blind political thought to the very nature of political reality as it occurs in the lives of men and women.

Christian Bay noted in 1965, that Lipset's "replacing political ideology with sociological analysis" was implicitly a kind of conservative acceptance of the status quo.[78] Further, Bay was concerned that comparative government studies which concentrated on the booming field of development often were beginning to conclude that democracy was not the best form of government if development be the goal of politics. What concerned Professor Bay was the anti-political level of this kind of behaviorist thinking, though, it must be remembered, socialist theory had long ago arrived substantially at this view that the need of development can put in abeyance the problems of democracy. Thus, Bay wrote:

What was anti-political was the

301

assumption, explicit or implicit, that
politics, or at any rate American politics,
is and must always remain primarily a system
of rules for peaceful battles between
conflicting private interests, and not an
area for struggle toward a more humane and
more rationally organized society.[79]

Politics must again rediscover a vision. "... The
human goals of politics should be conceived in terms
of maximalizing human freedom.... Politics exists for
the purpose of progressively removing the most
stultifying obstacles to a free human development with
a priority for the worst obstacles."[80] In
restrospect, it sees curious and ironical that this is
also the essential function political theology began
to claim for itself.[81] The reasons may not be
entirely coincidental.

Out of a criticism of the very method of
sociological and behavioral political theory,
therefore, a moral reaction arose which sought to
reintroduce the classical question of what ought to be
the form and content of the public order within the
dimension of the human social good. J. Peter Euben's
perceptive remarks upon the limits of scientific and
rational methodology underscored the degree to which
descriptive political thought carried a bias against
an ethical politics that would account for those who
did not share justly in the public order.

Believing that our propositions capture
reality, we sometimes forgot that any theory
of politics and modes of political
organization favors certain values,
life-styles, and people at the expense of
others. Material abundance does not alter
this situation. The promise of such
abundance is not itself material. To be
rich and yet desperate seems yet somehow
absurd. That it is not absurd remains an
unanswered and at least potentially a
political challenge. The recognition that
there are many poor and despairing, without
dignity, commitments, or self-respect, is a
prerequisite for escaping the intimidations
of liberal politics and scholarship without
ignoring their significance.[82]

By a kind of circular logic, then, the end of ideology
has led to a resurgence of political considerations

302

that seem near to ideology itself as the major program for contemporary political theory. Indeed, Professor Euben's proof for the inadequacy of liberal and behavioral theory is little more than a reaffirmation of the Gospels -- concern for the poor, the downtrodden, and the weak -- in a current context. Thus, the Christianity which Professor Lipset saw being driven out of the Third World as the last vestige of colonialism made its reappearance on the theoretical level as the consensus of radical politics. In this sense, the ease with which many theologians have embraced radical political positions is not surprising or unexpected, however dubious the capacity of the ideologies to reach the quasi-religious ends so proclaimed.

Zbigniew Brzezinski, however, saw this so-called ethical and planetary consciousness of radical politics to be, at best, "a form of hedonism and narcissism." This self-proclaimed "high-minded rhetoric" was really deficient because it did not engage the intellectual and scientific structures needed to bring it about.[83] Brzezinski saw the new "technetronic" age, as he called it, which he saw potentially capable of meeting the admitted material requirements of mankind, creating by its very complexity a new age of confusion and chaos in comparison with which the cold war will be seen to have been a time of relative order.

"The real danger of the 1970's and 80's is a world-wide disintegration of social and political order: in brief, a planetary fragmentation of peoples and states."[84] This was to happen, presumably, because the supposedly idealistic young had merely passion and enthusiasm to sustain their visions. They had little "long-term commitment," or conceptual tools to understand the requirements of a new ethical and political order. In other words, the current rediscovery of an ethical or spiritual politics has a moral root in hedonism on the part of the rich and in envy on the part of the poor, both of which stand to ruin any possibility that man will use his intelligence in a sane technical and political fashion.[85]

Thus, the reappearance of ideology at the international level runs up against a despair and violence on the part of the poor and a skepticism in the developed nations against the potential of science and technology.[86] What is lacking is a theory or an

intelligence that could ground the possibility of
development or liberation for the poor in a concept of
man that can accept science and technology without
denying objective human values in freedom. It is into
this theoretical breach that political theology sees
its place in political theory, a place a revived
classical and medieval political theory suspects is
neither effective to achieve the ends desired nor
protective of what religion stands for in the energies
and destiny of mankind.

IX. FROM THE POLITICAL TO THE CONTEMPLATIVE.

The struggle going on within political theology
today is about transforming its purpose so that it
might become an active force and guide to fill the
spiritual lacuna that has arisen in modern political
theory. The danger of this way of posing the problem,
especially in the Third World where much of this
impetus for political theology lies, consists in its
failure to account for the terms of classical theory
as well as older Christianity which were both most
reluctant to identify the religious task with the
political. Indeed, this politicization of theology
strikes the older theory as abandoning that higher
level of reality and morality which preserves the
dignity of man by insisting that politics is not his
ultimate destiny.

Likewise, the question for contemporary political
theory vis-a-vis the spiritual comes back to the
issues posed in earlier history about the place of the
spiritual in politics. It is clear that the spiritual
has a place in the public order. It is not a purely
private affair as much of modern theory has held. But
politics has its proper autonomy that cannot and
should not become a vehicle for man's metaphysical and
religious drives. In one sense, the spiritual has
always been more powerful than the temporal. There
are many indications today that we are again proving
this point.

What is required is a theoretical effort to
regain the validity of man's scientific,
technological, and economic capacities within a world
that is broader than politics. The first step in this
process, it would appear, must be a recognition on the
part of religion that its main and sole justification
is not worldly success seen in terms of human

304

alleviation. It is quite true that at the origins of modern health care, hospitality, care of the poor and orphans lies a spontaneous religious impulse to do something about the weak of this world. (See Chapter XII) The Gospels clearly teach this to be a major sign of Christianity. The modern state has subsumed most of these voluntary functions into itself as a normal part of its competence.

Yet, all of this is not and cannot be what religion is "for." The other side of modern economic development and growth is abundance and leisure which seem, in the long-run, to be our real future.[87] But both leisure and the care of the poor are signs that man as a person transcends the political and cannot be wholly absorbed in it. What is curious about much of Christian political and revolutionary literature -- something pointed out by the more perceptive of critics -- is its failure to protect precisely the spiritual in man because it overly identifies religion with the worldly task.[88]

In conclusion, political theology is today claiming a place in the history of political theory. Political theory itself, moreover, has more and more come to recognize both theoretically and practically that its modern evolution from Machiavelli has been deficient and vulnerable because of its underestimating of man's spiritual desires and realities. At first sight, this appears like a happy coincidence for both. Yet, what seems more obvious, from a longer look at political theory beginning with the classical and Christian tradition, is that political theology has not been so far able to preserve its own proper mission as theology. Christianity is not a pure spirituality, to be sure, as Marsilius tried to make it. But its major task is to distinguish the public life of the world with its admittedly spiritual depth from full identification with the Kingdom of God.[89]

Since Christian theologians tend to confuse the two, they are prone to undervalue and underestimate the properly political questions that legitimately belong to the public order. Furthermore, in this effort to sanctify the existing political regimes, especially the socialist ones, or transform by revolution corrupt regimes into holy ones, they seem to have forgotten the political implications of evil which classical and especially Augustinian politics recognized. The result of this is both a failure to

305

confront the theoretical problem of the transpolitical destiny of man (even in this world) and to ignore the kinds of specifically worldly threats that do arise in the political order. The danger and trend of political theology today, it seems, is the re-erection of a new style "Byzantine" theory, this time with none of the subtleties of independence that even Byzantium preserved.

The lesson of all of this is the need to rethink the whole origin of modern political thought so that political philosophy does not have, as it does for modern theory, a totalist tendency which absorbs into itself all that is of man, both here and hereafter. The recovery of moderation from classical theory is evidently a principal avenue along which the enormous practical future of man in the world lies. But classical political theory itself, even to remain itself, needs the added contribution of medieval theory which clarified and located the proper objects of man and his society. Political theology, in its present form, must be looked upon not as a continuation of classical or medieval theory, but rather an extension of modern theory.

The confusion this causes is, no doubt, enormous. What political theology has lost, much to the detriment of man's future, is the pragmatic sense that owes much of its grounding to the particularities of medieval theory as to the tradition associated with Burke in modern experience. As a result of the ideological bent of political theology, we do not find enthusiasm and talent being poured into the pedestrian daily affairs of suffering, inventive man. Out of this alone progress can arise, but progress must be seen within its true limits as understood by classical and medieval theory. The careful empirical accounting for what happens to ideological and religious enthusiasms, which we find in Russian dissidents such as Solzhenitsyn, as in neo-capitalist thinkers such as Gilder, Novak, Bauer, Macrae, Jeane Kirkpatrick, and others, has a theoretical link to the nature of medieval political theory.

For many, however, what is now sought is a sudden political solution that would eliminate once and for all man's plight. The validity of classical and medieval political theory seems to be found here, in the reminder to both theology and contemporary political reflection that the way of man is still through the evils and hardships and turmoil of man's desires and finiteness. The other side of this theory is a sense of freedom and accomplishment which recognizes that man is precarious, yet capable of producing a nobility that is properly his, but not one which conceives itself to be totally autonomous. When Aristotle ended the _Politics_ with a discussion of leisure, he reminded man that the end of politics is contemplation.[90] This still remains the most radical single notion in all political thought. Medieval theory advances this classical position in that it gives content and shape to what such contemplation might ultimately be about, how it related to the city of man, to politics, to friendship, to the worst and to the best forms of civility men could expect.

Contemplation, thus, remains the essential connection between political theory and political theology. Medieval political theory persists to account for man's presence in the world as a political animal _and_ his presence in the universe as the being given the internal life of God as his ultimate happiness. This is why, in the end, spirituality will always be, in some basic sense, also a public question, why action will always remain subordinate to prayer and contemplation. This remains the medieval legacy reaffirmed by the results of modern political theory and the political theology based on it.

Footnotes:

1. Leo Strauss, "What Is Political Philosophy?" _Journal of Politics_, #3, 1957, Reprinted in _Contemporary Political Thought_, J. Gould, ed., New York, Holt, Rinehart and Winston, 1969, pp. 58-59, and Glencoe, Free Press, 1956.

2. Strauss, _ibid._, p. 64.

3. See E. Voegelin, "Was Ist Politische Realität?" _Anamnesis_, München, Piper, 1966, pp. 287-88.

4. "... Sicut praecepta legis humanae ordinant hominem ad quandam communitatem humanam, ita praecepta legis divinae ordinant hominem ad quandam communitatem seu rempublicam hominum sub Deo." _Summa Theologica_, I-II, 100, 5.

5. "Legis enim humanae finis est temporalis tranquilitas civitatis, ad quem fines pervenit lex cohibendo exteriores actus, quantum ad illa mala quae possunt perturbare pacificum statum civitatis. Finis autem legis divinae est perducere hominem ad finem felicitatis aeternae; qui quidem finis impeditur per quodcumque peccatum, et non solum per actus exteriores, sed etiam per interiores." I-II, 98, 1.

6. Jonathan Swift, _Gulliver's Travels_, R. Quintana, Editor, New York, Modern Library, 1955, p. xxiv.

7. "By the state, remember, St. Augustine does not mean any given city or kingdom. When he speaks of the _civitas terrena_, the city of the earth, which he also calls the _civitas diaboli_, the diabolical city, he means all who through all the centuries have striven for the sort of goods I have described. It began in Adam's time, with the first fratricide, Cain, and continues through the time of Remus and Romulus, the reconstituted fratricide, down to the present. All of these people who strive for self-satisfaction in this way, as they are grouped in different states, under different rulers, constitute the city of the devil. God in His mercy has given them ... this utilitarian suggestion or insight: give up that boundless lust for wealth, come to terms.... And when men, following this utilitarian suggestion, agree to give up their absolute lust, to accept a share of the common good, and to punish those who exceed their

shares, we call the result a state -- an association
dictated by utility for the purpose of enabling a
group of people to enjoy, without destroying one
another, whatever goods they like best. Some people
will like one thing and some will like another. We
will have, therefore, a hierarchy of states, some not
as bad as others, yet all corrupt to some degree, for
the original sin contaminates them all...." Dino
Bigongiari, "The Political Ideas of St. Augustine,"
The Political Writings of St. Augustine, H. Paolucci,
Editor, Chicago, Regnery-Gateway, 1962, Appendix, pp.
349-50.

8. Steven Runciman, Byzantine Civilization, New
York, Meridian, 1956, p. 87.

9. In Colonial American Writing, R. N. Pearce,
Editor, New York, Holt, Rinehart and Winston, 1962,
pp. 138-39.

10. See Carl L. Becker, The Heavenly City of the
Eighteenth Century Philosophers, Yale Paperback, 1957;
J. B. Bury, The Idea of Progress, New York, Dover,
1955; Sydney E. Ahlstrom, "The American National
Faith," Religion and the Humanizing of Man, J.
Robinson, Editor, Los Angeles, The Council on the
Study of Religion, 1972, pp. 87-100; Will Herberg,
"America's Civil Religion," Modern Age, Summer, 1973,
pp. 226-33; Stanley Rothman and S. Robert Lichter,
Roots of Radicalism: Christians and the New Left, New
York, Oxford, 1983.

11. Juan-Carlos Scannone, "La théologie de la
libération en Amérique Latine," Christus, Paris, June,
1972, p. 346. (Author's translations unless
indicated). See James V. Schall, Liberation Theology
in Latin America, San Francisco, Ignatius Press, 1982.

12. "It becomes obvious why Christians and
secular men who speak the language of political
humanism find themselves so often side by side. They
participate in a fundamental refusal to be absorbed by
systems that require adaptation to given structures.
They both deny the legitimacy of all structures --
either structures that claim to be based in nature, or
structures that claim to represent transcendent
eternal values, or structures that claim to represent
the truth of technological efficiency -- as the
determining and final context for man's action. With
their common passion for, and vision of, human
deliverance, they agree that integration in systems is

309

a form of domestication that trades security for freedom, goods for a critical consciousness, a full stomach for man's vision of a new tomorrow. The problem of humanization cannot be thus equated with economy or economic development (the great temptation of the poor nations of the world!) Humanization is not the gift either of the gods of futility or of their resurrected form today, the gods of technology. Both agree that man does not live by bread alone. The fundamental issue at stake is whether man is free to create his own future...." Ruben A. Alves, A Theology of Human Hope, Washington, Corpus Books, 1969, p. 83. See J. Moltmann, Theology of Hope, J. Leitch, trans., New York, Harper, 1965.

13. See Marx's, "Excerpt from the Critique of Hegel's Philosophy of Right," in Marx & Engels, Basic Writings on Politics and Philosophy, L. Feuer, ed., Doubleday Anchor, 1959, pp. 262-66.

14. See J. Metz, "An Eschatological View of the Church and the World," Theology of the World, W. Glen-Doepel, trans., New York, Herder and Herder, pp.81-100; Carl E. Braaten, "Toward a Theology of Hope," New Theology, #5, M. Marty, ed., New York, Macmillan, 1968, pp. 90-110.

15. See O. Cullmann, The State in the New Testament, New York, Scribner's, 1956; Jesus and the Revolutionaries, New York, Harper's, 1970.

16. The contrast between the more recent forms of political theology and the pre-conciliar discussions on religious liberty and the necessity of religion to grant an autonomy to the state can nowhere become more graphic than by a rereading of John Courtney Murray's We Hold These Truths, Sheed and Ward, 1960.

17. Harold Mattingly, Man in the Roman Street, New York, Norton, 1966, pp. 156-56.

18. Dean M. Kelly argued, on the other hand, that the failure of the so-called traditional Protestant churches along with, more recently, the Roman Catholic Church to provide an abiding context of religious worship and meaning has caused them to decline, while the more conservative and sect type churches which retain a very strict code and belief are growing. See Why Conservative Churches Are Growing, New York, Harper, 1972.

19. See Ernest Cassirer, "Crisis of Man's Knowledge of Himself," An Essay on Man, Doubleday Anchor, 1946, pp. 15-40; C. N. R. McCoy, The Structure of Political Thought, New York, McGraw-Hill, 1963, pp. 73-98; George Sabine, A History of Political Theory, New York, Holt, Rinehart and Winston, 1963, pp. 123-40; Mulford Q. Sibley, Political Ideas and Ideology, New York, Harper, 1970, Chapter 6 and 7.

20. See McCoy, ibid., p. 99 ff.

21. See Warren Winiarski, "Niccolo Machiavelli," in History of Political Philosophy, L. Strauss, ed., Chicago, Rand McNally, 1963, pp. 247-76; McCoy, ibid., pp. 147-186; J. R. Hale, "Machiavelli and the Self-Sufficient State," in Political Ideas, D. Thompson, ed., Baltimore, Penguin, 1966, pp. 22-33.

22. "Indeed the modern world has increasingly seen political activities as autonomous. Not only practically but also theoretically the acquiring, maintaining and exercise of power admitted every possible means. Politics was become a law unto itself. Injustice at the service of the political was committed not only without bad conscience, but even from a certain sense of 'duty.' Machiavelli was the first to express this independent 'morality' in the political realm...." R. Guardini, The End of the Modern World, J. Theman, trans., New York, Sheed and Ward, 1956, pp. 47-48; see Leo Strauss, Thoughts on Machiavelli, Glencoe, Free Press, 1959.

23. See Leo Strauss, "Marsilius of Padua," History of Political Philosophy, pp. 227-46; Sabine, p. 287 ff; Alasdair MacIntyre, After Virtue, Notre Dame, University of Notre Dame Press, 1981.

24. See James V. Schall, "Cartesianism and Political Theory," The Review of Politics, April, 1962; Christianity and Politics, Boston, St. Paul Editions, 1981.

25. "It is now that Aristotle's non-ecclesiastical or pre-ecclesiastical thought begins to show its full implications in the justification of a purely civil commonwealth, perhaps Roman but not Papal, and to show them by the pen of Marsiglio, citizen of the city-state of Padua, exponent of mixed imperial and city-state philosophy, almost Greek. The process now begins -- while

311

eviscerating the State of that ethical content with which Aristotle had endowed the Polis -- of making for it all the ethical claims on the individual which the great Greeks presumed for their own intimate and cultural community." George Catlin, The Story of the Political Philosophers, New York, Tudor, 1939, p. 181.

26. See Sabine, ibid., p. 141 ff.

27. See Wolfhart Pannenberg, "The Church and the Eschatological Kingdom," in Spirit, Faith, and Church, Philadelphia, Westminster, 1970, p. 118 ff.

"In the chaos in which we try to think out ways and means of hoisting ourselves on to the level of that phenomenal change that is taking place in this 20th century, I offer a few reflections on what non-Christians expect the Church to do in the field of public morality, and these reflections can be reduced basically to three precise demands:

1. Recognition of the autonomy of human values in the fields of knowledge and action;

2. The embracing of man's Promethean ambition for a continuous creation of the world and of man by man;

3. A clear decision to enfranchise the word and reality of socialism as the condition for the unbounded development of all men and the whole of man.

We are anxiously and hopefully waiting for this step to be taken because our common future depends on it. We do not ask any Christian to be less Christian but rather to be more fully Christian -- that is, to contribute a Christian response to the problems of our time and in the spirit of our time. We are profoundly convinced of the fact that communism cannot fully succeed without integrating the best of the Christian contribution to the image of man." Roger Garaudy, "What Does a Non-Christian Expect of the Church?" Concilium, #35, New York, Paulist, 1968, pp. 44-45; Ernest Bloch, Atheism and Christianity, New York, Herder, 1972; Roger Garaudy, From Anathema to Dialogue, London, Collins, 1967.

28. See B. Mondin, L'Eresia del Nostro Secolo, Torino, Borla, 1971; Paul Goodman, The New

Reformation, New York, Random House, 1970; E. Voegelin, The New Science of Politics, Chicago, University of Chicago Press, 1952, pp. 107-32; also James V. Schall, "From Politics to Enthusiasm, Some Reflections on Atheism, Heresy, and Sanity in the Waning Years of the Twentieth Century," Homiletic and Pastoral Review, October and November, 1971.

29. "The Role of Political Theology in Relation to the Liberation of Man," Religion and the Humanizing of Man, ibid., p. 132.

30. See The Revolutionary Writings of Father Camilo Torres, M. Zeitlin, ed., Harper Colophon, 1969; François Francou, "Le Chili, le Socialisme et l'Eglise," Cahiers de l'actualité religieuse et sociale, 15, mars 1972, pp. 181-85; Jose Ramos, Quaderni di azione sociale, Gennaio, 1971, pp. 31-46; A. Zenteno, "Justicia: Denuncia-Annuncio-Compromiso en Medellín," Christus, Mexico, Julio, 1971, p. 39 ff.; Jose-Maria Gonzales-Ruiz, "The Public Character of the Christian Message and of Contemporary Society," Concilium, #36, pp. 54-62; "Options politiques de l'église," Lumière et Vie, # 105, novembre-décembre, 1971; What the Religious Revolutionaries Are Saying, E. Smith, ed., Philadelphia, Fortress, 1971; Enrique Dussel, History and the Theology of Liberation, Maryknoll, Orbis, 1976.

31. See Edward McNall Burns, Ideas in Conflict, New York, Norton, 1960, pp. 543-65; James Petras, "Ideology and United States Political Scientists," Apolitical Politics, C. McCoy, ed., New York, Crowell, 1967, pp. 76-98; Lee Cameron McDonald, Western Political Theory, New York, Harcourt, 1968, pp. 606-11; Dante Germino, Political Philosophy and the Open Society, Baton Rouge, Louisiana State University Press, 1982.

32. See Sanford Levinson, "On 'Teaching' Political 'Science'," Power and Community, P. Green, ed., New York, Vintage, 1970, pp. 59-84; Eugene Rabinowitch, "The Student Rebellion: The Aimless Revolution," The Bulletin of the Atomic Scientists, September, 1968.

33. See Gilles Martinet, "La Jeunesse Révolutionnaire et les Partis Communistes," Le Monde Diplomatique, avril, 1972, p. 13; Laszek Kolakowski, "The Concept of the Left," The New Left Reader, D. Oglesby, ed., New York, Grove, 1969, pp. 144-60.

"From the perspective of intellectual history, it is striking that the issue of development in its economic, social, and political guises arose to challenge the social scientists just at the time when we thought we had buried the presumably old-fashioned and innocent concept of progress. Although earlier social theorists had certainly given support to the notion of human progress and social evolution, modern social scientists have generally been somewhat embarassed by this popular Western and peculiarly American article of faith. With the rise of the dictators and the holocaust of World War II, the mood of social science was at best agnostic and skeptical to any suggestion about either the inevitability or even the desirability of progress. With this as a background, the social sciences were hardly ready to embrace enthusiastically the concept of 'development' as applied to the non-Western world." Lucian W. Pye, Aspects of Political Development, Boston, Little, Brown, 1966, p. 51.

34. See Willi Oelmuller, "Ethics and Politics Today: Philosophical Foundation," Concilium, #36, pp. 40-53.

Of essential importance in understanding the relation of the issues of political theory, its terms and evolution, with the kinds of enthusiasm and values embraced in political theology is the discussion of Charles N. R. McCoy, "On the Revival of Classical Political Philosophy," The Review of Politics, April, 1973, pp. 161-79. It is also important to recognize that much of the current expansion of theology into politics has little awareness of the thoroughness with which this sort of a question has been treated in classical political theory.

35. See Michael Harrington, The Accidental Century, Penguin, 1967, pp. 275-306; Richard Shaull, "The New Challenge Before the Younger Churches," Christianity and World Revolution, E. Rian, ed., New York, Harper's, 1963, pp. 190-208; N. Greinacher and A. Muller, The Poor and the Church, New York, Seabury - Concilium, # 104, 1977.

36. See Herman Kahn, "Interview," Intellectual Digest, September, 1972, pp. 16-19. See Peter Berger, "Speaking to the Third World," Commentary, October, 1981, pp. 29-36; P. T. Bauer, Reason and Rhetoric, Cambridge, Harvard University Press, 1984.

37. See James V. Schall, *Human Dignity and Human Numbers*, Alba House, 1971, Chapter I; *Christianity and Life*, San Francisco, Ignatius Press, 1981.

38. See Ramos, *ibid.*, p. 35.

39. See R. Laurentin, *Liberation, Development and Salvation*, C. Quinn, trans., Orbis, 1972; Gonzales-Ruiz, p. 56; Olov Hartman, "Development and Liberation," *Lutheran World*, #2, 1973, pp. 133-40; Giulio Girardi, *Marxism and Christianity*, New York, Macmillan, 1968.

40. "The Church's mission is to be a sacrament, that is, an effective sign of salvation. If the construction of the just society is part of salvation history, the Church has her proper role to play in building this new order. This role can be described as a double function:

1. Hermeneutic function: to interpret the signs of the times and orientate the purpose of human action so that it conforms with the plan of salvation.

2. Critical function: to denounce absolutism and any deviation from the plan of salvation; the criterion will be her eschatological consciousness; to draw attention to the temporary nature of every historical situation ....

The Church is critical because she predicts the plan of salvation, as well as man's place and role in this plan." Jesus Garcia Gonzalez, "Development and/or Liberation," *Lumen Vitae*, Louvain, #1, 1972, p. 26.

"The socio-critical attitude of the Church cannot consist in the proclamation of one definite social order as the norm for our pluralistic society. It can only consist in that the Church operates its critical and liberating function in society and applies it to this society. The task of the Church is not a systematic social doctrine, but a social criticism." Johannes B. Metz, "The Church and 'Political Theology'," *Concilium*, #36, p. 17.

41. An example of the overall flavor of much of this kind of thinking can be seen in the following

"Manifesto" of a Mexican group called "Priests for the People":

"As believers in Christ and heralds of the gospel, we radically oppose capitalism because:

- It protects the strategic power of the dominant class through an economy organized for profit, for individual gain, for excessive concentration of wealth.

- It looks on work as merchandise; it is an enslaving subordination of the worker, who is obliged by the system to sell his labor.

- The private ownership of the means of production that it defends inevitably divides society into oppressors and oppressed, and leads to the horrible system of domination of man by man.

- Most of the population lives in grinding poverty, because there is no chance for a fair distribution of income. Prices are based not on production costs, but on what the market will bear.

- Internationally, it brings about a dependence on imperialism that hamstrings the underdeveloped countries, which are more and more invaded by 'international' corporations.

... As we see the socio-political reality, a new type of production is coming, one without exploitation or excessive wealth, and it will be the basis for a new society...."IDOC, North America, March, 1973, pp. 24-25. See D. Mieth and J. Pohier, Christian Ethics and Economics: The North-South Conflict, New York, Seabury - Concilium #140, 1980.

42. See Brian Wicker, First the Political Kingdom, Notre Dame, University of Notre Dame Press, 1968.

"If action is the midwife of the future, then human activity can add the new to the world. It can indeed be an act of creation. God's grace, instead of making human creativity superfluous or impossible, is therefore the politics that make it possible and human. This is so because in the context of the politics of human liberation man encounters a God who remains open, who has not yet arrived, who is

316

determined and helped by human activity. God needs man for the creation of his future." Alves, p. 136. See Gustavo Gutierrez, A Theology of Liberation, Maryknoll, Orbis, 1973.

43. "Reactionary governments in the Western World may once have considered Christianity their subservient ally against revolution. But today, when unpredictable change is a sort of predictable constant, there are some theologians who keep urging Christianity to abandon its role as the docile supporter and sanctifier of the status quo. They urge, instead, that it join forces with leftwing radicalism in the fight for a remade society. Thus a new movement, a theology of revolution, is moving within the orbit of Christendom. While not yet a homogeneous school, it holds that the chief function of Christianity is to spearhead radical change for the sake of freedom and justice." Vernon G. Grounds, Revolution and the Christian Faith, Philadelphia, Lippincott, 1971, p. 13. See also Giuseppe Vaccari, Teologia della Rivoluzione, Milano, Feltrinelli, 1969; Hans-Jurgen Prien, "Liberation and Development in Latin America," Lutheran World, #2, 1973, pp. 114-32.

44. See Johannes Metz, "Creative Hope," New Theology, pp. 130-141; Christianity and the Bourgeoise, New York, Seabury - Concilium, #125, 1979.

45. See Joseph Comblin, "Secularization: Myths and Real Issues," Concilium, #47, pp. 121-133.

"From one point of view, the Christian now lives in the curse and judgment of existence in a Godless world. However, from another perspective, the very profane Existenz which our destiny has unveiled may yet prove to be a path to a universal form of faith. The very fact that our present is so detached from its past, from Christendom, with its corollary that an acceptance of the present demands a negation of Christendom, of the Christian God, can mean that the horizon of our present will open into a future epiphany of faith that will draw all things into itself." Thomas J. J. Altizer, "America and the Future of Theology," Radical Theology and the Death of God, T. Altizer, Editor, Indianapolis, Bobbs-Merrill, 1966, p. 20. See L. Boff, Jesus Christ Liberator, Maryknoll, Orbis, 1978.

46. "At the same time, as God gave man, through the interplay of cosmic evolution, intelligence,

317

freedom, love, in one word, a soul, God also
completely and fully gave an extension of his temporal
destiny in a divine dimension. He called mankind to
an age capable of gathering together in him, in a
simultaneity of fullness, the totality of his fleeting
existence. In short, he calls man and mankind to an
everlasting fulfillment." Laurentin, p. 213. See
also J. B. Metz, Concilium, #26, pp. 2-18.

47. "Insoluto e pero rimasto il problema della
violenza, che si e continuato a definire
sostanzialmente non evangelica, ma senza affatto
chiarire l'equivoco contenuto nel termine e che da
tempo si vorrebbe chiarito, cioe se violenza delle
istituzioni, contra la quale sarebbe quindi legittima
e perfino doverosa una reazione di difesa, anche, al
limite, di carattere violento." Gianpaolo Salvini,
"Il Sinodo e la Giustizia nel Mondo," Aggiornamenti
Sociali, Milano, Febbraio, 1972, p. 95.

48. In the older notion, providence was a divine
attribute which meant that it could not be simply
political. The combination of providence with
politics or the reading of politics through providence
makes the divinity more controllable.

49. This is the real danger of identifying "sin"
with social sin. For it means that the guilty are not
any longer individual human beings who have done
something wrong, but members of a class or group.
This is the reappearance of a kind of corporate sin.
See again the reading of Footnote #41 for an example
of the way this mentality appears in popular
literature. See E. Feil, "The Theology of Revolution:
A Critique," Theology Digest, Autumn, 1971, pp.
220-24.

50. "Political theology preaches, celebrates,
meditates, dialogues, demonstrates, protests,
worships, confronts, listens, and looks. Its content
is revolutionary, its methodology is
multi-dimensional, its voice is the voice of protest
... In short, the work of political theology is social
change, and in the long run, radical social change."
Joseph M. Petulla, Christian Political Theology: A
Marxian Guide, Maryknoll, Orbis, 1972, pp. 30-31.

51. See James V. Schall, "The Significance of
Post-Aristotelian Thought in Political Theory,"
Cithara, November, 1963.

52. "Machiavelli overturned the tradition of classical political thought; he effected a revolution from the dominion of Plato and Aristotle, who had taught men what they ought to do. Machiavelli teaches what men do -- herein lies his revolution, our debt, and his triumph." Winiarski,ibid., p. 247.

53. Jacques Ellul, The Political Illusion, K. Kellen, trans., New York, Vintage, 1972, p. 21.

54. "With the decline of religious faith the problem which the Prophet defined in the Bible, 'Wherefore doth the way of the wicked suffer?' received a new interpretation. Before, the question could be considered on the transcendental plane: one had the assurance that the account would be settled in the hereafter, in another place. Once religious belief was undermined, however, the evils and injustices of this life could no longer be regarded as merely temporary or temporal; therefore, they ceased to be tolerable, and men began to put their faith in the achievement of perfect justice and the settling of accounts in this world, not the next." J. L. Talmon, "Utopianism and Politics," Utopia, G. Kateb, ed., New York, Atherton, 1971, p. 94.

55. See Friedrich Heer, The Intellectual History of Europe, J. Steinberg, trans., London, Weidenfeld and Nicolson, 1966, pp. 1-25. See also James V. Schall, "The Urgency and the Waiting," World Justice, Louvain, #4, 1969-1970, pp. 435-59.

56. See Metz, Concilium, ibid., p. 12.

57. "Then, with the ordinary conventions of civilized life thrown into confusion, human nature, always ready to offend even where laws exist, showed itself proudly in its true colours, as something incapable of controlling passion, insubordinate to the idea of justice, the enemy of anything superior to itself...." Thucydides, The Peloponnesian War, R. Warner, trans., Penguin, Bk. 3, p. 211.

58. See Samuel P. Huntington, "Political Order and Political Decay," Political Order in Changing Societies, New Haven, Yale University Press, pp. 1-92.

59. This was in fact what the methodology of Hobbes proposed at the origins of modern theory. It is no accident Hobbes was a translator of Thucydides.

60. Hannah Arendt, <u>The Human Condition</u>, Doubleday Anchor, 1959, p. 156 ff.

61. See for example Herbert Marcuse, <u>One-Dimensional Man</u>, Boston, Beacon, 1967.

62. See Metz, <u>Concilium</u>, <u>ibid</u>., p. 14.

63. See for example, R. Buckminster Fuller, <u>Utopia or Oblivion</u>, New York, Bantam, 1969; R. L. Sinsheimer, "Genetic Engineering, the Modification of Man," <u>Impact of Science on Society</u>, October-December, 1970, pp. 279-91; "Genetic Science and Man," <u>Theological Studies</u>, September, 1972; John McHale, <u>World Facts and Trends</u>, New York, Macmillan, 1972; <u>The New Revolutionaries</u>, T. Ali, ed., New York, Morrow, 1969.

64. "This article will first recapitulate a widely held skepticism about the criteria for the 'good man' who is the aim of eugenic policy." Joshua Lederberg, "Experimental Genetics and Human Evolution," in <u>Beyond Left and Right</u>, R. Kostelanetz, ed., New York, Morrow, 1968, p. 180.

"I am convinced that all sovereign nations and all political theories and realized political systems, class warfaring, and charity are obsolete because they were all invented as ways for special groups of organized humans to survive a little bit better under the fundamental working assumption that there did not exist and never would exist enough metabolic sustenance to permit more than a minority of humanity to survive and live out its potential lifespan of years." Fuller, <u>ibid</u>., p. 210; see also p. 178.

From the standpoint of political theory, these passages and similar ones are of great significance as they claim a solution for the problem of the good life not in either politics or theology but in biology or technology.

65. See A. Toffler, <u>Future Shock</u>, Bantam, 1970.

66. See Sabine,<u>ibid</u>., p. 141.

67. Daniel Bell, "The Passing of Fanaticism," in <u>The Decline of Ideology</u>, M. Rejai, Chicago, Aldine-Athenaeum, 1971, pp. 40, 44.

68. The Bishops of Peru, "Justice in the World," _Lumen Vitae_, #1, 1972, p. 36. See also the series in _Lumiere et Vie_, entitled, "Ambiguites du Progres," #111, janvier-mars, 1973.

69. _Encounter_, November, 1955.

70. See _The Christian-Marxist Dialogue_, P. Oestreicher, Editor, London, Macmillan, 1969; Petulla, _ibid_.

71. Seymour Martin Lipset, _Political Man_, Doubleday Anchor, 1963, p. 439. Italics added.

72. In his _Imperialism_, Lenin projected the internal failures of the Marxist analysis onto the structure of colonialism.

73. Lipset, _ibid_., pp. 453-54.

74. _Ibid_., p. 454.

75. _Ibid_., pp. 454-55.

76. _Ibid_., p. 456.

77. See _To Free a Generation_, D. Cooper, Editor, New York, Collier, 1968. See Todd Gitlin, "The Future of an Effusion: How Young Activists Will Get to 1984," _1984 Revisited_, R. Wolff, Editor, New York, Knopf, 1973, pp. 11-39; Tom Hayden, "The Politics of 'The Movement,'" _The Radical Papers_, I. Howe, Editor, Doubleday Anchor, 1966, pp. 362-77.

78. Christian Bay, "Politics and Pseudopolitics: A Critical Evaluation of Some Behavioral Literature," _Apolitical Politics_, p. 23. See Lipset's own reaction to this in the Introduction of the Doubleday Anchor edition of _Political Man_.

79. _Ibid_., p. 23.

80. _Ibid_., pp. 37, 41.

81. In this regard, it is interesting that Alexander Solzhenitsyn's complaint against the religious leaders of the Russian Orthodox Church is precisely that they do not protest: "We are robbing our children when we deprive them of something which they can never experience again -- the pure angelic protection of worship which as adults they can never

recapture, nor even realize what they have missed. The right to continue the faith of their fathers is annulled, as is the right of parents to bring up their children in their own outlook on life -- while you, hierarchs of the Church, have accommodated yourselves to this, even abetting it and finding in it a true sign of freedom of religion." "Letter to Pimen, Patriarch of All Russia," The Tablet, London, April 15, 1972, p. 360.

82. J. Peter Euben, "Political Science and Political Silence," Power and Community, pp. 45-46.

83. Zbigniew Brzezinski, "The International and the Planetary," Encounter, August, 1972, p. 52.

84. Ibid., p. 54.

85. Ibid., p. 54.

86. See Philip Handler, "Science in America," U.S. News, January 18, 1971, pp. 32-33.

87. See Theodore Roszak, Where the Wasteland Ends: Politics and Transcendence in Postindustrial Society, Doubleday; John Naisbitt, Megatrends, New York, Warner, 1982.

88. See E. L. Mascall, Theology and the Future, New York, Morehouse-Barlow, 1968.From the side of a development theorist, David Apter has also warned of the temptation to identify religion and politics into some kind of unified form. See his "Political Religion in the New Nations," Some Conceptual Approaches to the Study of Modernization, Prentice-Hall, 1968, pp. 193-233.

89. Ivan Vallier has perceptively noted the danger of radical politics which attempt to theologize the public order: "The distinctive feature of this radicalism is that the office of the priest, including its symbolism and charisma, is injected into civic life as a type of political authority. This is a very old and traditional kind of action, with deep roots in the caesaropapist infrastructure of Latin America. Clerical radicalism is an appropriation of an old means in the service of new goals. It is an implicit refusal to acknowledge that civil and ecclesiastical spheres should be differentiated." "Radical Priests and Revolution," Changing Latin America, D. Chalmers, ed., New York, Columbia, 1972, p. 17. For a rather

opposite view, see Yves Vaillancourt, "Les politisés chrétiens et la libération," <u>Relations</u>, Montréal, mai, 1972, pp. 141-45.

90. See James V. Schall, <u>Far Too Easily Pleased: A Theology of Contemplation, Play, and Festivity</u>, Los Angeles, Benziger-Macmillan, 1976.

CONCLUSION

In "Isaiah Revisited," Jane Sharp began, in The Bulletin of the Atomic Scientists, a rather one-sided advocacy for disarmament by citing the great Hebrew prophet's famous "pounding swords into ploughshares."(Isaiah, 2:4)[1] Everyone, undoubtedly, is tempted to quote scripture for his own purposes. Yet, this very citing of an apocalyptic passage as a symbol of contemporary Armageddon, for the "hell" of nuclear war itself, evidently the "worst" evil conceivable by the modern popular and scientific mind, serves to recapitulate the thesis of this book. The principal justification for Christian and medieval political theory lies in the need to distinguish moral and physical destruction.

"We should recognize that utopian hopes for total nuclear disarmament cannot excuse a Western failure to defend its independence soberly without using reckless threats," Albert Wohlstetter wrote in an essay which properly distinguishes these two levels.[2] Isaiah himself was not merely talking about a politically peaceable world, nor, more especially, was he dealing with a peaceful world produced exclusively by "political" means. To use Isaiah in this fashion is, no doubt, the easiest way to avoid the main issue presented to political theory by the Judaeo-Christian tradition. This is the issue of the locus of beatitude as that goal has been formulated in the history of political theory, from The Republic of Plato himself.

Professor Douglas Sturm has argued, in his perceptive essay, "Politics and Divinity: Three Approaches in American Political Science," that God did have a necessary and legitimate place in political theory in the behavioralist, traditionalist, and post-behaviorialist schools which have dominated American political science in recent decades. Sturm himself went on to make a case for uniting activist humanism with religious concepts of God and His action in the world. He emphasized, as did the scriptures, that a concern for the weak and the needy is the principle by which political theory, in some sense, ought to operate. Professor Sturm went on to conclude, by citing Professor Arnold Brecht's remark,

325

that political science ought not to ignore the divine alternative and the light it might shed on political events when they cannot be fully explained by the social sciences.[3]

The three main approaches to the study of politics, however, might well suggest different ways to present the problem of the divinity in political science. "In the first correlation -- between behavioralism and the cosmological approach," Professor Sturm wrote,

> God may be a principle of intelligibility required to explain certain observable features of the world, but the study of political realities may and need never reach that point. In the second correlation -- between traditionalism and the ontological approach -- God may be the transcendent source of the order of being and the ultimate standard for the order of politics, but the more directly and completely one approaches the contemplation of divine reality as the ground and fulfillment of one's personal being, the more distant becomes one's concern for the world of politics. In the third correlation -- between post-behavioralism and the anthropological approach -- apprehensions of divine and political realities are in principle both part and parcel of one's lived-experience of the world. Thus, from the final perspective, theology and political science are complementary forms of understanding both intended to shed light on the character of human experience and to provide direction for human action.[4]

What is to be noted here, however, is the way politics comes to be used as a criterion of the divine and a corresponding criterion of the human, itself now subject to ideology and its political definition of the best and worst form of life.[5] Freedom in politics is placed over being as the standard of value to select the proper mode of unifying politics and divinity. What is lacking here is a proper goal that is not itself political, yet still open to the human.

This is, essentially, what the classics sought to do with the distinction between ethics and metaphysics. Revelation is then something addressed

326

to ethics, politics, and metaphysics in the sense that the human intellect is open to receive it. The rational creature is understood to be capable of receiving revelation freely. This is why it is not, ultimately, an "alienation" that a complete knowledge of man find its source outside human capacity as such, but not outside its capacity to know and receive knowledge from what is more than merely human, though with the incarnation, also human.

The Christian and medieval traditions, I have argued in these reflections, remain abiding and necessary elements in political theory itself. They are persistent because they have an intellectual principle which allows them freedom to remain subject to the kind of being man is created to be -- from nature in Aristotle, from God in Aquinas. At first sight, this will seem paradoxical. Nevertheless, the impasse reached in the modernizers of classical political theory, like Voegelin and Strauss, in contrast with the activism of the post-behavioralists, continues because of the limits of political theory itself. And these limits are the substance of the classical Christian contribution to political theory. These limits constantly appear when they are not acknowledged and thought about as such.

The concern for a just order in this world -- the "freedom" project of the post-behavioralists -- as well as the rational limits of classical thought, confront, in their own ways, the problem of what is the purpose of man in the universe and how does politics relate to it.[6] Jacques Pohier wrote, in this connection:

> Our conception of God is closely linked with the way we use sin to explain man ... Man's view of his condition and God's creative and saving design do not necessarily coincide. In fact, there is good reason to think that they differ notably.
>
> My working hypothesis, therefore, is that sin serves to explain that the reality of man does not coincide with man's view of himself.[7]

Such theological observations, it appears, lie close to the root of the problem constantly recurring in political theory. This is the problem of whether politics is an ultimate explanation, or at least, an avenue to it.

The assumption, however, that a perfectly man-made, "just" political order is the way of God, the argument implied by Professor Sturm and much activist theology, leaves aside the classic problem of "The City of God," of whether the non-existence of a just order means also that men cannot and do not achieve "happiness" in any sense. This was the consideration with which Aristotle began the _Ethics_. On the other hand, it is possible to achieve a relatively good political system and still lack ultimate happiness. How is mankind to confront this situation which arises, in a way, directly out of political theory itself? Such was the sort of issue that was at the roots of medieval political theory.

Christian theory itself began not with the death of Nicias, nor with the death of Socrates, those deaths with which political theory began, but with the death of Christ. Those who knew of the death of Christ also knew of the death of Socrates. This has meant that the darker side of the human condition not only requires explanation -- hell and evil and all that is less than perfect -- but also that its political consequences be accounted for. Classical theory understood this as a fact, with its description of the decline of regimes.

Christian theory, on the other hand, understood it also in its causes, in what was called original sin and pride, something that appeared in each human being so that no reformation of a political system as such would remove the dangers lurking to mankind through a disordered human heart. This remains in some basic sense the gulf that separates modern from classical and medieval political theory. The only way to overcome this separation is to deny the metaphysics upon which it is based, to make the "reality of society" to be substantial while reducing the individual to an incident in the on-going species. (Chapter XII)

The Greek question of the best state and the Christian doctrine of resurrection with ultimate beatitude before the Triune God, consequently, are also related. Yet, Hannah Arendt was right in sensing that the properly political questions are to be kept free of those belonging to _The Life of the Mind_.[8] It is not necessary to deny that God has an "interest" in the things of this world to maintain that politics is not of the substance of the higher things to which, as Aristotle said, we should be devoted insofar as we can. In this sense, the great contribution of medieval political theory lies in its insistence that all orders of human reality, of reality itself, the lowest with the highest, reason and revelation, are legitimate. At the same time, this theory can admit a proper, unique place for politics, without granting to the civil order either the lowest nor the highest positions, both of which distort and destroy politics itself when it is confused with them.

Reminiscent of what has been argued about the Christian guardians and the tradition of institutions that were formed by the medieval experience in answer to philosophical and political questions, Professor Alasdair MacIntyre concluded his book After Virtue:

> What (early and medieval Christians) set themselves to achieve instead -- often not recognizing fully what they were doing -- was the construction of new forms of community within which the moral life could be sustained so that both morality and civility might survive the coming ages of barbarism and darkness. If my account of the moral condition is correct, we ought also to conclude that for some time now we too have reached that turning point. What matters at this stage is the construction of local forms of community within which civility and the intellectual and moral life can be sustained through the new dark ages which are already upon us.

> And if the tradition of the virtues was able to survive the horrors of the last dark ages, we are not entirely without grounds for hope. This time however the barbarians are not waiting beyond the frontiers; they have already been governing us for quite some time. And it is our lack of consciousness of this that constitutes part of our predicament. We are waiting not for a Godot, but for another -- doubtless very different -- St. Benedict.[9]

What does this mean, to wait not for a Godot but for a St. Benedict? Clearly, here medieval theory is seen to be directly pertinent to what modern political

philosophy has not been able to resolve. How virtue
can exist in a philosophic system which denies its
pertinence is no doubt fundamental.

But why not recall Aristotle, rather than St.
Benedict? Medieval political practice and theory have
led us to suspect that the sensibility of Aristotle,
vast as it is, will not arise solely from natural
sources. What is new is not the thesis of Aquinas
about reason being addressed by revelation, but the
worrisome outlines of a pseudo-revelation that
presents itself in the form of the contemporary
ideologies. The struggle for the validity of
revelation itself is involved in the tradition which
sees that politics is not the proper object of
revelation, nor is revelation an ideology.

The enterprise of political theory, then, remains
a crucial one. As the scriptural tradition taught,
politics is the most likely area in which to make and
remake all of the human in man's own original image,
to replace, thereby, any natural or divine signs of
what man is. When Plato finally argued in The Laws,
against the Greek Protagorean tradition, that God, not
man, was the measure of all things, he witnessed to
the essential freedom that politics exists to
preserve.(716a) This is the idea that man's nobility
is not so much that he created himself, but that, as
Genesis said, he is created. His human conscious
experience is rather the discovery and living out of a
real good already objectively found in him, in his
history, in his fellow men, in his being itself, in
Being itself. Metaphysics remains prior to politics.
The opposite is also true. Political theory likewise
includes a reflection of how real evil is lived out,
of what is the worst state. The meaning and
definition of this evil, formally, is opposed to the
human good seen as a reason, a gift already placed in
man, but a good open to deviation by the human will
from its proper end.

The genius of Aquinas' theory of law, therefore,
its firm insistence on preventing law, civil law, from
coercing all virtues and preventing all vices, is that
it allows man's ultimate hopes and, yes, damnation to
take place, without making these directly political,
while not denying that the political participates in
some sense in both glory and rejection. The political
is limited for its own good. Without the
clarification of the kinds of states or regimes
available to men, without likewise St. Augustine's

ultimate City of God, political theory is tempted, even up to the post-behavioralists, to recreate man and his society, the former by the latter, because it can find no other goal but an earthly Isaiahan kind of kingdom.

Ultimately, this is what political theory is about -- about the locus of this kingdom, and its opposite, about what man can expect being what he is, both reasonable and graced. The long tradition of political theory, even to current speculative considerations, seems to suggest that without classical Christian reflection, men, even Christian men, will try to erect a perfect kingdom in this world, that political science and methodology can easily become instrumental to this purpose even to the point of justifying the worst regime as the best.

Christian and medieval theory, therefore, is not merely an historical account of certain out-dated philosophers and theologians, but an essential foundation for political thought itself. It is something that persists in almost everything that we do in the social world. This is the theoretical foundation that prevents politics from claiming what it cannot deliver. This is the basis that allows politics to remain itself, that is, politics, without simultaneously denying in its name those realities beyond politics, those realities that do correspond to the ends, desires, and hopes man does, on political and metaphysical reflection, find in himself.

Footnotes:

1. Jane M. O. Sharp, "Isaiah Revisited," _The Bulletin of the Atomic Scientists_, Part I, April 1978; Part II, June, 1978.

2. Albert Wohlstetter, "Bishops, Statesmen, and Other Strategists On the Bombing of Innocents," _Commentary_, June, 1983, p. 34. See also the Pastoral Letters of the German and French Bishops on Peace and War, San Francisco, Ignatius Press, 1984; Patrick Glynn, "Why an American Arms Build-up Is Morally Necessary," _Commentary_, February, 1984, pp. 17-28.

3. Douglas Sturm, "Politics and Divinity: Three Approaches in American Political Science," _Thought_, December, 1977, p. 365; see also Dante Germino, _Political Philosophy and the Open Society_, Baton Rouge, Louisiana State University Press, 1983.

4. Sturm, _ibid_.

5. _Ibid._, pp. 354-63.

6. See James V. Schall, "Atheism and Politics," _Christianity and Politics_, Boston, St. Paul Editions, 1981, Chapter IV, pp. 94-117.

7. Jacques Pohier, "What Purpose Does Sin Serve?" _Theology Digest_, Spring, 1978, pp. 27-28.

8. Hannah Arendt, _The Life of the Mind_, New York, Harcourt, 1978, 2 Vols.; see also Leo Strauss, _The City and Man_, Chicago, University of Chicago Press, 1964, Chapter I.

9. Alasdair MacIntyre, _After Virtue_, Notre Dame, University of Notre Dame Press, 1981, pp. 244-45. See Christopher Derrick, _The Rule of Peace_, St. Bede's Publications.

GENERAL INDEX

Common Good, 32, 242, 243.

Contemplation (Speculative Order), viii, 52, 59, 73, 76, 77.

Creation, vii, 6, 10, 58, 92, 114, 223, 224, 257, 279.

Death, vii, 84, 99, 122, 132, 133, 142, 149, 194.

Development (Modernization), 50, 92, 132, 138,150, 158, 160, 290, 296-98, 300, 301, 306.

Ecology, 138, 230, 238.

Evil, vii, 6, 25, 30, 32, 49, 54, 56, 77, 86, 88, 90, 92, 99-101, 107-11, 113-24, 129, 157, 162, 194, 196, 198, 205, 206, 222, 325, 328, 330.

Fall (Original Sin), 26, 29, 32, 49, 73, 99, 107, 110-12, 137, 172.

Forgiveness, 24, 113, 125, 270.

Hell, 30, 83, 85-7, 89-95, 98-101, 108, 129, 134, 157, 194, 253, 325, 328.

Human Dignity, 8, 53, 54, 163.

Ideology, 43, 57, 99, 123, 133, 148-50, 266, 272, 297-301, 303, 326, 330.

Immortality, 27, 28, 70, 74, 85, 101, 174, 179, 221, 222.

Judaeo-Christian Tradition, vii, viii, 13, 39, 129, 271, 325.

Justice, xvi, 29, 31, 58, 74, 79, 85, 87-9, 97-9, 130, 135, 139, 141, 143, 146, 162, 165, 170, 237, 260, 265, 286.

Law, vii, xiv, 3, 13, 14, 32, 88, 94, 122, 129, 130, 135, 139-41, 144, 145, 149-52, 157, 177, 194, 196, 221, 229, 236, 237, 253, 280, 330.

333

Medicine (Health), 130, 131.

23, 26, 30, 33, 51, 58, 60, 83, 87, 100, 109, 111, 120, 137, 139, 147, 161, 169, 183, 197, 199, 208, 236, 254, 270, 271, 286, 294, 305.

Political Philosophy, Roman (Cicero), 12, 22, 32, 52, 54, 56, 57, 144, 145, 170, 171, 265, 266, 270.

Practical Sciences, xiv, 164, 167, 169, 219.

Property, 26, 32, 68, 69, 72, 75, 77, 78, 99, 111, 172, 176, 263, 269.

Regime, (Form of Rule, Government, Polity), Best, 6, 26, 53, 57, 58, 60, 79, 84, 110, 135, 142, 157, 161, 162, 166-68, 175, 179, 199, 280, 328; Second-Best, 26, 53, 111, 129, 140, 147, 166, 168, 178, 181, 182, 185; Worst, 26, 52, 53, 84, 90, 109, 123, 161, 164, 181, 193-95, 197, 198, 200-02, 204, 209, 210, 212, 213; Distinction of, 159, 162, 195, 214, 286, 330; Mixed, 169, 177-80.

Religion, -- and Politics, vii, viii, xiv, 8, 9, 28, 40, 143, 148, 174, 195, 200, 204, 207, 212, 282, 293, 302, 304, 307; -- as Politicized, 45, 76, 99, 151, 182, 222, 260, 262, 279, 283, 285, 286, 289-91, 298, 304-06.

Revelation and Reason, (grace and nature), 5, 12, 51, 69, 70, 88, 94, 96, 97, 100, 101, 115, 123, 137, 164, 173, 174, 196, 219, 220, 254, 255, 257, 260, 261, 265, 266, 269-71, 296, 326, 330.

Roman Law, 140, 141.

Socialism, 69, 72, 138, 237, 290, 291, 305.

Theology, -- and Politics, xv, 3, 4, 13, 30, 148, 157, 263, 267, 271, 284, 288-90, 292, 294, 297, 302, 306.

Totalitarianism, (Absolutism, Tyranny), xvi, 13, 25, 30, 43, 48, 49, 71, 84, 91, 93, 96, 100, 120, 136, 140, 163, 181, 184, 195, 196, 199, 211, 219, 260.

War, 108, 134, 193, 195, 198, 200, 205, 214, 325.

INDEX OF NAMES IN TEXT

285, 286.

Calvin, John, 3.
Cassirer, Ernest, 170.
Chesterton, G. K., 100, 107, 115, 124.
Churchill, Winston, 206, 212.
Christ, (Jesus), 22-4, 26-33, 39, 41, 49, 59, 67, 69,
83, 96, 97, 122, 142, 146, 195, 328.

Cicero, 23, 26, 57, 129, 170, 171, 175.
Cioran, E. M., 151.
Cranston, Maurice, 267.
Cullmann, Oscar, 30

Daniélou, Jean, 13.
Dante, 83.
Dawson, Christopher, 40, 68.
Deane, Herbert, 46.
deJouvenel, Bertrand, 22.
Descartes, Rene, 288.
Dostoyevsky, Fedor, 92.

East, John, 47.
Ellul, Jacques, 96, 98, 294.
Euben, J. Peter, 302, 303.

Finnis, John, 29.
Fromm, Eric, 3.

Galbraith, John Kenneth, 181, 299.
Garaudy, Roger, 289.
Gaylin, Willard, 97, 99.
Gierke, Otto von, 236, 237, 239.
Gilder, George, 306.
Gilson, Etienne, 266.
Gregory the Great, 43.
Grotius, Hugo, 288.
Guitton, Jean, 41.
Gulliver, Lemuel, (Jonathan Swift), 281.
Gurian, Waldemar, 108

Hallowell, John, 95, 96, 100.
Hegel, George F. W., 4, 42, 85, 121, 179, 235, 247,
279, 288.

Hessen, Robert, 239-41.
Hitler, Adolph, 85, 206, 209.
Hobbes, 6, 43, 90, 175, 184, 200, 210, 213, 263, 279,
282, 288.

Homer, 85.

Isaiah, 8, 325, 331.

James, St., 142, 152, 181.
Jeremiah, 8, 9.
Joachim of Flora, 32, 85, 112, 172, 175, 178.
John the Baptist, 70.

Kant, Immanuel, 42.

John XXIII, 134.
Johnson, Samuel, 157.

Kirk, Russell, 129.
Kirkpatrick, Jeane, 306.
Kolakowski, Lezek, 30-32, 99, 100.
Kreyche, Robert, 90.
Kristol, Irving, 150.

Laszlo, Ervin, 239.
Lehman, John, 208.
Lenin, V. I., 292, 293, 300.
Lewis, C. S., 151, 202, 259, 266, 269.
Lincoln, Abraham, 165.
Lippmann, Walter, xii.
Lipset, Seymour M., 299-301, 303.
Locke, John, 279.
Luther, Martin, 67, 133.
Luttwak, Edward, 204.

McCoy, Charles N. R., 1, 169.
McIlwain, Charles H., xi.
McInerny, Ralph, 254.
Machiavelli, Nicolo, x, 33, 43, 48, 138, 145, 175, 200, 201, 253, 261, 268, 269, 279, 287, 289, 294, 305.

MacIntyre, Alasdair, 329.
Macpherson, C. B., 26.
Macrae, Norman, 306.
Madison, James, 179, 180.
Maimonides, Moses, 1, 3.
Manson, Charles, 121.
Maritain, Jacques, 96, 134, 266.
Markus, R. A., 39.
Marsilius of Padua, 85, 173, 175, 238, 288, 305.
Marx, Karl, xi, xvi, 2, 4, 32, 50, 78, 138, 158, 159, 180, 197, 202, 209, 237, 238, 284, 288, 290, 299, 300.

Mascall, Eric, 266.
Mather, Cotton, 284.

Mattingley, Sir Harold, 285.
Mertes, Alois, 203.
Mill, John Stuart, vi, 144.
Miller, Stephen, xv, xvi.
Minogue, Kenneth, 29, 181.
Montesquieu, 179.
Moore, Barrington, 44.
Moynihan, Daniel, 158, 183.

Nader, Ralph, 239, 240.
Nelson, Michael, 29.
Neuhaus, Richard, 206.
Newman, John Henry, 114, 115, 117, 118.
Nicias, 295, 296.
Niebuhr, Reinhold, 44.
Nietzsche, Frederick, 121.
Nkrumah, K., 135.
Novak, Michael, 306.
Nozick, Robert, 240, 241.

Orwell, George, 193.

Pargetter, Robert, 117, 118.
Partridge, P. H., 159.
Paul of Tarsus, 13, 25-7, 101, 141, 170, 180, 292.
Pegis, Anton, 266.
Persig, Robert, 161.
Peter, St., 24, 27, 170, 219.
Philo, 3.
Pieper, Josef, 68, 254.
Pilate, Pontius, 21, 22, 24, 27, 32, 142.
Pius, XII, 48.
Plamenetz, John, 183.
Plato, xiv, 5, 6, 8, 11, 12, 21, 23, 25, 27-9, 42, 52-4, 59, 67-79, 86-9, 94, 95, 101, 109, 110, 114, 129, 130, 139, 140, 142, 144, 158, 166, 171-4, 177, 180, 193, 195, 200, 220, 237, 264, 265, 267-70, 286, 290, 296, 325, 330.

Pohier, Jacques, 327.
Polybius, 169, 179.
Popper, Karl, 71.
Puritans, 3, 5, 16.
Rahner, Karl, 228.
Rawls, John, xiii, 29, 98, 237.
Rostow, W. W., 299.
Rousseau, Jean-Jacques, 6, 90, 179, 279, 288.

Sabine, George, 297.
Saint-Simon, Henri de, 160, 178.
Sakharov, Andrei, 204.

Salk, Jonas, 238, 239.
Schlesky, Helmut, 145.
Shafarevich, Igor, 69, 202.
Sharp, Jane, 325.
Shils, Edward, 298, 299, 301.
Sobran, Joseph, 258, 268.
Socrates, vi, 6, 21-3, 27, 28, 32, 41, 58, 59, 70, 78, 83, 85, 109, 158, 161, 174, 183, 194.

Solle, Dorothy, 289.
Solzhenitsyn, Alexander, 112, 123, 149, 163, 164, 180, 183, 202, 204, 305.

Sophocles, 24, 85, 296.
Stoics, 6, 25, 54, 55, 85, 169, 170, 286.
Strauss, Leo, vii, 3, 33, 93-6, 100, 115, 173, 183, 258, 260, 265, 271, 279, 327.

Sturm, Douglas, 325, 326, 328.

Tacitus, 296.
Tawney, R. H., 97.
Thatcher, Margaret, 202.
Thucydides, 25, 88, 110, 164-66, 174, 180, 295, 296.
Tinder, Glenn, vii.
Tocqueville, Alexis de, 158, 178, 179.

Valadier, Paul, 107.
Veatch, Henry, xiii.
Vergil, 84.
Voegelin, Eric, 33, 46, 49, 93, 173, 264, 271, 272, 280, 327.

Von Balthasar, Hans Urs, 3, 267.
Von Braun, Werner, 221.

Walzer, Michael, xii, 211.
Wattenberg, Ben, 177.
Weber, Max, 3, 75.
White, David, 118, 119.
Wildavsky, Aaron, 2.
Wohlstetter, Albert, 325.
Wolfe, Christopher, 279.
Wolin, Sheldon, vii.
Wynn, Wilton, 134.

Yahweh, 7-13, 16, 21.

Zaehner, R. C., 120, 121.

ABOUT THE AUTHOR:

James V. Schall is an Associate Professor in the Department of Government in Georgetown University in Washington, D. C. Previously, he taught at the Istituto Sociale in the Gregorian University in Rome and in the Department of Government in the University of San Francisco. He is a priest, belonging to the California Province of the Society of Jesus. Formerly, he was a consultor on the Pontifical Commission for Justice and Peace.

His previous books include: Redeeming the Time, New York, Sheed & Ward, 1968; Play On: From Games to Celebrations, Philadelphia, Fortress Press, 1971; Human Dignity and Human Numbers, Staten Island, Alba House, 1971; Far Too Easily Pleased: A Theology of Play, Festivity, and Contemplation, Los Angeles, Benziger-Macmillan, 1976; Welcome Number 4,000,000,000, Canfield, Ohio, Alba Books, 1977; The Sixth Paul, Canfield, Ohio, Alba Books, 1977; The Praise of 'Sons of Bitches': On the Worship of God by Fallen Men, Slough, England, St. Paul Publications, 1978; Christianity and Life, San Francisco, Ignatius Press, 1981; Christianity and Politics, Boston, St. Paul Editions, 1981; Church, State, and Society in the Thought of John Paul II, Chicago, Franciscan Herald Press, 1982; Liberation Theology, San Francisco, Ignatius Press, 1982; The Distinctiveness of Christianity, San Francisco, Ignatius Press, 1983. He does a regular column, 'Sense and Nonsense' in Catholicism-in-Crisis.